SETTLING ACCOUNTS

DATE DUE

EDITORS

Sherry B. Ortner, Nicholas B. Dirks, Geoff Eley

A LIST OF TITLES

IN THIS SERIES APPEARS

AT THE BACK OF

THE BOOK

PRINCETON STUDIES IN
CULTURE / POWER / HISTORY

SETTLING ACCOUNTS

VIOLENCE, JUSTICE, AND ACCOUNTABILITY IN POSTSOCIALIST EUROPE

John Borneman

PRINCETON UNIVERSITY PRESS
PRINCETON, NEW JERSEY

Copyright © 1997 by Princeton University Press
Published by Princeton University Press, 41 William Street,
Princeton, New Jersey 08540
In the United Kingdom: Princeton University Press,
Chichester, West Sussex
All Rights Reserved

Library of Congress Cataloging-in-Publication Data
Borneman, John, 1952–
Settling accounts : violence, justice, and accountability in
postsocialist Europe / John Borneman.
p.   cm. — (Princeton studies in culture/power/history)
Includes bibliographical references and index.
ISBN 0-691-01682-8 (cloth : alk. paper)
ISBN 0-691-01681-X (pbk. : alk. paper)
1. Post-communism—Europe, Eastern.   2. Rule of law—Europe,
Eastern.   3. Reparation—Europe, Eastern.   4. Political crimes
and offenses—Europe, Eastern.   5. Retribution.   6. Social
justice—Europe, Eastern.   7. Europe, Eastern—Social policy.
8. Europe, Eastern—Politics and government—1989–
I. Title. II. Series.
HN380.7.A8B67 1997
306.2'0947—dc21   97-12041   CIP

This book has been composed in Palatino

Princeton University Press books are printed
on acid-free paper and meet the guidelines
for permanence and durability of the Committee
on Production Guidelines for Book Longevity
of the Council on Library Resources

http://pup.princeton.edu

Printed in the United States of America

1 3 5 7 9 10 8 6 4 2

1 3 5 7 9 10 8 6 4 2
(pbk.)

Contents

I BEGAN the research for *Settling Accounts* on a trip to Berlin in March 1990. Funded by the German Marshall Fund, I went as an anthropologist to observe the first free, multiparty elections in East Germany since 1946. I had just finished a study of everyday life during the Cold War in the divided Berlin, and I was a few months away from completing a book about Germany's first steps toward national unification. In my search for the key issues in the radical transformations of culture, society, and politics, I was struck by public demands, often bordering on hysteria, for justice. These demands ranged from requests for rehabilitation of one's name or reputation to calls for the prosecution of members of the old elite. Initially they had little to do with fights over the return or redistribution of property, which has since occupied the attention of so many intellectuals. Much public attention was focused on what legal theorists call "moral injuries"—deeds, like attempted murder, that did not result in actual harm but were nonetheless wrong. People seemed united that the "actually existing socialist" regimes were illegitimate and that their elites had behaved unethically, if not criminally. In this transformative moment, the burning issues in public discourse, not only in East Germany but throughout much of East-Central Europe, became: how and for what should people be held accountable, and how could past wrongs be set right? It appeared that the immediate legitimacy of the new postsocialist states of the former East bloc rested largely on formulating adequate responses to what all agreed were intractable problems of rectifying perceived injustice under the old regimes. Most of this book is devoted to evaluating the performance of these new states in reckoning with their criminal pasts in the first five years after the revolutionary change of regimes. This reckoning has involved an attempt to invoke the principles of the rule of law.

Now, as I close this study, the relevance of the initial topic that interested me is no longer limited to the losers of the Cold War, to the former socialist regimes of East and Central Europe. From Western Europe to Latin America to Asia, even the regimes of the capitalist victors and their allies have been unsettled by demands for accountability and justice. An extraordinary anti-Mafia campaign continues to shake the foundations of postwar Italian political culture; Chilean and Argentinian officers responsible for terrorizing and killing political opponents have been tried and imprisoned; two past presidents of South Korea were recently convicted on charges of ordering a massacre. Although it is unlikely that many of these campaigns will result in convictions or imprisonment (or that general amnesties will be declared, as has already happened in Chile and Argentina), the performative effect of the state's effort should not be ignored. What began quite narrowly as a study of the transformation of East bloc socialist regimes now appears relevant outside the European context. Indeed, it is perhaps the beginning of a particular kind of History. We are witnessing a world movement for retributive justice: the conviction of wrongdoers and the restoration of the dignity of victims.

Unlike distributive justice, which is concerned with giving each his/her proper share, or corrective justice, which is intent on rectifying harms, retributive justice deals primarily with moral injuries, wrongs that frequently do not result in material injury or harm. In current usage, *retribution* has come to be associated solely with punishment for offenses, yet etymologically the meaning of the word includes rewarding for good deeds. Only in the course of the twentieth century has the meaning of retribution been reduced to a manifestation of revenge motives. Up until the late-nineteenth century, it has always been part of a settling of accounts that necessarily both punishes evil and rewards good.

The relevance of retributive justice in the contemporary context goes far beyond the fate of individual criminals and victims; its increasing importance is part of a global ritual purification of the center of political regimes that seek democratic legitimacy. Not all states, of course, seek democratic legitimacy, and those which fail, despite positive intentions, to achieve democratic political form will likely turn to dictatorial means of assuring their domination. For them, retributive justice will likely not be justice at all. But for those that do seek democratic legitimacy, only with this purification can the "rule of law" be successfully invoked. Only with an appeal to principles embodied in public "rule by law" instead of in personal "rule by men" can these new states in East-Central Europe establish democratic legitimacy. The invocation of the rule of law is not a one-shot injection of justice into former state socialist settings, a return of errant governments to political normality; regime purification is necessarily a periodic process.

To invoke the rule of law has always meant different things to different people. Some analysts see it as a set of procedures to protect individuals from arbitrary rule, while others view it as the progressive march of reason and rationality. The former tend to focus on human rights and political liberties, the latter on contract and property rights. Historically the two perspectives have been difficult to disentangle theoretically and empirically, partly because private property rights and political liberties coexist everywhere in a sometimes complementary, sometimes antagonistic relationship. The distinctive claims and interconnectedness of the two perspectives was illustrated again in 1989 in Tiananmen Square by Chinese demonstrators, who took the rule of law to mean political liberties and freedoms—whereas Deng Xiaoping and other members of the political elite saw it as the importation of foreign, Western individualism. Subsequently many of these demonstrators have reportedly become capitalists, joining the political elite in its progrowth economic goals. Yet in order to reach these economic goals, Western banks and lending institutions have forced the elite to enact, if only formally, contract law—hence invoking at least some basic tenets of the rule of law. The new legislation will undoubtedly have an effect on political liberties and on principles of accountability. Precisely what that effect will be remains to be seen.

This study emphasizes another, frequently neglected aspect of the rule of law: its principles of accountability, which, I maintain, are intrinsic to the legitimation of democratic states and theoretically prior to conceptions of human and property rights. In this, it deviates from most contemporary perspectives on the rule of law. I am, however, not alone in my focus on accountability. In literary criticism, for example, Derrida-inspired deconstruction has been concerned with locating the authority of representation. Hence it has focused largely on questions about "from where" one speaks or writes in order to hold authorities accountable for their representations. In the history of science, questions about medical ethics, the role of profits in drug research and use, and the regulation of biogenetic experiments have become central. What unites the humanities and social sciences today is a fundamental concern with renewing and reinvigorating principles of accountability in a fluid and decentered international order. I hope that such a focus will also become a central concern of legal and political studies.

My own views on law have changed considerably in the course of my research for this book. When I began, I thought it was presumptuous to assume that the discredited socialist states needed the rule of law in order to reestablish their legitimacy. To be sure, most of these states seemed to have lost their monopoly on the legitimate use of violence, but I remained unconvinced that invoking the rule of law would bring about a more peaceful public order. Moreover, the sudden attempt to install a new system of formal procedures and rules entailed a rejection of the entire system of socialist legality, not only of its rules but also frequently of the people representing and enforcing them *tout court*, without consideration of individual responsibility. In any case, most social theorists at that time were not talking about the rule of law and retributive justice but about constitutions, property rights, and the extension of Western markets into East-Central Europe. Their interest in the installation of specific institutional arrangements, I thought, would meet the same fate as other attempts to insert a global ideology, such as the fate of "development" in the Third World: it would fail, even measured by its own terms, but not without leaving permanent traces of an international property regime. Five years later, I have concluded that one must distinguish between the installation of institutional arrangements and invocation of the principles of the rule of law; this invocation is not only desirable but also a prerequisite for internal and external legitimacy.

I now think that this invocation is not only part of a global ideology that is spreading to the East bloc, but that the rule of law also consists of ritual performances such as trials for wrongdoers and public vindications. These performances are in fact transnational practices and processes, and they are intrinsic to maintaining the legitimacy of all states that claim democratic form. While the principles of the rule of law share with other jural types a function of ritual purification—establishing moral principles through the identification of wrongdoing and the righting of wrong—the rule of law has proven itself to be a superior set of such principles. Contrary to many pundits who claim that economic growth or acts of reconciliation alone will legitimate the transformed East bloc states or quell the violence that has accompanied the transitions, I conclude that failure to rectify past injustices will undermine the legitimacy of new states. I now think that democratic states require the reiteration of principles of accountability to reestablish themselves as moral authorities that can claim to represent entire communities.

Most anthropological studies of legal regimes closely follow the emic conceptions of those regimes (or of scholars or elites within them) and assume the autonomy of either folk or national legal categories and cultures. The little ethnographic research on law during the transformation of socialist legal regimes has also focused on specific conflicts within national legal cultures—assumed to be separate, holistic, and bounded—without adequately addressing the increasing internationality of all conflict and culture. I am arguing against extending such a cultural relativism, however well intentioned, to the analysis of legal systems, and seek instead an encounter between the empirical detail of how the principles of the rule of law work in specific places and what their claims are to universal validity.

Settling Accounts therefore presents itself as a blurred genre: part ethnography of ritual purification under the rule of law in the former East Germany, part history of a global legal transformation, part essay in comparative political-legal anthropology, part moral philosophy. In the dynamic circumstances of the current transformations in East-Central Europe, invocation of the principles of the rule of law is, I would think, a global chance for a more democratic, more accountable, and less violent world. Its success will depend on factors such as the cultural and historical particularities of power structures, the kinds of social groups emerging, and the range of interests considered expressible.

Some readers may be uncomfortable with my prescriptive conclusion, especially set out in the preface to a book. They may remain skeptical, even after reading this book—and I think they should, for my prescriptions may prove wrong. Rectifying injustice is a continuous process and will remain an *aporia*, an insoluble problem. And perhaps I am overly optimistic in assuming that within the principles of accountability political liberties might counterbalance the corrosive power of property rights. But I am not satisfied with a response that merely describes conditions of injustice in order to maintain the proper ironic and relativistic stance to categories of wrongdoing. It is my conviction that since we as scientists are engaged not only in describing our objects but also in constituting them, we are obligated to engage in this more self-consciously—especially if we might thereby help to mitigate conditions that produce violence. This is best done, I believe, not by proposing a normative and universal theory of justice that begins with ideal conditions but instead by maintaining a dialogue between the propagation of certain norms and the reconstruction of actual and diverse conditions. That said, my intent here is not to minimize the significance of the many other factors influencing the production of violence; but for reasons of parsimony, I will be focusing solely on jural process.

Chapter 1 frames the methodological, interpretive, and disciplinary issues presented by the replacement of socialist legality with the principles of the rule of law; it argues for a theory of democratic accountability that is predicated on retributive justice and the rule of law. Chapter 2 suggests how one might engage in a comparative sociology of regime transformations in East-Central Europe; it attempts what I call "a skeptical description" of legal and governmental reforms in four states between 1989 and 1993. Chapter 3 seeks to historicize the legal transformations by placing them in the context of the development of Western legal traditions and of its most recent bifurcation into the two Germanys during the Cold War. Chapter 4 engages in a detailed analysis of the invocation of the rule of law in East Germany, with a focus on the creation of a domain of criminality called *governmental and unification criminality*. Chapter 5 examines the issue of accountability through the prism of a single extortion trial, that of Professor Wolfgang Vogel. Chapter 6 analyzes the efficacy of such trials in terms of the theory of democratic accountability outlined in chapter 2. Chapter 7 examines retributive justice from the perspective of the victim, focusing on the work of a Commission of Vindication. Chapter 8 makes a final comparison of regime transformations and democratic accountability in eight East-Central European states. Unless otherwise indicated, all translations from foreign languages are mine.

Acknowledgments

OVER the last five years, many individuals and institutions have provided support for the research that went into this book. Foremost, I wish to thank the National Council on Soviet and East European Research for major travel and research support from 1992 to 1994, and the Fulbright Foundation for a research/teaching grant in Berlin in 1994–95. Also, I am grateful for support from the Wenner-Gren Foundation, an American Council of Learned Scholars and German Academic Exchange Service grant for German-American cooperation, a MacArthur Foundation grant to Cornell University's Peace Studies Program, Cornell University's Institute for European Studies, and the German Marshall Fund. Among the people I wish to thank, most of all I am indebted to Stefan Senders for discussions, criticisms, and help in preparing the manuscript, to Jack Skarbinski for research assistance, to Michael Weck for discussions and research assistance, and to Professor Ilona Stolpe, who provided me with indispensable support and criticism in all aspects of the research. I am also grateful for the opportunity to present parts of this material in talks at Stockholm University, the University of Bergen, the University of Oslo, the University of Copenhagen, the Queen's University of Belfast, the University of Hannover, the University of Texas at Austin, Cornell University, the University of Texas at Austin, the University of Michigan, and Humboldt University in Berlin. Last, my debts to all those jural and political officials in Germany for interviews and materials are too numerous to list, as are those to friends in Berlin who listened to my ramblings and answered my questions. I thank them all.

Part One

FRAMING, COMPARING, HISTORICIZING

CHAPTER 1

Framing the Rule of Law in East-Central Europe

ACCOUNTABILITY AND RETRIBUTIVE JUSTICE

In theory, democratic form distinguishes itself from all other political forms in one major respect: its leaders are accountable to the public over which they rule. By contrast, in other political forms such as monarchies and dictatorships, leaders are held accountable to no one but themselves. The principles of German *Rechtsstaatlichkeit*, or in English the "rule of law," represent an attempt to institutionalize this theory of accountability. These principles, elaborated over the last nine centuries, are not formally dependent on the democratic form alongside which they developed; they can coexist with other forms of political representation. However, principles of accountability are necessary to a democracy in a way they are not to other political forms. These principles make transparent and predictable the relation of the sovereign to the ruled, a process fundamental to all democracies. They include such axioms of government as separation of powers, the principle of legality, the demand that statute law find general application, the prohibition of excesses of state authority, assurances for an independent judiciary, and a ban on retroactive legislation (see chap. 3). They set forth the minimal conditions necessary to secure the democratic state's monopoly on the legitimate use of violence. In the following, I will be arguing that democratic legitimacy depends above all on a system of political and personal accountability that is institutionalized in the principles of the rule of law.

The opening of the Berlin Wall on November 9, 1989, was part of a chain reaction, and by no means the original link, wherein the entire system of political communities of "actually existing socialist states" in East-Central Europe, colloquially called the "East bloc," collapsed. It has been followed, at least formally, by the invocation of the rule of law, or the German *Rechtsstaat* tradition, that characterizes Western Europe. Although jural reform has varied from state to state in scope, intensity, and duration, everywhere it is seen as more than a parochial or national event. Indeed, the current restructuring is part of a larger, transcontinental process of transformation that is redefining the nature of all political communities, creating new rules for accountability and membership as well as new categories of victims and criminals. Some commentators, such as Bernard Schlink (1994: 433–37), liken this process to a period of "revolutionary justice" following the end of the Cold War international order (cf. Blumenwitz 1992; Lüderssen 1992).

Among the most controversial aspects of this restructuring are the trials and criminalizations of former political elites in East-Central Europe. In many ways, they are comparable to the Nuremberg trials following World War II. At Nuremberg and in other war trials, thousands of individuals were tried and convicted, hundreds executed. At the time, the trials were considered of dubious legality and were conducted without precedent. The usual interpretation given to the legacy of Nuremberg has been that the trials set a precedent for the extension of human rights (cf. Janis 1993: 241–72). But today the Nuremberg trials stand out in another respect: as landmark legal processes of world historical significance in holding governmental officials accountable for wrongdoing.

Prior to these trials, a ruling elite's violation of community norms to an unbearable degree usually resulted in either their exile or death, frequently without any pretense to a fair trial. The Nuremberg prosecutions were a historical novelty, an attempt to judge lawmakers and other responsible individuals by mostly noncodified but implicitly agreed upon international legal norms of human rights. They relied on theories of "natural law" that posit a distinction between "the law" and "morality"—with morality being superior to and the legitimation for law and legal order. Although such theories have always been integral to Western legal systems, most jurists in the postwar period, especially those working in the West German Rechtsstaat tradition, have followed a theory of "legal positivism" that equates law with what is right.[1] "What was *Recht* [law/right] yesterday cannot be *Unrecht* [illegal/wrong] today" became the positivist-inspired, postwar dictum repeated in self-defense by judges and politicians who were accomplices in Nazi criminality. Such a reliance on positivism has made it extremely difficult to locate criminality in the political center of any regime where the laws—the right—is legislated. Many of the problems encountered by judges and prosecutors in coming to terms with the German Democratic Republic's (GDR's) past are directly related to the understandable difficulties postwar jurists encounter when they try to reckon adequately with the wrongs committed during the Third Reich.

Largely because postwar democracies have tended to rely on legal positivism, they also have tended to displace criminality from the center to the margins, away from political leaders to border regions and provincial actors. Or they redefine the border regions and margins, in turn, as those areas that include whatever is considered criminal. Hence, it was not uncommon (and not without some truth) that Germans after the war repeated the slogan "The little guy hangs, the big ones go free." Nuremberg was the first major exception to this displacement of accountability, but it has been followed by other "exceptions"—for example, the Watergate impeachment process and trials in the U.S. in the early 1970s, the anti-Mafia campaign in Italy that began in 1992, and, finally, the continued indictment of political leaders throughout much of Western Europe. As well, the international tribunals set up by the United Nations to prosecute the architects of genocide in Bosnia and Rwanda follow the Nuremberg precedent. The trend, moreover, has not been limited to Europe and Africa: In 1995 and 1996, anticorruption campaigns took their toll on high officials in China, two former heads of state were convicted for rights violations in South Korea, and public passion in Argentina reached a peak in the demand for an accounting by officials responsible for the disappearance of more than nine thousand people between 1976 and 1983. In each case, criminality is traced to the heart of government and authority itself. Such a process of bringing criminality home, so to speak, of locating crime in and not outside of government, could have enduring consequences for international legal regimes and for legal process in different democracies. To locate criminality in the center is to suggest that responsibility and accountability must be situated there also. Resistance to such attempts is massive, but the potentially enduring lessons of this attempt for the world's ruling elites cannot be underestimated. Seven years after the revolutionary change of regimes in East-Central Europe, how might we evaluate the performance of the new states in reckoning with their criminal pasts and the rectification of injustices?

First, we must note an apparent paradox. Where there has been little or no attempt to prosecute former authorities for wrongdoing in East bloc states, these societies have been marked by a cycle of violence and counterviolence, motivated by revenge and supported by some of the old elite, who have frequently resumed power under a nationalist platform. Surely, this violence is directly linked to the trauma of the communist epoch as well as to the revolution directed against its aborted utopia. Certainly, the memories of unaddressed wrongs from the the two world wars are also significant factors in some countries. By contrast, in those states where there have been successful prosecutions of former authorities for wrongdoing, the trials have frequently provoked sympathy for the convicted and scorn for the original victim's moral claims. Moreover, where such trials have occurred, the people's initial passion for retributive justice appears to have substantially subsided, if not altogether disappeared. Many analysts make the perverse claim that such prosecutions actually delegitimate new states. It does seem as if in all of the former socialist states, including East Germany, the possibility for a criminalization of the old elite and retributive justice, for jural reform generally, existed for a period of only several years after the regime change. Yet, in most of the new states where some retributive justice has been pursued, the potential for violence seems to have been peacefully, if precariously and perhaps only temporarily, dampened or diverted. On the other hand, the states with the most violence are those where there was no attempt at retributive justice.

The question is: What does a relative failure to continue public prosecution of criminality undertaken by the old regime and public indifference to the fate of past victims mean? In what context should it be interpreted? Is it because people are more fundamentally concerned with wealth and prosperity (problems associated with the economy) than with justice and morality (problems associated with legal security)? Does this indicate, as Stephen Holmes of the University of Chicago (1994: 33–36) and the Polish scholar Wiktor Osiatynski (1994: 36–41) concluded, a desire to close "the books on the crimes of the past"? Are we to evaluate, along with Osiatynski (36), "the failure of decommunization and resistance to the retributive phase of the revolution—with its predictable violence, injustice, and destructiveness— . . . [as] one of the most important successes of the postcommunist transformation"?

This book is a sustained argument in another direction. It contends both that a successful reckoning with the criminal past obligates the state to seek retributive justice and that a failure to pursue retributive justice will likely lead to cycles of retributive violence. For historical reasons, many languages do not allow the clear distinction that I am making here between retribution and retaliation. In Germany, for example, since the end of World War I, *Vergeltungsjustiz*, a term narrowly associated with revenge, retaliation, and victor's justice, would be the most likely translation of retributive justice. Yet *ausgleichende Gerechtigkeit* is also within the semantic reach of Vergeltung, and this concept points toward fairness as a form of justice, to be attained through a rebalancing such as requital, expiation, or repayment. The difficulty in finding a translatable word for "righting a wrong" whose semantics has not been fixed or polemicized by an unjust political experience indicates the fundamental significance of the problem that I am addressing.

Legal theorists, following Aristotle, usually divide justice into two types: distributive and corrective. Clearly, what I am dealing with here is not distributive justice; the wrongs cannot be righted by dividing up the pie, by dealing each person his/her proper share. As well, retributive justice should not to be confused with corrective justice, a distinction Jean Hampton (1992: 1701), philosopher at the University of Arizona, has clarified. Corrective justice is concerned to "compensate victims for harms," meaning that a jural authority acts only when an actual injury or harm is suffered by a particular person, who is then identified as the victim deserving of remedy.[2] This remedy is corrective justice: it corrects the injury by compensating the victim for the harm suffered. By contrast, retributive justice seeks to "compensate victims for moral injuries." A moral injury is an agreed-upon wrong but need not necessarily result in a specific harm. The immorality of the deed lies not in the degree of harm suffered by the victim but in the wrongness of the deed itself. Attempted murder, for example, results in no harm but is nonetheless a wrong or a moral injury. In the case of a moral injury, the jural system focuses not on correcting a harm but on righting a wrong. It holds the wrongdoer accountable, and by righting the wrong reestablishes the dignity of victims. Such victims can be groups or individuals (insofar as they exist and can be identified or created), or they can be the entire moral community that has been injured.

In contrast to the dominant scholarly opinion among criminal justice experts, I argue that the two conditions—righting the wrong and reestablishing the dignity of the victim—are linked, and that both are necessary to prevent cycles of retributive violence. In former socialist states where there has been no retributive justice, however, one can witness and even predict cycles of retributive violence. My concern here is to determine under what conditions it is possible to stop long-term cycles of violence, which, as history shows, are always latent in any group. If the principles of the rule of law are not invoked and ritually reaffirmed, a society will be confronted with a potentially endless cycle of violent retaliations.

Although retribution is "neither the exclusive, nor perhaps even the primary, responsibility of the state . . . , [the state is] an impartial moral agent of the entire community. [It has] greater capacity to recognize the moral facts than any involved individual citizen" (Hampton 1992: 1693). Therefore, if the state wants to establish itself as a moral agent with legitimacy in the entire community, it has an obligation to pursue retribution where wrongdoing has occurred. In this chapter, I begin a comparisons of regimes and their jural restructurings, which will be developed more fully in the final chapter, and I examine political theory and its relation to jural restructuring. I then look at these cases in terms of an anthropology of law, and finally, I suggest a theory that can account for the different effects of jural restructurings in East-Central Europe.

COMPARISON OF REGIME TRANSFORMATIONS

The jural restructurings in East-Central Europe can be divided into three basic types of transformations: radical regime change and some retributive justice, little regime change and little retributive justice, radical regime change and extensive retributive justice. A first type is where the legal regime has changed abruptly yet smoothly, with some restitution for victims of the old regime but little or no reckoning with wrongdoing committed in the past—this has been the case in Slovenia, Poland, and Hungary, and to a large degree in the Czech Republic, though there for different reasons. In Slovenia, Poland, and Hungary the regimes themselves initiated reform that enabled the participation of the opposition, making it difficult if not impossible to purge or prosecute former officials or public employees, or to review judges for past misdeeds. One of the first acts of the newly installed Slovenian government in March 1990 was to stage a public ceremony where it apologized for past violations. In contradistinction to the other republics in the former Yugoslavia, its demands for self-determination were accompanied by the systematic enactment of legislation formulated to protect minority rights according to Parliament of Europe norms (Minnich 1993: 91). In Poland, there has been to date only one prosecution and trial, for the murder of a priest. In Hungary, there were several prosecutions of individuals responsible for putting down the 1956 revolution, no imprisonments, and no trials against officials for actions committed after 1956.

In the former Czechoslovakia, President Václav Havel sought to prevent such a reckoning, arguing instead for a form of collective guilt: since all Czechs were complicitous, singling out any individuals for punishment would be unfair and unproductive. Thus government form initially changed while personnel, except at the very top, remained substantially the same. Judicial personnel were screened for secret police complicity, resulting in about 10 percent of the judges leaving service, with a smaller number of state prosecutors demoted but not fired. Individuals working in state agencies have also been vetted, but the severest penalty has been demotion to a lesser position of authority; many of these cases have been appealed and most individuals reinstated. After 1992, the split between the Czech and Slovak republics distracted attention from internal cleansing, as wrongdoing was displaced onto an exteriorized other. In 1994 and 1995, however, Czech prosecutors made additional indictments and completed some trials.

A second type of transformation, where regime change, especially in the legal domain, has been more apparent than substantive, where there has been minimal recognition of victims and very little or no prosecution of wrongdoers, has taken place in Serbia, Croatia, Romania, and Russia, and perhaps all of the former Soviet Republics except the Baltic states. Yugoslavia disintegrated into a genocidal war, centered in Bosnia, victimizing most of the population in an attempt to create ethnically homogeneous territorial and political units modeled after Croat and Serb ethnicities. In Romania, the Ceaucescu couple were executed, their son put in jail, and the remaining members of the Politburo given sentences from fifteen to twenty years for a planned "genocide," as it was called, referring to the final Politburo meeting where plans were made to squash the demonstrations in the fall of 1989. These acts of revolutionary justice against a small elite served as a substitute for any further cleansing; the same government, state security, and public officials serve as before. In Russia, a new political class has arisen to compete with the old *nomenklatura*, but there has been no dismissal of judges or state prosecutors and no purge of officials. The Communist Party was declared illegal, but that act served, as in Romania, as a substitute victim, an alibi to prevent or delay further recriminations against persons or structures actually responsible for past wrongs.

A third type of transformation characterizes the Baltic states—Bulgaria, Albania, and Germany. In these states, there has been radical regime change, substantial compensation to former victims, and extensive prosecution of the old elite. In Bulgaria, several top government officials were put on trial, including three former prime ministers, who all went to prison. In the spring and summer of 1992, there was a widespread purge of former party officials from the civil service and academic institutions and the vetting of thousands of others (Smollett 1993: 13). As elsewhere in the East bloc, this reckoning stopped abruptly when former communists, now nationalists and private property owners, returned to power. In Albania, a number of former high officials and symbolically prominent persons, such as Nexhmije Hoxha, the wife of the former dictator, were arrested and tried in a relatively late wave of trials in 1993 and 1994. And in a new labor reform, the government dismissed tens of thousands of people. Initially these trials and dismissals were widely interpreted through local idioms: as acts of personal revenge or ways of demobilizing lawful opposition, rather than as attempts to rectify past harms (Imholz 1995: 54–60). Given Albanian isolation from the international legal regime during the Cold War, such interpretations were to be expected. The majority of Germans after World War II held similar opinions of the Nuremberg trials and began revising their judgments only fifteen years after the actual event. Hence for Albanians, this historical reckoning might form the basis for future reinterpretations of the transfomation. Jural reforms in the Baltic states differ from state to state, and they continue to be in a state of flux because they have been intricately tied to an ongoing separation from the Soviet Union and from internal ethnic Russian (among other) "minorities." But all three Baltic states have engaged in substantial retributive justice. The German transition has involved a reckoning with the past surpassing those of other states in scope and scale. I devote the middle chapters of this book to Germany and then return to a comparison with other regimes in the final chapter. Before going into the German reforms, let me detour to discuss possible frameworks for understanding these jural transformations.

JUSTICE AND POLITICAL THEORY

At least since the eighteenth century, the Enlightenment ideals of universal rationality, individual freedom and choice, and continuous progress have been central to the development of European legal systems and international law. As we approach the end of the twentieth century, many intellectuals have questioned the viability and universal validity of these ideals (see Judt 1994: 1–20). The principles of the rule of law have not escaped this general questioning of Enlightenment ideals. Most legal criticism, in particular by scholars working in Critical Legal Studies (Kennedy 1979; Trubek 1984; Unger 1983), has taken one of two paths. One criticism focuses on the hidden assumptions and categories within particular legal doctrines in order to make explicit their thematic commitments and persuasive authority. It often reproaches legal regimes for poor performance with respect to their own ideals, especially with regard to the class-based nature of jural administration. Along these lines, it can be argued that legal regimes of any type do not eliminate criminality but at most define, control, and direct crime into class- or race-based categories.

A second criticism analyzes the relation of principles and counterprinciples within specific legal domains in order to uncover and propose alternative visions and possibilities. Even after acknowledging the validity of these two critiques, we are left with no clear position on the possibility of prescriptive argument in law. And none of these scholars has proposed an alternative to the principles of the rule of law. Moreover, the argument of Critical Legal Studies tends to attribute violence within rule-of-law regimes not to the principles but to a lack of effective commitment to these principles and to their unintended effects as they operate in a world constituted by pernicious hierarchies. There remains widespread agreement that the rule of law, primarily along the model of the German Rechtsstaat, is a positive good that should be invoked not only in the former socialist states of Central and Eastern Europe but throughout the world. Indeed, it seems as if the rule of law is integral to the process of reestablishing legitimate authority, stability, and a system of international security in the post–Cold War order. At the same time, the rule of law is no perfect jural order; it always functions within political structures and therefore is never neutral or immune to power.

The thematic commitment of the rule of law is to a particular set of institutional and procedural guidelines, which in turn are premised on a set of moral principles for determining both the conditions under which individuals can be held accountable and the possibilities for punishment of wrongdoing. Whereas the legitimacy of nondemocratic forms of government does not depend on principles of responsibility and accountability, the legitimacy of a democratic polity does. Therefore a democratic polity needs as a minimal condition a commitment to the principles of the rule of law. Historically prior to and independent of democratic form, these principles remain a precondition for contemporary democracies. They assert that political leaders within democracies cannot put themselves above the laws even though they make them.

The new states of East-Central Europe, however, often assert democratic political form before the rule of law can be invoked. For them, it is not a question of merely renewing or reaffirming guidelines and principles of accountability, as it is today in post–World War II Western European democracies. Having developed over several centuries as part of Western European political and civil cultures, these principles are now being invoked in other contexts literally overnight. This new systemic transformation of what was called "socialist legality" is placing unusual theoretical and practical demands on the immediate performance of the rule of law, specifically on its ability to withstand democratic political manipulation. While this problem holds for all political regimes, it is particularly pronounced in the context of legitimation crises of the late twentieth century. The contemporary state lacks both the political-economic sovereignty and the monopoly on the legitimate use (and the means) of violence it arguably had in the first half of this century. Above all, the violence accompanying the moment of the rule of law's invocation threatens to undermine its promise of future justice. Trust in the procedures and principles of the rule of law has yet to be established, and without it there is no legitimacy. Without legitimate rule, insecurity tends to become institutionalized in patterned violence between states and between states and their residents.

Even if we grant the Enlightenment premise that the rule of a law is a superior set of procedural guarantees and techniques for addressing crime and punishment, this premise holds empirically only for Western Europe today. Only there has trust in the legal system been established, on the basis of which legal regimes and states are conferred legitimacy. The catch is that the same premise becomes a possibility for the varied polities of East-Central Europe only after trust in the principles has been established. But this trust will not initially develop out of an affirmation of the procedural guarantees alone, for these guarantees must first be invoked. Hence the claim made by Jürgen Habermas (1988: 277) in his Tanner Lectures on Human Rights, that the rule of law "draws its legitimacy from a rationality of legislative and judicial procedures guaranteeing impartiality," cannot be extended to the present context in East-Central Europe. By contrast, Foucault (1977) has criticized this pretext of impartiality, claiming that, as political authorities distance themselves from the responsibility for and machineries of violence through the institutionalization of rational procedures, these procedures tend to lead to more minute and indirect forms of practical domination. Along these lines, Michael Herzfeld (1992: 156) argues that the modern state's bureaucracy is fundamentally involved in the "production of indifference," a process wherein "the state itself becomes a massive machine for the evasion of responsibility, while arguing that people should 'pay' for their crimes." Differences notwithstanding, all three writers share in common a concern for the difficulty inherent in turning the principles of accountability into actual practices.

A way out of this tangle, at least theoretically, may be to follow Judith Shklar, who in *The Faces of Injustice* shifts the focus by arguing that the core question of legitimacy addressed by jural systems is not impartiality per se but a specific kind of moral response to perceived injustice. In other words, a jural system's validity does not rest primarily on its neutrality or objectivity (though I do not mean to minimize the significance of the perception of objectivity), but on the appropriateness of the response to the violation in question. What specific kind of moral response to perceived injustice is called for? The perception of injustice, writes Shklar (1990: 89), is "the one natural core of our morality. It is our most basic claim to dignity." Because injustice is an enduring feature of human life, the appropriate response is to address this "natural core" of morality by reaffirming our "most basic claim to dignity." Hence "dignity" is not something about which the modern state can remain neutral if it is to establish itself as the ultimate arbiter in deciding what is right and wrong. Does this mean that the modern state must be partial in addressing crime?

The answer here is an unqualified yes. Regardless of how rational the modern state is in its legislation or impartial in its jural procedures, the state legitimates itself through a prior decision: where it locates criminality and accountability. That decision, of what kinds of injustices to recognize and whom to hold accountable, is far from a neutral or procedural one. It is a moral and political choice, and its correctness is measured by varied social criteria of appropriateness and dignity. Habermas is of course correct that democratically enacted laws ("rationality of legislative procedures") and procedural rules and technologies of justice ("rationality of . . . judicial procedures") are crucial for producing legitimate outcomes in legal processes. However, he is talking about the reaffirmation of principles in an already installed and institutionalized democratic Rechtsstaat, where there already exists a social consensus about the dignity of the person and about what constitutes crime. Habermas (1996) does complicate this view in his most recent work, insisting that "liberal virtue" will result from the interpenetration of legal form and a deliberative, democratic politics. But the kind of consensus about which he writes does not exist in most states in the world, and specifically not in the case of former socialist states. There, the legitimacy of the rule of law as both an ideology and practice rests less with its procedures, rules, and regulations than with the prior decision as to what makes a conflict adjudicable in the first place. And, without a "rationalized lifeworld" of the sort Habermas describes, what makes conflict adjudicable depends on the "perception of injustice," on establishing a "natural core of morality" based on some fundamental distinctions about rights and wrongs and what constitutes "human dignity." Moreover, since the definition of human dignity varies culturally and temporally, states will never arrive at a final set of distinctions for themselves nor at a final, universal moral order. Nor can they ever be fully confident that their order of laws corresponds exactly with moral order. Nonetheless, all states are constantly compelled to take sides and to strive continually to implement a moral world in which "the natural core of morality" is given precise definition.

When jural systems propose possible remedies for losses (whether harms or moral injuries), they give both specific definitions to wrongs and establish a principle of accountability for crime. The dual process of identifying legitimate victims and defining wrongdoing does more than settle conflicts; it also constitutes the political community as a moral community. It defines or reaffirms a particular vision of dignity—in Max Weber's words, the "values toward which associational conduct might be oriented" (1978: 902). A jural system, then, defines the proper moral response of the political community to the continuous problem of perceived injustice.

Weber and Durkheim offer us alternative, though by no means incompatible, insights into the relation of the political community to morality. A long list of political theorists, from Aristotle to Rousseau, from Adam Smith to Carl Schmitt, have argued that the political community is always first a moral community. Contrary to a narrowly economistic position, a common, or class-based, interest in economics is itself insufficient to form a political community. "Prosperity" is nowhere an absolute but always a relative value, meaning that it alone cannot serve as a social glue. For some people, however, economics may become the domain accorded the highest moral value, so that identification with the accumulation of private property becomes one of or even the core of human dignity. Many prewar East-Central European owners whose property was expropriated after 1945 have made such a claim. Property rights, they argue, are at the core of their human dignity. This line of argument has been extremely divisive within former socialist states; nowhere has it served to unite the people (cf. Verdery 1996). Contrariwise, the precondition for a political community as such, Weber insists, is a "value system ordering matters other than the directly economic disposition of goods and services." In addition to a "territory" and to "the availability of physical force for its domination," the "political," he continues, is constituted by "values toward which associational conduct might be oriented" (1978: 902). But from where do the values come that determine with whom one is to associate?

Durkheim asked this question, and his answer was: religion and the sacred. Everything emanates from religion and returns to it—especially in periods of intense social conflict. The heart of religion, according to Durkheim, is performative ritual in which all oppositions are reconciled and the group, if not fully united, at least reaches a provisional consensus. In this act of group unification, sacrality is established and differences are lost, effaced, or eliminated. Durkheim's insight must be amended in two ways: first, this loss of difference is never total, and therefore unity is always partial; second, even when in the service of harmony, the elimination of difference is necessarily violent, and all acts of violence are potentially contagious; they have the potential to lead to cycles of escalating violence. To avoid this contagion, the violence must either be displaced or concealed. The rule of law as part of the democratic nation-state is a response to this particular human aporia; it both appropriates violence for itself as the moral authority responsible for maintaining the conditions necessary for "peaceful conflict resolution," and it displaces or conceals that initial and continuous violent appropriation. Herein rests the major challenge in the invocation of the rule of law, for, as Derrida (1992: 10) has argued, law "cannot become justice legitimately . . . except by withholding force or rather by appealing to force from its first moment."

Before I continue along these lines, let me first deal with another argument of Weber's, for which he is perhaps better known, one that leads away from Durkheim. Weber viewed the development of the rule of law since the sixteenth century as a prime example of the increasing rationalization of the Western world, a movement from religious to secular practices, with concern for predictability and calculability, systematization through writing, more professional and standardized judicial recruitment, more consistent and impartial application of the law. In short, an increase in "formal rationality." Hence Weber (1978: 976–78) consistently contrasts the modern law with *Kadi-justice*, the arbitrariness or informality associated with either patrimonial or traditional authority. When the rule of law is promoted today as a superior form of jural organization, as Habermas does in the text cited above, it is with a focus on Weber's description of rationality and secularization. Weber, however, placed his theory of rationalization in a wider framework of ideology or orienting values. If we follow his lead there, the Rechtsstaat has to be understood not only in terms of progressive "formal rationality," but also in terms of the ethical values motivating it, the "substantive rationality" of Christian "inner-worldly aestheticism." This aestheticism generated institutions whose goal was to transform the world, and it supported processes whereby theological doctrines became effective social controls. The zealous and self-denying daily activities that Weber observed in the economic life of Protestants can also be taken to describe the twofold response of the Rechtsstaat mentioned above: its active appropriation of violence (in order to transform) and displacement/concealment of violence (in order to control).

Weber's formal definition of the state as the institution having a "monopoly on the legitimate use of violence" needs to be broken down into two additional questions: How does this monopoly come about? How is this monopoly maintained so as to legitimate itself? Both of these questions return us again to the Durkheimian theorization of how group unity is achieved—to ritual performance. For a state can legitimately use force, or legitimately dominate in the more general Weberian sense, only when its violence is sanctioned by a group ethos that the state purports to represent, and when that group submits to the state's representation of itself. Such an ethos is the concern of ritual—for example, elections, trials, ceremonies—where issues of unity and cohesion are performed and "resolved." Thus how groups unify and maintain unity is a question that must always precede and accompany that of how they are administered (an issue of rationality). My focus in this monograph will be on law not as a set of rules, procedures, and technical devices for getting things done, a rational choice game whose rules can be perfected (which, considering law's shortcomings in getting things done, can hardly be the criterion for its status as universal ideology), but as a set of ritual practices performed in the belief that the performance itself will establish what is right. Such a secular morality rests on a symbolic core, and it is part of a modern ideology of social unity and state legitimacy.

From this perspective, the entire history of Western law is rooted not in reason serving reason, as one Hegelian school might suggest, but in reason serving the deepest emotions of the people. In his history of the Western legal tradition, Berman locates these emotions in "the fear of purgatory and the hope of the Last Judgment" (1983: 558). Theoretically, secular verdicts are homologous to religious last judgments; both are "final" truths as opposed to an eternal situation of moral ambiguity. Verdicts are, in a sense, much like purgatory, a particular displaced response to the trauma of evil. They are an expiation for wrongdoing, an assignation for and relief from guilt. To be effective, the response to perceived injustice need not, however, present itself as a final closing of the books—surely an illusionary view derived from a belief in the end of history. Regardless of how one deals with crime, wrongdoing and injustice will continue. Instead, the rule of law establishes hope that there is a process toward a continuous Last Judgment, and this process entails establishing this-worldly accountability, a moral authority that can stop the individual vendetta or revenge killing. When socialist states dissolved, socialist normative systems went with them. What followed was an agonistic period of tremendous ambiguity about judgment and guilt, a delegitimation of legal systems with a corresponding increase in criminality at every level of the society. At stake in the invocation of the rule of law in former socialist states is the possibility for the establishment of legitimate moral judgments valid for the entire community. These moral judgments are political decisions, they involve violence, and they either displace or conceal that initial moment of violence.

THE STUDY OF LEGAL REFORM AND ANTHROPOLOGY

What does an anthropology of law have to say about the jural transformations in East-Central Europe? Traditionally, anthropologists of law have worked within an evolutionary model that posits two kinds of societies: those with and those without a state. Moreover, most have viewed the state as a foreign and unfriendly transplant onto a native population that had its own "customary law" to regulate social conflict or, according to some theorists, had no law at all. The nonstate communities were, in Lévi-Strauss's well-known formulation, "cold societies," while the state communities were "hot societies," meaning dynamic and historically changing. Most ethnographic study of law has dealt with what were classified as pre-state jural systems and the nonsystematic transformation of customary law or its integration into state systems. Two seemingly opposed scholarly traditions have informed this work. On the one hand, inspired by the foundational work of Lewis Henry Morgan and Sir Henry Maine, anthropologists saw law in a developmental sequence, as part of the social evolution of human groups and institutions. On the other hand, British functionalists were wary of any sort of historicism and therefore embraced the cold society perspective, turning toward synchronic, functionalist interpretations. Bronislaw Malinowski's concern with law as social control and A. R. Radcliffe-Brown's concern with the rules of dispute settlement were the pioneering studies of the functionalist school. Both evolutionists and functionalists viewed jural systems through the same model of a "society": legal systems were a set of enclosed, hermetically self-contained, rule-governed thought systems. Both also viewed jural systems as dividing into distinct types that were either premodern or modern. The American culturalist tradition inspired by Franz Boas did not substantially modify this framework.[3] Not until Max Gluckman's work in the 1950s on the influence of the colonial state on customary law in Africa did the research questions substantially change.

Those anthropologists who studied legal systems within state structures most often carried with them the ahistorical, functionalist assumptions about reproduction and continuity over time, about spatial closure, that had been held in the study of jural systems among peoples without states. This kind of academic consensus accorded well with the commonsense assumptions of politicians and state administrators, whose continuous production of formal rules was legitimated by the theoretical argument that legal systems were part of an evolutionary continuum, properly demarcated spatially (by national geographic maps; cf. Gellner 1983) and temporally (by an assumption of their own autopoetic functioning systematicity; Luhmann 1985).[4] In the 1970s, the focus shifted, following Gluckman (1965a, 1965b), to disputing processes. While questioning much legal dogma (such as the impartiality of judges or dispute settlers, the class-based nature of justice), these studies also tended toward an involution by working within self-understood folk or national legal frameworks. If legal systems existed either outside of time or in their own time bubbles, and in well-demarcated spaces, then the mix of legal systems was always theorized as a fight for dominance between two separate, reified entities, between custom and law, stateless and state, cold and hot, traditional and colonial systems. By the 1980s, anthropologists generally no longer assumed that colonial law simply replaced or would replace customary law, since they had too frequently observed the opposite trend: a reinvented indigenous law reasserting itself over national law in historically and culturally specific ways. Even within this relation between the national and the indigenous, however, it was supposed that the new law could be understood as part of the new cultural system, and this culture was that which had already established itself, or would soon, as an enclosed, systemic, rule-governed, moral order. By 1989, Starr and Collier (1), in summarizing new directions in the field, proposed that anthropologists make "asymmetrical power relations and world historical time essential to their analysis."

East-Central European legal transformations present us with a new set of problems and comparisons that few disciplines, let alone legal anthropology, are prepared to describe and explain. The problems encountered in the (re)invocation of legal principles assumed to have been either dormant or rejected, but in any case not totally foreign, have not yet been adequately theorized. What we do know from legal anthropology is that no homogeneous, global jural system will result from this invocation. Each appropriation of the principles of the rule of law will involve a different kind of local invocation, yet all such democratic states are interrelated. Most often, the success of one state depends on the success of others with which it has the most contact. My own analysis owes a great deal to Sally Falk Moore (1978, 1986), whose work has focused on the creation of asymmetries in sequential time. Rather than understand legal systems in terms of a functionalist model of separate cultural systems, Moore emphasizes the temporality of law in its formulation, implementation, and effects. From this perspective, the political and economic context is not exterior to the law but itself part of a cultural form to which law gives a certain expression. It follows that the distinction between inside and outside—native and foreign, colonial law and custom, national and international—is an effect of the process by which asymmetries are created, not prior to and fixed before conflict appears in legal form.

Applied to the jural reform in East-Central Europe, then, the Rechtsstaat's installation is not external or foreign to "socialist law," nor is it an enclosed system of rules and procedures that former socialist states adopt in a fixed form—even though the case can be made that this happened *formally* with the unification of the two Germanies. The assumptions that the Rechtsstaat was foreign to former socialist states is invariable in form are effects of Cold War representations. They are products of a regime of knowledge that organized the world into Eastern European "area studies" and Western European "national histories" (see Geyer 1989: 316–42). In practice, the principles of the rule of law were constantly used as utopic or dystopic measures—to conform to or deviate from—by legal practitioners in socialist and capitalist states. It is more accurate to understand the possibilities for the rule of law today not as the importation of foreign principles but as having always been present in former socialist states, though often transfigured, perverted, or abjected.

This is not an argument for *legal pluralism*, a descriptive term opposed to *legal centralism*. That term came into common use during the 1970s and has since been embraced by a wide range of critical theorists, postmodernists, feminists, systems theorists, and legal anthropologists (e.g., Merry 1993, 1990; Yngvesson and Harrington 1990). It widened the area of the social world marked out by state law to include, in its most expansive expression by the systems theorist Niklas Luhmann (1985: 1), all of the rules that shape directly or indirectly "all collective human life." It also marked a conscious attempt to recover previously marginalized spheres of reglementation and to give voice to individuals or groups ordinarily excluded from legal discourse. What motivates the pluralists to subsume all rules into law is, I suspect, a desire to democratize law by adding more voices to the choir. But while democracies require the rule of law, the reverse is not true; law does not require democratization. Though law necessarily involves participation, the validity of its principles are not dependent on either majoritarian ideals or the extent of participation. Ideally, law holds the community up to the highest moral standards available. Its function is not democracy but justice or fairness, which necessitates an entirely different relation to plurality.

A second and related problem with legal pluralism is a confusion of the level at which plurality is identified. Certainly, in the domain of legal practice—legal content, mechanisms, norms, procedures, local understandings—plurality in East-Central Europe exists. However, my concern is with the principles of the rule of law that regulate such plurality. I propose not a conceptual enlargement of the legal domain—the pluralization or homogenization of normative orders—but a specification of what constitutes a proper state law. The perspective of this study, then, also assumes that the new invocation of the rule of law is not merely a set of independent national projects but also part of a global process in the formation of interconnected political communities following the end of the Cold War.

VIOLENCE, ACCOUNTABILITY, DIGNITY

Several other concerns that have been central to anthropology can also help to frame these jural restructurings. Here I will demonstrate one link between the regulation of violence as it relates to a principle of accountability and to the role of the victim's dignity. Let us begin with a discussion of rituals of sacrifice and their relation to judicial systems and state legitimation.

Perhaps the most ambitious attempt to theorize the relation of violence to justice is that of René Girard. He makes a distinction between societies that practice sacrifice and those that invoke the rule of law. The former societies, which have been most intensively studied by anthropologists and on which Girard (1977: 120) concentrates, practice ritual sacrifice of substitute victims. "The king's sovereignty—real or imagined, permanent or temporary—seems to derive from an original, generative act of violence inflicted on a surrogate victim." This generative act is repeated in ritual, is reenacted especially "when the fear of falling into interminable violence is most intense" (120). A spirit of revenge animates the victim, whose desire to spill the blood of the perpetrator threatens to turn into an interminable process of vendettas and blood feuds that could infect the whole social body, setting "off a chain reaction whose consequences will quickly prove fatal to any society of modest size" (15).

The "fundamental difference between primitive societies and our own," Girard (14) asserts, is that sacrifice is "a specific ailment to which we are immune." "For us," he continues, "the circle [of vengeance] has been broken. We owe our good fortune to one of our social institutions above all: our judicial system, which serves to deflect the menace of vengeance. The system does not suppress vengeance; rather, it effectively limits it to a single act of reprisal, enacted by a sovereign authority specializing in this particular function. The decisions of the judiciary are invariably presented as the final word on vengeance" (15). The private vengeance of the sacrifice is replaced by the public vengeance of the trial. In principle, private and public vengeance do not differ, "but on the social level, the difference is enormous. Under the public system, an act of vengeance is no longer avenged; the process is terminated, the danger of escalation averted" (15–16).

The modern judicial system, acting for the state as a sovereign and independent body, removes the possibility for reprisal from the hands of the victim and those near to him/her, "taking the place of the injured party and taking upon itself the responsibility for revenge" (17). Primitive societies, as he calls them, have elaborate "preventive measures," the most important of which is the concept of sacrifice, which, in turn, is embedded in religious practices. In such societies, "the rites of sacrifice serve to polarize the community's aggressive impulses and redirect them toward victims that may be actual or figurative, animate or inanimate, but that are always incapable of propagating further vengeance. The sacrificial process furnishes an outlet for those violent impulses that cannot be mastered by self-restraint. . . . The sacrificial process prevents the spread of violence by keeping vengeance in check" (18).

This framework has much to offer in explaining the current invocation of the rule of law in former socialist states. Let me propose several amendments to Girard's framework for the analysis of sacrifice, justice, and violence under the rule of law. First, Girard's analysis of violence in "primitive" societies rests on a psychology of innate aggression and revenge that is asserted and never proven. In the last several decades, theories of instinct-driven human behavior have been criticized precisely because they have been unable to locate the instinct. Even when one employs the less biological term *drives* and assumes one can identify them, one must grant their historical and cultural variability. As well, Girard's (Christian) evolutionary scheme, carried over from Hubert and Mauss (1964), which posits a "primitive precursor of the disinterested self-sacrifice of the deity" (Bloch 1992: 29)[5] has also been harshly critiqued (Detienne 1979). Indeed, when Girard (1977: 33) states that "Western civilization . . . has enjoyed until this day a mysterious immunity from the virulent forms of violence," one wonders where he has been living, for the most recent wave of genocides in the Balkans, as well as the Mafia murders in Italy, had many Western predecessors before he completed this book.

Rather than assume a universal human "instinct" of aggression that results in violence, we should give more weight to politically motivated violence and thereby to sociological explanations. It seems as if much of the 1990s' exteriorization and sacrifice of ethnic groups justified on quasi-religious grounds (for example, the Chechen by the Russians, the Bosnian Muslims by the Serbs) is primarily the result of instrumental decisions by political elites made in order to maintain power. Also, since the "group" for Girard is an undifferentiated, ahistorical whole, we cannot account for the choice of whom to sacrifice. His theory insists on a nearly random, indiscriminate victim for sacrifice. In the regime changes following 1989, the choices of sacrificial groups have been predictable and hardly random: most often gypsies, Jews, and perceived foreigners. As well, association with "communism" has served as a symbolic reservoir for pollution and therefore a target for purification. A sociologically informed explanation for sacrifice would make it unnecessary to hold to an (untenable) instinct of personal revenge to explain what motivates societies to construct jural systems for regulating violence. Rather, jural systems are a response to the group's search for a moral authority, and this authority is attained in part through retributive justice, by righting a wrong in such a way that the victim's dignity—always socially defined—is reestablished.

Girard notes that many societies, from the ancient Greeks to the South American Aztecs, to the African Dinka and Ndembu, to medieval Germanic groups, have practiced sacrifice as a purification rite. "The function of ritual," he writes, "is to 'purify' violence; that is, to 'trick' violence into spending itself on victims whose death will provoke no reprisals" (36). Here he seems to be arguing that sacrifice is not a response to revenge motives but a social scapegoating intended to redirect potential violence away from the actual perpetrator. Its function is to identify an individual to kill, symbolically or actually, in order to purify and unite the affected group, to absolve the group of any further responsibility to seek redress for the initial crime. At this very general level, one can identify two dimensions to the sacrificial process that hold for each of the new East-Central European regimes: (1) identifying possible culprits to hold accountable, who then are vetted for complicity with the secret police, tried for crimes, or simply vilified in media campaigns, and (2) assuaging injured parties through rehabilitation, compensatory payments, publication of their stories, or similar measures.

Hence, and this is my second point, modern judicial systems in democratic states are not immune from sacrificial rites, but instead, especially during this period of (re)invocation, they rely on sacrifices in order to fight corruption, open institutions to renewal, and assuage victims of the old regimes. In fact, periodic regime change itself, through elections might be understood as such a rite. But systems with the rule of law differ in a crucial respect from all others: The core of their legitimacy rests in identifying the actual perpetrator, or at least in a theory that a good-faith effort is made to identify the actual perpetrator. Sacrifices legitimate the Rechtsstaat only if they do not involve a substitute victim. Alternatively, when societies without the rule of law seek someone to hold accountable for the initial offense, the first suspect is often replaced by another, and another, in a chain of substitutes. A substitute is actually preferred, notes Girard, since it avoids the principle of perfect reciprocity—an eye for an eye—and therefore the necessity for a cycle of reciprocal acts of revenge that would unleash violence and lead ultimately to a sacrifice of the entire group. This substitute requires a "certain degree of misunderstanding," even deception, so that it appears the god himself is demanding the new (and final) victim. The sacrifice "serves to protect the entire community from its own violence" by suppressing dissensions, rivalries, jealousies, and quarrels. It stems the tide of indiscriminate substitutions and redirects violence into 'proper' channels," meaning outside the community and toward some exteriorized individual or group that "lacks a champion" (8, 10). A substitute victim absolves the group of any further responsibility to seek redress for the initial crime.

For modern judicial systems, the substitute victim is not enough. Now violence must fall on the "right" wrongdoer—"with such resounding authority, that no retort is possible" (Girard 1977: 22). The problem for the Rechtsstaat is that the actual perpetrator may be too powerful, or it may be too unpalatable politically to prosecute him. In that case, the perpetrator cannot be readily exteriorized, cannot be placed "outside" the society. Hence, a major problem for a Rechtsstaat is determining not only who committed the crime, but also who is it politically possible to exteriorize, to place outside the group? Which ethnic group, political elite, nation, minority group, or individual can be held accountable for committed wrongdoings without dividing the political community? Since 1989, every East-Central European society has been struggling with this question, and the answer determines which offenses are held to be criminal and therefore worthy of prosecution. It is my thesis that in those states where there occurred a debate about moral responsibility and where there was no immediate exteriorization of guilt, the new Rechtsstaat performed a successful "final judgment," in the religious sense, a performance that would ultimately enable the state itself to function as a moral agent and keep settling accounts. The definition of the collectivity provided by the state at this moment of transition is likely to occasion more conflict than consensus (Kertzer 1988; 1980: 131–68). But it is not the level of conflict but the belief in its fair arbitration that is the key to a peaceful outcome. As Nicholas Dirks (1994: 488) writes about ritual generally, such ritual performances come at a moment of social liminality, when "all relations of power (and powerlessness) are up for grabs as a time for the reconstitution and celebration of a highly political (and thus disorderly) ritual order." Yet without such provisional moments of public struggle over self-definition, no claims whatsoever to legitimate democratic authority can be made.

Alternately, in those places where the individual or group held accountable was not a purification from an acknowledged inside, where no internal cleansing and only scapegoating of already exteriorized others occurred, then further cycles of retributive violence are likely to follow. Cycles of violence will follow either as new waves of internal purges (of exteriorized others) or as foreign wars. Maurice Bloch (1992: 6) makes a very similar claim in his account of the politics of religious experience, noting that the "final consumption [of a 'native vitality'] is outwardly directed toward other species," or alternately, is "merely a preliminary to expansionist violence against neighbors."

To describe the absence of retributive justice—the failure to acknowledge victims, prosecute regime-related crime, and establish standards of moral accountability—as a sign of "one of the most important successes of the postcommunist transformation" (Osiatynski 1994: 36) effaces the actual efforts made in all of former socialist states to invoke the Rechtsstaat as a moral authority. If ongoing efforts to introduce standards of political accountability and responsibility fail, defenses of the newly invoked principles will be reduced to arguments for a set of superior procedural techniques for getting things done.[6] But, as I have been arguing, the legitimacy of getting things done through democratic political form rests on a prior invocation of the principles of the rule of law. Often this defense of the new East-Central European regimes is further reduced to a kind of cargo cult argument about the new regime's ability to bring home the bacon, to generate wealth and private prosperity by respecting capitalist property laws: let bygones be bygones, and let's all get wealthy together[7]. But who is buying that today? The single most significant and immediately noticeable result of the regime changes has been a massive redistribution of property and the creation of a wider range of economic class differences than previously existed. In those states where retributive justice had no hearing, proponents of the revolutions of 1989 have lost or are losing their moral authority, and members of the old apparatus have reasserted former privileges and prerogatives as well as have often become the primary benefactors of the property reforms. Contrary to Habermas's early writings, a political community cannot legitimate itself on the basis of procedural impartiality and technical rationality alone. Nor is it sufficient, as he argues in his most recent work (1996), to focus on institutional design and discursive procedures. A moral community also requires belief in a superior morality of politics, a politics that is perceived as just.

The other side of the coin to the question of accountability is that of the place of the victim. Efforts to vindicate or rehabilitate victims seek to reestablish their self-worth and value through the staging of an "event" that publicly repudiates the message of superiority or dominance that initially caused the diminishment in the victim's worth. "Whatever decisions we do make will, however, be unjust," Shklar (1990: 126) reminds us, "unless we take the victim's view into full account and give her voice its full weight. Anything less is not only unfair, it is also politically dangerous." Cycles of violence can ultimately destroy the group; certainly they create conditions of permanent insecurity and instability. What discredits the legal system is its inability to displace violence onto itself. This displacement is successful only when a system of accountability is established whereby wrongdoers are punished and the dignity of victims is reestablished so that the injured party does not feel compelled to turn to violence to exact retribution.

If I am correct in following a long line of political theorists who maintain that the state strives not for moral neutrality but, as Hampton writes (1992: 1693), "to implement a moral world" through its decisions to punish or not to punish wrongdoers, then our next question concerns which crimes are the state's business to punish? And what are the justifications for these criminalizations? Law, in this view, does not exclude politics but requires a set of political decisions that reinforces a particular vision of dignity. The end of the Cold War has renewed debates about the prevailing definitions of human "dignity" that were embedded in the Cold War order. Invocation of the principles of the rule of law with the corresponding symbolic meanings involves defining which crimes are the state's business to punish, who to rectify, and who to hold accountable for injustices that, though now concentrated in the "socialist past," are continuous and ongoing. The jural reform in East-Central Europe, then, though ostensibly about eliminating past injustices, is more centrally about defining the future parameters along which the legitimate state not only has moral obligations but can itself claim to represent morality.

CHAPTER 2

Comparing: Decommunization—
Recommunization—Reform?

EVERYONE AGREES that much has changed economically, politically, and culturally, since the collapse of "actually existing socialist regimes" in East-Central Europe. But there is no agreement on how to best characterize these changes, which theoretical frameworks or descriptive terms to apply, and even more fundamentally, what caused them. In his authoritative reporting of events surrounding the collapse, Timothy Garton Ash (1990) coined the word *refolution*, claiming that regime changes had aspects of both revolution and reform. Others have since picked up on this term. For purposes of analysis, however, revolution and reform are already ambiguous concepts that are only further obscured by merging them. Leaving aside the more academic question of whether the initial events were willful revolutions (I am convinced that they were; see Borneman 1991, 1997), we still cannot take for granted that subsequent changes in specific regimes, or in the economies and societies of the East bloc generally, are a result of intended reforms or, alternately, the effects of global structural changes largely outside of human agency. Given the ruins in which "communism"—the great Utopian project of this century—lies, it might be wise to remain skeptical of attempts to attribute general intentions and specific outcomes to reform projects. Here I will be content to begin a "skeptical description" of current regime change in East-Central Europe, which, I hope to show, is a necessary first step toward an analysis.

DECOMMUNIZATION AND RECOMMUNIZATION

Before beginning this positive project, let me briefly critique what has become perhaps the dominant descriptive framework for analysis of regime changes and current reform. Many analysts, especially those working in the United States, have adopted the descriptive label *decommunization* to describe post-1989 reforms (Holmes 1994: 33–36; Osiatynski 1994: 36–40). Sometimes they use *recommunization* to describe the return to power through reelection of former communists (Holmes 1994: 33–36). Decommunization is understood as positive reform, recommunization as a rejection of reform. Among the many reasons to avoid the use of these labels, the most compelling are that these terms are both descriptively false and analytically misleading; and that they mythologize reform processes by emptying them of their complexity, giving them the simplicity of essences, endowing them with what Roland Barthes (1972: 143) called "a blissful clarity."

Why are these terms so misleading? First, one can only decommunize what was already communist, yet the particular form of economic and political organization that one associates with the ideology of communism existed nowhere in the former East bloc, nor, by the 1980s, did any of the regimes within this bloc seriously aspire to it. Misleading, too, is the term *recommunization*, as it infers from the reentry to high office of former members of now-defunct socialist or communist parties that these elected officials are propagating "communist" goals or party platforms. More often than not the opposite is true: most of the former nomenklatura who have remained or reentered office are adamant nationalists and free marketeers, an ideological mix that is, if anything, an inversion of communist ideology.

Second, even if one understands *communism* as a Cold War shorthand for (the former) "actually existing socialism," marked by command economies, politically dependent judiciaries, and puppet legislative branches, the term is clearly inapplicable to most of the current regimes. The organizational forms proposed and explored by former communists bear little resemblance to those of their Cold War predecessors. In those republics that do retain many of the features of former communist states, such as Romania and Russia, for example, most former leaders do not advocate a return to state control and ownership of the means of production, the central criterion of communism. Alternately, decommunization does not always result in reform. Where there has been a radical decommunization, such as declaring the communist party illegal, as in Russia, former party members have retained their positions as well as most of their privileges, in most cases using capitalist reforms to improve upon their prior economic (and often political) status.

A more accurate description of the processes of judicial, political, and economic change should first take into account the historical specificity and elasticity of the term *reform*. It must also allow for a more detailed acknowledgment of the differences both within and between former socialist states. Ethnographic descriptions of native terms, practices, and processes will necessarily lead to better assessments of where change is coming from and in what direction it is going. We should pay particular attention to the *type, intensity,* and *duration* of specific changes and their relation to reforms—in other words, to the local effects of changes of economic, political, and social regimes over time (see Verdery 1996). In what follows, I shall focus on local descriptions of jural reforms, paying close attention to the ways jural reform is either linked to or detached from other changes, such as redistributions in wealth, economic restructuring, or democratization. I concentrate on four postsocialist countries in some detail, paying closest attention to the German transition.[1] Finally, I use this description to address the widely expressed (and often heralded) desire attributed to most East-Central Europeans to "close the books on the crimes of the past." Is this desire also revealed in a more detailed analysis of terms and concepts used to describe jural and political reform?

SKEPTICAL DESCRIPTIONS OF REFORM

Russia

Reform began in 1985 in the former Soviet Union, or so they say in contemporary Russia. At that time, Gorbachev initiated a widely publicized *perestroika* (economic reorganization or liberalization) and *glasnost* (public transparency of politics). Glasnost has long since disappeared from use, not because of recommunization but because of its success: Russia has a relatively free press, public debate, and a public sphere where past and present actions are contested. Perestroika, on the other hand, is a term still utilized, but it is often used to refer to separate processes of *reformy* (reform), *privatizatsiya* (privatization), and *demokraticheskiye reformy/demokratizatsiya obshchestva* (democratic reforms/democratization of society—this term specifies processes also associated with glasnost).

The most recent privatization is understood in the context of a history of attempts at economic reform, the many (failed) perestroikas since the 1917 revolution. In this light, some Russians differentiate between a first, or Khrushchev-directed, perestroika (omitting Lenin's New Economic Policy altogether), and a second, or Gorbachev-directed, one; neither of these restructurings entailed *privatization* as the term is used today. Many Russians claim that the Boris Yeltsin–directed privatization of the last several years has been primarily a transfer of ownership from the state to Yeltsin's friends, whom he rewarded for loyalty to him with industrial firms, hotels, and the like. The word often used for this is *prikhvatizatsiya*, meaning "expropriation and plunder," the giving away of government wealth to well-connected and unscrupulous businessmen and bankers. To express their ambivalence about this process, in colloquial Russian the word *prevratizatsiya*, which means "making depraved," has been coined from the word *prevratiza* (privatization). It appears, then, that privatization is both an expropriation or transfer of ownership from state to private (mostly Russian national) hands and a form of moral degeneration.

Both *perestroika* and *democratization* have been endowed with new meanings in response to the empirical experiences of the present. For example, in explaining the reasons for the war in Chechnya, the populist Russian general Alexander Lebed said, "Early this year we are celebrating the tenth birthday of perestroika, which has degenerated into *perestrelka* [an exchange of fire], and about whose victims there is still no *pereklichka* (account)" ("Wenn Verteidigungsminister lügen," *Die Zeit*, January 13, 1995, 3). In this reformulation of perestroika, economic reorganization has resulted in civil wars and uncounted victims.

When the term *democratization* is used, people refer to a wide array of both positive and negative processes. It may refer to the development of a free and critical press, or be viewed as the cause of collapsing social values and an authority crisis. "Democracy" is also seen as "endangered" by the war in Chechnya, by neofascists, by violations of human rights, or by Yeltsin's disrespect for the principles of legality. Alternately, the democratizing reforms initiated by Gorbachev in the early 1980s resulted in the formal breakup of the Soviet empire into autonomous republics, a breakup that has often given birth to even more autocratic structures within particular communities, regions, and states than existed before. Although the Russian federation adopted a constitution in 1993 that guaranteed the rule of law, including protection of basic human rights, the provisions of this constitution have been blatantly violated by the president, the Duma, regional and local political authorities, and the police. Moreover, the state has clearly lost its monopoly on the legitimate use of violence as well as its control of economic life to both internal and external agents. Organized extralegal and criminal groups have stepped into one power void, making "crime" and its control a more urgent political issue for most people than democratization. International agencies and nongovernmental organizations (NGOs), such as the North Atlantic Treaty Organization and the International Monetary Fund, have also stepped in to dismantle and in part restructure the military-industrial complex and financial institutions.

The absence of a consensus around the principles of legality and legal norms tends to strengthen forces supporting a fascist political form that promises to eliminate chaos and guarantee order. Largely because law enforcement officials often do not see it as their duty to enforce judges' decisions, the judicial system has not been an important factor in the transformations to date. To nearly all of the Russians with whom

I talked, the principles of legal security and trust continue to ring hollow. In response to my questions, each person immediately gave me a different example of continued disrespect for or arbitrary enforcement of legal decisions by police and bureaucrats. At the same time, however, nobody related to me examples of the excessive illegalities that one associates with Stalinism.

Neither judges nor state prosecutors have been reviewed for past illegalities, and not a single judge or prosecutor has been dismissed on the basis of criminal activity. I was told that over 90 percent of all former judges are still serving, the rest having retired or moved to private business. Among a small circle of politicians and political activists there has been a debate on the utility of *lustratsiya* (cleansing/sacrifice/review/disqualification), but most Russians, I was assured, would not even know what the word means. (A similar word, *lustrace*, was used in the Czech Republic, but the process there actually resulted in demotions and was used to "cleanse" some former collaborators from public office, many of whom were later reinstated [Cepl 1992a: 24–26].) Judges frequently complain about their relatively low pay, and judicial buildings are delapidated and neglected in comparison to buildings of the executive or legislative branches. In cases where state prosecutors or police have successfully built a case against some criminal activity, I was told that an estimated 80 percent of the accused are released within a day of the arrest. Judges apparently fear becoming victims of organized crime (although to date it has been journalists who have been murdered and who are under attack). The effects of Leninist political philosophy seem to endure at least in the lack of differentiation between the executive and judicial domains. Judicial independence, therefore, has yet to be established as a credible doctrine, and judges are also not widely known for their civil courage. The Supreme Soviet existed in the same form, with the same members, until the October 1993 elections, with a great deal of continuity in personnel even after these elections. Moreover, since a "cleansing" has never taken place and reform has been incremental, the notion of a "thick line" between past and present and a "closing of the books" makes no sense whatsoever. Nowhere in Russia is the term *recommunization* employed to describe the present transformation.

Hungary

In Hungary, too, communization (de- or re-) is not used to characterize the changes and reforms of the last decade. The most frequently employed terms to describe economic transformations are *szerkezetváltás*, meaning "macro- and microrestructuring," and *uj növekedéski pálya*, meaning "new growth path," understood as the attempt to put an end to economic stagnation. From 1989 through 1993, the ruling coalition justified its reforms in terms of the goal *új magyar tulajdonosi középosztály*, creating a Hungarian (*sic*, not international) middle class of private owners. Whatever measurable success in economic reforms, it has been counterbalanced by a growing sector of poor people. With regard to privatization, Hungarians attach to the term a variety of prefixes and adjectives that differentiate between the kinds of property transformation: (*elő*) of small enterprises and services (*központosított*) of large, state-owned firms, (*decentralizált* or *ön-*) self-privatization by managers of state-owned firms, and, finally, the infamous *spontán privatizáció* (spontaneous privatization), characteristic of the period between 1989 and 1991 when managers transformed their firms into joint stock and limited liability companies before a corresponding legal form existed. (In Poland this last process is more pointedly called *nomenklatura privatization*.) In colloquial speech, two terms are frequently employed to critique these processes: *elkótyavetyélés* (the squandering of state-owned assets), and *átláthatóság* (the transparency of the process).

Restructuring the state and legal system in Hungary has been a gradual process (some claim it is two decades old), the most recent phase of which was initiated by the ruling socialist party itself around 1988. The goal of *jogállamiság* (more accurately translated in terms of the German model of *Rechtsstaatlichkeit* than of the Anglo-Saxon rule of law) involves a proper *hatalommegosztás* (division of power), *népsuveneritás* (sovereignty of the people), and, in the most significant innovation of the post-1988 reforms, a multiparty system that represents a plurality of interests. Opposition politicians refer to the prereform period as *pártállami idők* (party-state times), while in everyday speech the term used is a simple pejorative, *az átkosban* (during the [period of the] damned/accursed). The current ruling socialists refer to the post-1988 transition as a process of *modernizáció* (modernization), which they promise to pursue vigorously. Both opposition and ruling politicians argue that there has been insufficient reform, or *tisztogatás* (clearing), within the bureaucracy. In everyday speech, people differentiate between *régi* and *új káderek* (old and new cadres) and not between communists and anticommunists.

In Hungary, no thick line between past and present has been drawn, since it is generally assumed that Hungary has always been a Rechtsstaat, except for the violations occurring in 1956. The issue of *átvilágítás* (screening) of government employees, in particular the political elite, for complicity with the secret police remains unresolved. The post-1989 opposition-controlled government reviewed neither judges nor public prosecutors, and there have been no disqualifications in jural occupations. Parliament, however, passed a bill in 1990 controlling and disqualifying from responsible positions those who had been agents of the secret police. That process of review and disqualification is administered by a three-judge panel. About half of the individuals in leading positions in various governmental departments were initially subject to demotions, but only a select few were dismissed. Of those dismissed, however, about half have already returned to work in the government.

Poland

Poland is perhaps the best example among former socialist countries where the term *dekomunizacja* (decommunization) is widely used. Yet even here this term is misleading, and, for analytical purposes, other Polish terms may more accurately represent reform processes. Three concepts frame the contemporary Polish experience: *reforma* (reform), *demokracja* (democratization), and *kapitalizm* (capitalism). All three function as speech acts that simultaneously endorse as they constitute the objects they purport to describe. To oppose any of these processes one risks being demonized.

Reform comes in many colors, however, perhaps especially in Poland. First, there are those individuals or parties most solidly situated in the reform camp, *obóz reform* or *reformatorski*, as opposed to those who are against reform—which, of course, everyone insists they are not. Then, there are different types of reform: *reformy demokratyczne* (democratic reform) and *reformy gospodarcze* (economic reform), both entailing various microprocesses: *pluralistyczne społeczek'stwo* (pluralism, or multiparty system), *urynkowić* (creating markets), *samorząd* (self-governing). With the reform processes already five years underway, there are also terms to express ambivalences about these reforms. *Liberalne reformy* (liberal reform) is used descriptively to gloss economic reforms but, especially when used by the clergy, it also connotes a critique of these reforms—as antinational and antireligious. From this critical perspective, the reforms are amoral and unjust, resulting in moral relativism, consumerism, and Western European mass culture. In this vein, *tolerancja* (tolerance) is also used pejoratively, as a synonym for cosmopolitan ideas, moral relativism, and antinational sentiment.

As would be expected, there are also a variety of terms employed to differentiate aspects of economic reform. Capitalism is often referred to as *kapitalizm z ludzka twarza* (capitalism with a human face), playing on the reform slogan "socialism with a human face," used by party reformers after October 1956; it indicates general support for capitalist organization but also calls for adjustments to meet the needs of individuals (especially those most vulnerable). *Logika rynku* (the logic of the market) and *prawa gospodarki rynkowej* (laws of the market economy), concepts that around 1989 had quasi-theological import, are now used ironically to indicate their limited utility. In other words, some people insist that everything should not be submitted to this same logic, that there may be cultural or educational institutions that should be exempted from these so-called laws. *Prywatyzaja* (privatization), *reprywatyzacja* (reprivatization), and *powszechna prywatyzacja* (common privatization of state firms) refer technically to the reversion of state or collective property into private hands. The Polish term *uwłaszcennie nomenklatury* (privatization by the nomenklatura) is used to describe the so-called spontaneous privatization that the political and economic elite managed in 1989, turning collective property into their own private property before the passage of laws regulating such transformations. Some politicians, including Walesa, have recently begun contrasting this last term with "uwłaszczenie społeczeństwa," which refers to a privatization that returns the property to the hands of society with many ordinary people as individual owners.

The word *democratization* tends to be used generally to describe a Utopian situation and not specific practices. A democracy is a symbol for the best possible form of organization (including pluralism, free elections, self-government) and is often used ironically to critique the Polish situation (e.g., If we had a democracy, then we could expect things to function here.).

Finally, to describe the experience of former socialists being reelected or returning to power, the word *peerelizacja* has been coined. It is taken from the term *powrót PRL*, the PRL being the acronym for the former socialist Polish People's Republic, and means, again ironically, literally a return to the former socialist Poland. However, the former party members themselves tend to be dubbed *ex-komuna* (ex-communists) and the former ruling party *postkommunistyczne partie* (postcommunist party).

Germany

Like Russia, but unlike Hungary and Poland, the German Democratic Republic (GDR) represents an extreme case of an intended abrupt transition and radical break with the past. *Die Wendezeit* (the period of change/the time of the turn) is the concept most frequently used to describe the transition period, which began with the opening of the Wall in November 1989 but for many people has not ended yet. The words *die Reform* were initially associated with a "third way" between socialism and capitalism, the major proponent of which was the Party of Democratic Socialism (PDS), the renamed ruling party. When this third way was rejected, the word *reform* went with it. Instead, the plan was to radically restructure the East in a way that would entail as little as possible "reform" of the West. Economic and administrative change have been glossed by the term *die Abwicklung*, meaning a bringing to completion or closing of accounts. *Abwicklung*, which initially had a somewhat ambiguous connotation, has now become a solely negative term, especially, but not only, in the East. Business firms, child care centers, the secret police (Stasi), university institutes—all were *abgewickelt*. The *Treuhandanstalt*, a parapublic trust initially proposed in 1990 by the last GDR regime, was established to do the *Abwicklung*: to *privatisieren* (remove property from state ownership irrespective of to whom it goes), *sanieren* (clean up and make competitive or healthy), or close down state and party-owned property or enterprises. Use of the word *Treuhand* (guardian/literally, a faithful hand) in itself captures the ambiguity of establishing a centralized, lord-analogue that stands above all democratic controls and whose function is to secure the transformation of collective property into private forms.

This "privatization" has resulted in a massive transfer of property from East (national) to West (national and international), with 80 percent of all firms now in West German hands, an estimated 5 percent in East German hands. Most of the few East Germans who bought property through the Treuhand were members of the old elite, for they were the only ones with economic capital, or with the social connections necessary to obtain it. Privatization also eliminated three-fourths of all East German industrial jobs, causing widespread unemployment. Those who defend the Treuhand resort to a macroeconomic explanation about its effects: eastern Germany now has one of the highest growth rates in Europe (although this slowed considerably after 1994); its restructured industries have been modernized and are internationally competitive. Yet even this picture is disputed depending on which forecasts and past estimates are used.

The Treuhand dissolved itself as planned at the end of 1994, concluding that it had successfully completed its task in fewer than four years. The validity of the success story, however, depends on the criteria used to measure it. Klaus von Dohnanyi, the respected former mayor of Hamburg and an early critic of the Treuhand, has criticized it for deviating from its own goals; the Treuhand, he says, functioned as a daughter of the federal accounting agency (*Bundesrechnungshofes*), selling firms to the highest bidder without adequately considering the economic viability of the restructuring plan (cited in Jahberg 1994: 25). Other criticisms have been that East German industry was restructured according to the model of the highly subsidized West German industry, or that the Treuhand ignored pricing mechanisms in choosing buyers. Since the GDR used an entirely different (politically responsive and inaccurate) accounting system, the Treuhand found it impossible to determine the actual value of East German firms and therefore, working to privatize as quickly as possible, placed more importance on creditworthiness and the standing of buyers than on the "price" of GDR firms. This said, the controversies surrounding the work of the Treuhand have not led to a serious discussion of recommunization as an alternative, not even by the former socialist party (the PDS). With the closing of the Treuhand, the verb *abwickeln* also has dropped out of West German use as quickly as it had taken hold to describe reform in the East. However, East Germans continue to employ the word as a self-evident critical term for West German motivation and administration. Since many of the already privatized firms have gone bankrupt, or been gutted of their liquid assets by their new owners, or merely used to obtain subsidies for their western branches, an entirely new descriptive term has appeared: *second privatization.*

Democratisieren in the GDR was employed initially by the opposition and after 1989 by most active citizens to refer to the introduction of free elections and a multiparty system, and to guarantees of a free press and freedom of opinion. In this sense, the GDR has indeed been democratized. Across the East and West German political spectrum, the term is used descriptively as a blessing and as praise, though of course there are major philosophical differences among Germans as to how much democracy is desirable and on the relation of democracy to order. Still, democracy does not have the widespread ambivalence associated with the term in Russia. Considering how delegitimated democracy had become during the Weimar period, this trajectory in the meaning of the term is remarkable.

With regard to the judicial system, perhaps the most significant innovation has been the emergence of two related (and often conflated) types of crime: *Regierungskriminalität* (governmental criminality), a term coined to cover governmental criminality considered specific to the former GDR, and *Vereinigungskriminalität* (unification criminality), crimes associated with the processes leading to dissolution of the GDR and unification with the Federal Republic (for a detailed description and analysis, see chaps. 4 and 6). *Regierungskriminalität* has come to refer nearly exclusively to East German citizens and to include crimes such as shooting citizens on the border, election fraud, murder or kidnapping by the secret police (Stasi), spying on the Federal Republic, judicial illegality, abuse of public trust, doping of athletes, or damage to the environment. *Vereinigungskriminalität* refers to prosecutions, approximately half East, half West, of Germans for primarily economic crimes. Federal and state prosecutors in Berlin have justified their investigations and priorities as reactions to popular pressure for justice. The work in this area is to be completed by 1999.

Because of the rather poor conviction rates in prosecutions of these two areas of criminality, many prominent West Germans called for a general amnesty, a thick line between past and present. Instead, they called for *Versöhnung* (reconciliation) and contrasted this with *Vergeltung* (retaliation). Their sentiment was shared by several radically different groups of former East German citizens, including most prominently former nomenklatura and state functionaries. Focus on the calls for an amnesty deflected attention from the fact that the prosecutions by Berlin's Ministry of Justice were a response of a Rechtsstaat to citizen demands for justice, which in turn was a result of postunification processes of democratization. Moreover, while it has been difficult to obtain convictions for governmental criminality, federal and state prosecutors have had considerable success and have recovered billions of dollars in the area of unification criminality. As the state completes its cases against the former elite for governmental criminality, it has shifted its attention from jural personnel to economic crimes.

Added to the controversies around economic and political restructuring is another issue that has generated confused, if not hysterical, public discourse: cooperation with the East German State Security (Stasi) during the Cold War. The files of the former Stasi were initially opened up in early 1990 by an act of the last GDR parliament (with the agreement of all political factions, including the ruling socialists). The opening of the files was to provide "enlightenment," to enable citizens to have access to their own pasts. In practice, however, enlightenment often gave way to purgings; anyone found to have worked for the Stasi as an IM (unofficial coconspirator) was automatically dismissed from public service. This also happened frequently in private industry, even though private industry was not covered in any of the laws dealing with Stasi activities. The initial law regulating Stasi files was included in the Unity Treaty, against the wishes of many, if not most, West German politicians. This law was never thought of in terms of decommunization; as Joachim Gauck, who administers the files, has emphasized, "We didn't want to persecute communists, there is no decommunization [that is comparable to] de-Nazification" (Gauck 1995b: 10). In contrast to the process of "de-Nazification," the review of public servants after unification did not take into consideration party affiliation. The selective leaking of information from the files, however, has served to discredit both those individuals (not coincidentally, nearly all critics of the ruling West German coalition) placed under suspicion by the leaks and the function of the files themselves. Moreover, political reviews and disqualifications have frequently been misused to cast all East Germans as complicitous with the state (*Staatsnah*: "nearness to the state"—a category most conspicuously and arbitrarily used in adjusting some East German pensions)—although fewer than 1 percent of all East Germans had been actively working with the Stasi.

The two main reasons for dissatisfaction with the judicial restructuring since 1990 have been, first, resentment at the instrumentalization of the Stasi files and other issues of postunification criminality, and second, that there has been the perception of little equality before the law. Although before the twentieth century equality before the law was never one of the fundamental principles of Rechtsstaatlichkeit (a hierarchy of legal subjects and differentiated rules of standing have always existed), it is guaranteed in the Basic Law of 1949, and it was perhaps the major promise of socialism and therefore a general expectation of former GDR citizens. Judicial reviews, disqualifications, and prosecutions have been one-sided; the West German system and former West German citizens have not been subject to the same public scrutiny as those in the East, and the thoroughness of these processes varies from province to province. Only in the area of unification crime, as mentioned above, have about half of the public prosecutor's indictments been West Germans.

Given the foregoing analysis, one might well ask why, if not for a diffuse desire for a thick line or an amnesty, or at least a passive acceptance of recommunization, members of the PDS have been able to retain, and even gain, popularity in recent elections. Their appeal, I would insist, has little to do with this past. Rather, it is based primarily on lack of adequate representation for East German interests, on the sentiment that democracy has not gone far enough, and on the experience of inadequately rectified injustices or even the creation of new ones despite the installation of the Rechtsstaat. Over the last five years, there has been a general loss of faith in the ability of the Rechtsstaat to respond to and protect the weaker of the two parties (the East) in the unification process. As a result, the perception of present injustices has created sympathy for the PDS as a voice of the East versus the West. Despite this sympathy, only a small group of people, a minority even within the PDS, has reacted with nostalgia for communism as a means to rectify this East-West power asymmetry. Moreover, the relative success of the PDS must be viewed in the wider context of German party politics; in no province has the PDS received an absolute majority. The rejection of recommunization as a response to East-West injustices may be attributed to positive, if inadequate, accomplishments of the Rechtsstaat. Most important of these are the presence of legal security in the form of political accountability, and the protection of human rights and of the economic safeguards of the social welfare state. For many East Germans, the accomplishments of the Rechtsstaat are of course balanced against the limited legal protections provided in the area of labor law, and against the legalized abuse of the privatization and unification processes by many West Germans for their own enrichment.

To the extent East Germans do in fact experience legal security, some credit must be given to the initial review and disqualification of former members of the secret police as well as to the legal prosecution of nomenklatura. Legal security means not only predictability and continuity in application of the law (which, in fact, has not been the case, nor has it been the primary expectation) but also the confidence that one need not fear that the new state's power—especially in the judiciary, police, and bureaucracy—remains in the hands of former elites. In fact, public opinion polls indicate that East German confidence and trust in the judiciary and police has steadily grown since 1990, while that in other institutions like churches, political parties, or legislatures has wavered or declined (Gabriel 1993: 3–12).

Arguments for an amnesty in the German context appealed to "furthering unification," to "forgiveness" and "reconciliation," or to "reasonableness." In the ensuing climate, human rights activists, former oppositional leaders, and victims of the old regime were frequently branded as a hysterical minority that had lost touch with reality. (From 1990 to 1994, I frequently heard Bärbel Bohley, the "Joan of Arc" of the revolution, dubbed a *hysterische Kuh* [hysterical cow]!) As elsewhere in the East bloc, they lost much of their initial cultural capital. Instead of being acknowledged as actual victims of the socialist state who had legitimate claims for legal remedy, they were most often cynically figured as perpetrators of new injustices and obstacles to social harmony. Nonetheless, they remained a voice in a public discourse that was no longer underground and no longer silenceable. In fact, in 1995 and 1996, there were many indications that former opposition leaders throughout the former East bloc, including East Germany, had regained some of their lost public status. Because such minority discourses are now public and not private voices, the question of whether the East Germans *desire* to close the books on the crimes of the past is irrelevant. What they have in common with their former socialist neighbors in Russia, Poland, Hungary, and the Czech Republic is that they no longer have the ability to close the books. The society is already too open.

CODA

To recapitulate, I have made two overarching arguments that are basic to any anthropological science: (1) don't essentialize and (2) ask the natives. Because anthropology has had so little influence among the disciplines responsible for producing descriptions of East bloc transformations, these arguments have not been heard. I could go on to account for processes in other countries, but other examples will only support my general point about the importance of a skeptical, ethnographic description. By beginning with native terms one preserves the heterogeneity and temporal specificity of change and reform processes within and between countries. One is better positioned to accurately assess the type, duration, and intensity of current regime transformations—which vary greatly from place to place. Essentializing terms, such as *decommunization* or *recommunization*, may yield a blissful clarity, but their simplicity is analytically misleading. Social scientists should avoid using such terms, even when our colleagues in sociology and political science insist on their utility. Such terms presuppose the stability of described objects—in my example, judicial systems, ideologies, and nations—over time. Yet the opposite is true: our objects of investigation are always the result of syncretic and temporal social processes. Despite frequent appearances of stability, or even of a return to prior cultural forms, these legal and political systems are undergoing major transformations. Most Cold War analysts of Eastern Europe repeatedly committed the error of methodological essentializing—once a communist always a communist; some people and cultures never change; ghosts reappear and reproduce themselves in unaltered form. This is one of the major reasons why they were caught by surprise at the sudden and nonuniform revolutions in former socialist states. We should not repeat this error in analyzing reform.

Historicizing the Rule of Law

THIS CHAPTER makes an initial foray into the history of the German Rechtsstaat, concentrating on the progressive institutionalization of principles of accountability and responsibility. Neither a comprehensive inventory of events nor a complete chronology, it is a sketch that sacrifices depth for breadth. It looks at the development of principles of accountability from four perspectives: Western legal traditions, national histories, architectural symbolism, and the Cold War. These perspectives are units of different orders: ideal, spatial, material, and temporal. While they do not combine to give a total picture of the Rechtsstaat, they do move beyond a conventional law-as-ideas approach to present a more complex understanding of the different media in which the Rechtsstaat articulates its principles. I begin on the familiar terrain of the history of ideas of the Western legal tradition. Then I compare different spatial articulations of this Western tradition, focusing on national formulations of the principle of sovereignty. Third, I trace shifts in architectural symbolism of authority in jural buildings. Finally, I explicate the principles of Rechtsstaatlichkeit in the two Germanys during the Cold War by highlighting some of the key disputes about sovereignty up to the point of unification in 1990.

This summary history is intended to situate the reader so as to better understand the complexity of current conflicts surrounding, and the difficulties inherent in, the invocation of the principles of the rule of law in former socialist states. My focus on accountability and sovereignty should also help to clarify the historical relation of the rule of law to democratic form.

While scholars are not agreed on the desiderata that would define the Rechtsstaat, it still may be helpful to list the essential characteristics that have come to constitute this legal form over the course of the last nine centuries: (1) separation of powers within a state, in particular, the separation of the executive from the judicial branch; (2) the principle of legality (*formelles Gesetz*), implying that *(a)* the people's representatives adopt the law, *(b)* statutes find general application, and *(c)* the legislature itself is bound by the legislation; (3) sovereignty of (statute) law; (4) the prohibition of excesses of state authority (*Übermaßverbot*), or a principle of proportionality of crime to punishment; (5) an independent judiciary; (6) the principle that state action must be predictable in order to facilitate legal certainty, therefore forbidding retroactive legislation; (7) the principle of trust in the lack of arbitrariness in the law's application. These principles enumerate different aspects of institutional and political accountability, with the focus on making the relation of the sovereign to the ruled transparent, explicable, and predictable. In a comparison of the Rechtsstaat with the rule of law, Fuller (1969) and MacCormick (1984) reduce the above principles to four basic ideals: (1) separation of powers, (2) principle of legality, (3) prohibition on retroactive legislation, and (4) principle of trust in the legal system.

THE WESTERN LEGAL TRADITION

Historians generally date the beginning of European principles of the rule of law to the eleventh century. These principles developed not within isolated national experiences but in pan-European patterns that, of course, showed great regional and local variation. The national particularities (for example, French, German, Anglo-Saxon) in legal traditions that usually orient scholars were a late and gradual development, growing out of the territorialization of law following the Westphalian Peace of 1648, and then accentuated by nationalist movements in the eighteenth and nineteenth centuries. The German Rechtsstaat is part of this history, and it is the specific tradition with the most influence on contemporary developments in East-Central Europe.[1]

From approximately the sixth to the eleventh century, Germanic law was inseparable from political and religious life, embedded in the customs and morality of local communities. Folk, or customary, law was built around the blood feud and had a communitarian character based on the German concept of the *Gemeinschaft* (community), which, in turn, relied on shared notions of blood, soil, estate, and religious confession. Each *Stamm* (tribe) had its own law, with the patriarchal household serving as the legal unit. The blood feud, which revolves around the principles of honor and revenge, was eventually replaced (in much of Europe, not until the fifteenth century) by the principle of monetary compensation. What were perhaps the first courts, public assemblies or "moots" often met under linden trees, symbols of power and wisdom, to hear and decide disputes.

The Western legal tradition continually incorporated for its own purposes some of the traditions of Roman law (dated from the second century B.C. to the eighth century A.D.). Its perhaps most significant appropriation was the principle of the autonomy of law and politics, and this occurred following the split of the Eastern Church from the Western

Christian church, finalized in 1054. This Western movement, or the Papal Revolution, as it was called, made the bishop of Rome the sole head of the church, emancipated the clergy from the control of the kings, and sharply differentiated the church as a political and legal entity from secular politics. It culminated in the Gregorian reformation and Investiture Struggle (1075–1122) and gave rise to canon law (*jus novum*, taken from the Roman Catholic Church) and to new secular legal systems. Most important, it established the papacy as a visible, corporate legal unity, with a state structure governed by a single system of law. After 1122, writes Harold Berman in his general history of Western European law, "law came to be seen as a way of fulfilling the mission of Western Christendom to begin to achieve the kingdom of God on earth" (1983: 521). Thereafter, having violently separated itself from the secular order (which was viewed as plural and divided among various polities), Christianity employed canon law to realize a political and legal program for transforming life on earth. The Eastern Orthodox Church, along with political authorities in Muslim countries, did not participate in this reformation, though later Greece, Spain, and Russia also engaged in similar reforms.

From the period 1050 to about 1200, Western Europe saw the emergence of a system of feudal rights and obligations, a precocious "nationalization" of procedures with an emphasis on increasing precision, internal consistency, and generality of application. It remained largely customary law, however, and was less systematized than canon law, though strongly influenced by it. The drive for consistency and rationality in secular and ecclesiastical law also contributed to a view of law as continuously expanding and developing, as organically growing. Law was assumed to progress by means of ever greater codifications through the synthesis of opposed elements, a reconciling or elimination of differences and contradictions. Popes and kings both made laws and had inviolable rights, but they had to accept the other's limitation upon their own supremacy. In theory there remained but one legal authority, a common divine source for both popes and kings, expressed in the creed "God is the source of all law."

The tradition of the rule of law that grew out of the Papal Revolution meant both rule *by* law and rule *under* law. Rule *by* law referred to the fact that each governing body would rule by enacting laws and establishing judicial systems to interpret and administer them. Rule *under* law meant that the respective sovereigns were subordinate to the law that they themselves had enacted; they had to obey the law. It also meant that the sovereign's legislative power was subordinate to his judicial power. Finally, rule *of* law also meant that there was a plurality of legal jurisdictions, and each was bound by the law of other. The

English Magna Carta of 1215 and the Hungarian Golden Bull of 1222 were landmark documents in that they extended principles limiting the power of the sovereign and formulated more exact principles of accountability.

In Germany, the fragmented political power was replicated at the level of legal regimes, which varied not only by region or principality but also by city. A reconciliation of these legal codes came about only with the Bismarkian unification in 1871. The first example of a uniform criminal code among the Germanic principalities was the Carolingian (Peinliche Gerichtsordnung, literally, "legal order of penalties") of Emperor Karl V in 1532. But this codification was still based on feudal concepts of harm and punishment. In the sixteenth century, Luther and his followers in the Reformation provided impetus for a further secularization and objectification of law. Only in the early-eighteenth century, as the authoritarian state replaced the feudal one, did authorities begin new codifications that we might identify with the modern state.

Enlightenment thought influenced these developments, coupling the concept of "natural law" with appeals to "sound reason." Such a conviction in reason resulted in demands for differentiation, systematization, and ever more detailed codification of legal domains. It also reinforced the universalist aspirations of German law, for which it is known as exemplary among European traditions. One of the basic principles of the Rechtsstaat has been the Roman doctrine of *jus gentiun*, the incorporation of all elements of tradition that seem appropriate and universal in all traditions without regard to their origin. And since Roman law remains one of the pillars of pan-European identity, the attempt by German law to appropriate all traditions and to strive for universal application also marks German law as the "most European"—in other words, the least provincial of the various national legal systems of Europe. The Bavarian codification between 1751 and 1756 was the first such large reform in Continental Europe, followed by the Napoleonic Penal Code in 1791, a Prussian codification completed in 1794, and an Austrian in 1811. The Code of Criminal Law (*Reichsstrafgesetzbuch*), first promulgated in 1871, and the Code of Criminal Procedure (*Strafprozeßordnung*) of 1877 were both influenced by the ideas of the French Revolution. These two codes completed the unification of contemporary German criminal law under a uniform legal code.

The nineteenth century also saw changes in the intent and legitimation of criminal justice systems, with Prussia and Austria being the first states to abolish judicial torture. Anton Blok (1989: 31–54) writes that from the mid-eighteenth century on, an "enlightened elite" in northern Europe showed a growing concern with "dangerous classes" of individuals. This concern stemmed from moral and pragmatic concern with disorder, popular cultural expressions, and a recognition that judicial torture and theatrical punishment had run their course, if not become counterproductive. Other disciplinary mechanisms of the sort discussed by Michel Foucault in *Discipline and Punish* (1977) replaced them: the sovereign who could take life or let live was replaced by a regulatory state that confined, surveilled, and tried to reform prisoners, insisting on admissions of guilt and repentance. This shift in the philosophy of penalizing was exemplified in the architectural model of Panopticism, initially proposed by the British reformer Jeremy Bentham, then realized in the United States and reimported to Europe.

New correctional measures were rationalized by positivist thinking taken over from the natural sciences, including a belief in social engineering. A purposive rationality replaced the substantive goals of the criminal system; concern for the victim was replaced by a new focus on the criminal. In fact, the victim began to disappear altogether from rationalizations of law and punishment. Criminologists and legal theorists began to insist that the relation between perpetrator and victim was arbitrary, and therefore a system of penalties should address the (increasingly pathologized) state of the perpetrators alone. In a local case study, Aubert documents the transition from corporal punishment to confinement. The transition period, he writes, was marked by a legal tension between "the rule of law and legal reasoning, on the one hand, and the optimal pursuit of goals with the most effective means, on the other" (1989: 72). In other words, a standard of law as efficacious according to principles of legitimacy was compromised by the inability of the state to pay for it; the type of penalty was directly correlated with the ability of the state to finance it, not with the kind of crime it addressed, nor with the theory behind it. "[Thus] from the 1840s to the end of the century, there was a steady decline in the number of prisoners," although there was no decrease in the number of criminal suspects (70). Aubert concludes that an increasing number of suspended sentences were given to avoid imprisonment because the state had no money for it. This early "subsistence type of state control" (58), which employed fines, deportations, workhouse assignments, slavery, loss of property, death penalties, and corporal punishments such as branding, pillorying, whipping, and mutilation, eventually gave way to the reforms in criminal law at the end of the nineteenth century because, according to Aubert, the state's growing fiscal power made more expensive criminal sanctions such as imprisonment possible. Such legal reforms set the stage for the more profound reforms initiated by the postwar European welfare state. Especially influenced by German criminological theories, the shift from penalties to welfare, reform, and rehabilitation contributed to a further separation of the criminal from the victim, making it possible for the justice system to assume that the efficacy of criminal law could be measured by its impact on the criminal alone.

COMPARISON OF NATIONAL TRADITIONS:
ENGLAND, FRANCE, GERMANY

The breakdown of the absolutist state in Europe did not eliminate the search for transcendents. Rather, the belief in divine and natural justice was replaced by other kinds of transcendents, including human rights, democratic values, the national will, and positive law. The meaning of the rule of law has also changed, with differences in conceptual emphases in England, France, the United States, and Germany (see Blaau 1990: 76–96). In a comparison of these four national systems, Ulrich Preuß (1994a) usefully characterized the sovereign as parliament in England, *etat* in France, society in the United States,[2] and constitution in Germany. These differences developed during the adaptation of the same set of principles to varied local power configurations and in response to the growth of nationally inflected political communities. These communities developed not autonomously but in interaction with and often in opposition to each other. A brief comparison here might bring into sharper focus the German tradition.

As is well known, England has no written constitution but a system of common law and parliamentary rule with a complex set of mechanisms for representation. In seventeenth-century England, the rejection of absolutism resulted in the displacement of sovereignty from the monarch to a parliament whose supreme authority could be exercised only in the form of law. Yet, as Preuß points out, citizen's self-rule is the underlying principle of the English system, for it is the citizen "whose sovereignty the parliament exercises" (1994a: 15). Therefore legal practice, the experiential accumulation of precedents through case law in the courts, is more important in the English common law tradition than is any written or fixed body of legal norms.

In France following the Revolution of 1789, "the people" is conceived as a plurality of individuals that forms a national unity. Sovereignty rests with this nation, but the nation's common will is expressed only through a living population sharing a common government (envisioned as a "political body") within a territory. Therefore, a "constitution is only possible when one already has a state" and when that constitution aims to "protect the unity of the state and the integrity of its republican institutions in which the political energy of the French nation resides" (Preuß 1994a: 25; cf. Henkin 1994: 213–47).

The German constitutional movement was also tied to national and democratic principles but it developed later, in the nineteenth century. In Germany, as in England and France, the Rechtsstaat originated as a norm to discipline the absolutist authority of the state. But under the German doctrine of absolutism, the "state" was not constrained by law, nor checked by the people, but considered "außerrechtlich" (extralegal). The Rechtsstaat was conceived as a solution to this unchecked power of the sovereign state, the solution being another absolutism: a new omnipotence attributed to (statute) law guaranteed by a rigid, written constitution (*Verfassung*). The majority of German jurists in the period of the German Empire, 1871–1918, subscribed to the positivist legal doctrine which claimed that an administrative act carried its own legality; as a result there were no safeguards on the rule-making power of the executive to ensure proper exercise of authority. The Federal Republic rejected this doctrine in 1949, and safeguards were written into the Basic Law to reduce the area in which the executive was free to act outside the controlling influences of administrative law.

To summarize, the English rule of law is guaranteed not by a constitution but by the Parliament, whose function is to protect the rights of those whom it represents. Therefore parliamentary sovereignty fuses both individual and political freedom. The check on the power of the king (or the executive branch) did not imply, however, that the king or officials of his administration could be sued. The French etatist principle had a more immediately revolutionary function: to overcome the power of the estates and construct a system of egalitarian national citizenship. Though sovereignty derives from the people, it rests with the nation, a particular etatist representation of the common will. In Germany, the Rechtsstaat idea implied that the parliament, the people, even the executive organs, were subject to the constitution (or what is now the *Verfassungsgericht*, "constitutional court"), which, in turn, can be amended by the people. Thus the sovereign itself is subordinated to abstract, coherent, neutral legal principles, which are intended, in turn, to protect the *Volk* from itself, its laws, its leaders.

Preuß concludes, "British constitutionalism is genuinely political, American [genuinely] social, French genuinely etatist" (1994a: 25). To put Germany into this punchy and illuminating list would force Preuß into what he no doubts considers a tautology: German constitutionalism is "genuinely constitutional." By classical logic, tautologies are false statements, but this particular statement says something at the level not of classical but of German sociolinguistic logic. Unlike the British, American, or French versions of constitutionalism, the German version alone brings us into a hermeneutical circle from which there is no escape: the *Verfassung* is an opinion, a state, and a constitution. It is both the basic norm that is prior (the precondition for the state) and the after (the expression of the state). A redundancy, but not an untruth, is affected as each of these three meanings can be collapsed in the same German word, producing the semantically interesting phrase *Eine Verfassung verfasst die Verfassung* (a constitution constitutes the constitution). The question as to the noun and the predicate, as to the sovereign (opinion, state, or constitution), is fully ambiguous—but that does not make it false. To enter into one meaning, such as the opinion of the Volk, is to be already in a state with a constitution. All three instances of the sovereign are assumed to logically follow one another so that the possibility for a sovereign that is prior, separate, or outside of the state, opinion, and a constitution disappears semantically.

ARCHITECTURAL SYMBOLISM OF JUSTICE IN BERLIN

After a long period in which justice did not have its own buildings, but met under trees or in other nonjural settings, the city of Berlin erected its first legal building at end of the thirteenth century. It was attached to a town hall, at the corner of Königstraße (now Rathausstraße) and Spandauerstraße. In 1307 Berlin and Cölln (the two halves of the city) shared a common court for civil and criminal cases, which met under the *Gerichtslaube* (legal arcade), with one *Richter* (judge) and seven *Schöffen* (lay judges). The arcade was open on three sides so that the public could take part in the process, coming and going as it pleased. Often the sentence—for example, hanging, torture, public display— was carried out at the same place. The message of such judicial architecture was of a fluid border between public and private and of a temporal immediacy in the execution of justice. Each time the Berlin town hall burned down, as it did in 1380, 1484, and 1581, the Gerichtslaube was expanded and changed in form to reflect the increase in the role of publicity in the exercise of judicial power.

In 1495, governmental authorities created the *Reichskammergericht* (supreme court), which served until 1806 as the first court of legal appeal for the Holy Roman Empire of the German Nation. To this day, the Kammergericht has a special symbolic weight among German courts. For well over a hundred years, the Kammergericht met in different locations, depending on availability of space, and not until the seventeenth century was it given a permanent residence in the *alten Kollegienhaus* on Brüderstraße (now Berlinerstraße).

The eighteenth century saw a proliferation in the number of courts, few of which had a permanent residence. Many met in rented houses, even in *Hinterhofen*, the back courtyards where residency was shared with the poor and with industrial plants. At this time, the competency of the courts was defined by the status of the person involved: there were *Bürger Stadtgerichte* (burgher—city courts) for the *Adlige-* and *Priviligierte-Kammergerichte* (aristocratic and elite supreme courts), and the military courts for cases involving military infractions. And there were separate courts for the French colony of Huguenots, who had been invited to settle in Berlin with the edict of Potsdam in 1685. Their court system was initially established by an edict in 1690. A decree in 1702 defined the competency of these French courts as covering not only the French but any foreigner regardless of religion or ethnic status living within their colonies. Other large groups of immigrants, such as Jews or Bohemians or ethnic Germans from outside the Reich, were not given this privilege of having their own courts; instead, in cases of conflict, they had to appear before the Prussian courts according to their own status as *eximierte* or *Nichteximierte* (Kähne 1987: 9–26).

In the mid-nineteenth century, German governments created the institution of the public prosecutor to act for the "greater public good" (see chap. 4). A major demand of the civil opposition between the years 1830 and 1848 was for publicity (*Öffentlichkeit*), or performance in the public sphere. They called for the court to function as a "moral theater" with a "curative effect on all viewers" (Kähne 1987: 15). A law of July 17, 1846 brought the formal principles of procedure into Prussian criminal law, eliminating remnants of absolutism inherited from its role in the Inquisition. The court now was compelled to decide in a public and oral process (all evidence must still be read orally) on the basis of what the prosecutor presented before it. The first Prussian constitution, written in 1850, facilitated these processes of reform. Through the rest of the nineteenth century, a free press developed that often focused on courts and legal process. Trial reporting reached an apogee of sorts during the Weimar Republic, as the media extensively covered the many sensational and overtly political cases from partisan perspectives. This publicity increasingly undermined the authority of the courts, as each decision was evaluated as reflecting on the institutional legitimacy of the entire jural system.

German unification in 1871 was followed by plans for a consolidation of judicial authority. It resulted in a wave of new court-building projects unparalleled in history. The first completed structure was the mammoth Criminal Court in Berlin-Moabit, built between 1877 and 1882. This court incorporated elements of the Philadelphia model by making a prison a part of the whole, again uniting the judicial and penal in the same complex, as was the case with the fourteenth-century *Gerichtslaube*. This marked a turn away from the practice of attaching courts to town halls. In 1878 the courts in Berlin were integrated into a single system that united them with the regional courts. Between 1895 and 1915, Berlin authorities built seventeen new courts. Called "judicial palaces," their function was not only to intimidate but also to create spaces large enough for public participation in an enclosed, formally public arena. For example, the Moabit building has twenty-one courts that will seat one thousand spectators. No single architectural form dominated the style of these new buildings. They borrowed equally, for example, from Baroque and Renaissance styles, as well as from medieval forms. What they share in common are relatively forbidding, cold, formal external presences that contrast with the entries. Once inside, one stands in large, central, enclosed courtyards, with circular staircases that endlessly disappear and reappear, or steps that go dizzyingly upward. Such entrances encourage a feeling of verticality, if not vertigo, of spatial openness and limitlessness of power.

After 1910, there was little new building of courts. Overcrowding of dockets became common, and, with the increase in authoritarian sentiment and the rise of the Nazi Party in the Weimar period, courts lost much of their legitimacy. A proposal to build a central residence quarter for courts in one location in 1930 was never carried out. Rather than build new courts, the Nazis transformed old ones into *Volksgerichtshof* (People's Courts) with politically reliable judges and state prosecutors, which were to function "in accord with the legal sensibilities of the people." During their eleven years of existence in Berlin, from 1933 to 1945, the People's Courts tried sixteen thousand persons, of whom five thousand were given death sentences and executed (Kähne 1987: 25).

Following the defeat of the Third Reich in 1945, the Allies took over administration of the courts. Russian and American tensions led to an East-West division in 1949, which coincided with the founding of the two German states. This division resulted in a mass movement of legal personnel to the West. Of the 11 Senatspräsidenten of the Kammergericht, 9 moved West, to be followed by 19 judges who served on the Kammergericht. To illustrate the disproportionality of movement, of the 153 judges in Landgerichte (district courts) in the American sector, three went to the East (Kähne 1987: 26).

To recapitulate, toward the end of the nineteenth century, the legal system became more autonomous from the political sphere and opened itself up to public witness. This separation of the political and legal was reflected in the separation of courts from town halls, and in the building of judicial palaces that rivaled the grandeur of the buildings of other branches of government. At the same time, an increased public concern for crime was paralleled by a refocusing of judicial interest on the suspected criminal rather than on the victim. Some criminal courts, like Berlin-Moabit, were now attached to prisons, with a private entry to bring the accused from the prison to the court and back again. The court and prison becomes extensions of each other, a material unification of judgment, penalty, and punishment.

The publicity attracted by courts during the Weimar period undermined their legitimacy and contributed to an extreme politicization of issues of justice and judicial institutions. The Nazis institutionalized this politicization during the Third Reich, effectively making courts an arm of the executive branch (Müller 1991).

Following World War II, few new courts were built in the East or the West. The number of legal conflicts increased, however, with the result that many courts again have not had their own spaces and therefore have had to move around in rented spaces in other buildings. Of the new courts that have been built, their architectural style has been extremely modest in comparision to the fin de siècle architecture. The entrances no longer distinguish the courts from other public or private buildings; ceilings are low, the views from the staircases extend only to the next floor, the foyers are dull and functional, merely for the control of who enters and exits. If anything, the architectural styles indicate a lack of interest, bordering on disrespect, for the symbolism of judicial power and authority. By the 1980s, some new courts were built in West Berlin/West Germany in postmodern styles, not as new, separate buildings but attached to and eclectially integrated into other structures. These new structures are too few in number to allow us to draw any conclusions about tendencies, but in Berlin-Neukölln and in Munich two of the new courts were attached to a town hall and a shopping center.

THE TWO GERMANYS DURING THE COLD WAR

Reacting consciously to the collapse of the Weimar Republic (1918–33) and the criminalities of the National Socialist regime (1933–45), the Federal Republic of Germany (FRG) was founded in 1949 as a return to and renewal of the Rechtsstaat tradition. It was a constitutional order that is (1) a democratic state, (2) a Rechtsstaat, and (3) a welfare state.[3] Perceived weaknesses and abuses of a merely formal understanding of the Rechtsstaat, which had plagued the Weimar constitution, were supplemented by material (or substantive) aspects, often referred to as *Grundsätze*, "higher judicial norms," to prevent the formal framework of legality from being turned against the Western humanitarian tradition or proper ethical norms, as was the case with the Nazis. The theoretical distinction between the Rechtsstaat and political form (e.g., monarchy, democracy) was maintained; the Rechtsstaat in theory is an unchanging, perfect order while political form remains variable and imperfect. Whereas the liberal democratic state and its representatives (the government) are considered central to the constitutional order of the FRG, the political form is still conceptually separate from the Rechtsstaat. In a sense, "the political" is situated below or beneath the Rechtsstaat, since *the Constitution itself is the sovereign*.

The German Democratic Republic (GDR) was founded in 1949, a week after the FRG, and, like the FRG, initially relied on the constitution inherited from the Weimar Republic (minus many Nazi laws, which the Russians and other Allies had removed in the first several years of occupation). But from the beginning, it claimed to be not a Rechtsstaat but a "dictatorship of the proletariat," a revolutionary state that aspired to "socialist legality." Over the years, it increasingly drew from the Soviet tradition of constitutionalism at the height of its Stalinist version. For the GDR, sovereignty rested with the vanguard party (Socialist Unity Party), which acted in the name of a revolutionary "worker and farmer state" (later amended to include all active workers, regardless of status). While the FRG appealed to the bourgeois-liberal principles of Rechtsstaatlichkeit and parliamentary democracy, the GDR distanced itself from these principles, instead appealing to, in Walter Ulbricht's words, "the sense of actual justice and deep humanity" of its social order, whose legality was not in service of the Rechtsstaat but of "socialist relations of production" and a "socialist society" (cited in Müller 1992: 282). Accordingly, Ulbricht, the first head of state, radically instrumentalized law: law had no *Selbstzweck*; it was a tool in "the fight for the victory of socialism" (Alexy 1993: 209). The justification for such an educational function was construed from an unusual dialectical understanding of the double meanings of *Gesetzlichkeit* (juridical legality) and *Gesetzmäßigkeit* (according to the laws of history): socialist legality followed a notion of juridical legality that drew its purpose and justification from an understanding of the laws of history (Schroeder 1993: 204).

Opposed to what it termed the "mere formalism" of the FRG (which it also called petit bourgeois, demagogic, and illusionary), the GDR instead built on the radical reforms carried out by the Soviet Union under the mandate of the Potsdam Accords of 1944. It stressed the substantive aspects of the law, or, in other words, issues of substantive justice. Accordingly, GDR legal experts rewrote the civil and criminal codes inherited from the end of the nineteenth century, specifically rejecting the principles of division of power (in favor of a party dictatorship) and private property as the basis of the means of production (in favor of "total societal people's property"). At the same time, the basic legal code for civil law, the Bürgerliches Gesetz Buch (BGB), remained the same as in the Federal Republic until 1976, when the changes that had taken place in legal practice and interpretation were codified in the civil law code itself. In other words, legal practice usually far outran formal legal codes, which were then adjusted to practice in an ad hoc manner. During the 1980s the GDR moved toward defining itself as a Rechtsstaat, in 1988 coining the concept "socialist Rechtsstaat" for self-description.

The definitions of sovereignty changed in article 1 of three consecutive formulations of the GDR constitution: in 1949, "Germany is an indivisible democratic republic. She is constructing herself on German soil"; in 1968, "The GDR is a socialist state of the German nation"; in 1974, "The GDR is a socialist state of workers and farmers." Only the 1968 constitution was subject to a plebiscite, and people were obligated to vote. Ninety percent of all voters fulfilled this obligation, of which 92 percent voted for the proposed changes in the constitution. The sovereign throughout East German history was *the state*. Theoretically, that form of state was a dictatorship ruled by a hierarchical party that exercised its power in the name of the working class and its partners, but sovereignty ultimately rested with the Politburo.

West German legality followed an altogether different logic. The FRG alleged an "inner continuity" with German history, minus the years 1933–45. Although it claimed to be the successor state to the Third Reich, the FRG specifically reasserted links to legal developments and the constitution of the Weimar Period, enacting a provisional constitution, the Grundgesetz, or Basic Law, in 1949. Despite the FRG's initial emphasis on the formal aspects of the Rechtsstaat, it quickly incorporated substantive norms (embodied in what is colloquially called "the welfare state") into the legal system and the constitution. It did not claim to have access to the laws of history and therefore proceeded slowly with constitutional reform, retaining the Basic Law of 1949 to this day, even extending it unchanged in 1990 to the East German territories.[4]

Asymmetrical concepts of legality, justice, and sovereignty were major sources of conflict in structuring inter-German relations during the Cold War. The most relevant question for West German legal practice was whether East Germany was *Inland* or *Ausland* (a part of the FRG or a foreign country). Throughout the Cold War, the FRG refused to recognize the East German regime as a foreign, legal state, noting specifically that the GDR was not a Rechtsstaat but, as it referred to itself, a dictatorship. The Basic Law of 1949 included all East Germans under its jurisdiction and accordingly insisted on the eventual unification of the two temporary political regimes. Throughout the 1950s the FRG clearly insisted that the GDR was Inland and vehemently fought its existence, above all through the Hallstein Doctrine that forbid other states to recognize the GDR as a sovereign state.

Belligerent legal measures (such as a 1951 law that criminalized denunciations by GDR authorities, or a 1956 law criminalizing the West German communist party) and interpretations eventually gave way to milder opposition in the mid-1960s, beginning with the Vereinsgesetz (Law of Associations) of 1964, which restricted the criminal jurisdiction of West German laws to acts on West German territories alone. One of the problems with treating the GDR as Inland was that, according to the rules of "interlocal criminal law," German courts were required to recognize the validity of and to apply GDR law to crimes committed on East German territory. Yet, most scholars who held such a position were precisely interested in the opposite, in being able to pass judgment on and contest GDR law as a foreign law lacking political legitimacy, and hence contest recognition of the GDR as a sovereign state (Schroeder 1992: 12). Along these lines, the West German Supreme Court ruled in 1983 that the border between East and West Germany was not a "normal state border" but merely an administrative one.

As FRG legal scholars began noting a liberalization in legal practice within the GDR, which in turn continued and was supported by the warming trend in German-German relations accompanying the period of international détente in the 1970, many FRG courts began treating the GDR as Ausland (Müller 1992: 281). But legal decisions were inconsistent, and legal scholars remained divided. For example, while the West German Constitutional Court ruled (in the Grundlagenvertrag) that the GDR could not be viewed as Ausland, the West German Supreme Court, in a decision of the Third Criminal Senate for Criminal Law in 1980 (concerning a case of denunciation within the GDR), ruled that the GDR could not be viewed as Inland with respect to its criminal law (Schroeder 1992: 12).

Perhaps the most significant act in this warming trend of the 1970s was the signing by both German states of the 1975 Helsinki Agreement in the Conference on Security and Cooperation in Europe. In asserting that all human rights and fundamental freedoms "derive from the inherent dignity of the human person" (principle 7), this agreement made "rights" an inviolable, universal dogma whose source was no longer the political community but "dignity." Thereafter, states, such as the GDR, could not so easily hide behind assertions of national-territorial sovereignty when abridging the rights of their citizens, since they had explicitly agreed that certain "human" rights derive no longer from the political community but from a particular quality—dignity—inherent in the person.

In 1977, following an agreement signed by West German chancellor Helmut Schmidt and GDR head Erich Honecker, West German courts began more consistently treating the GDR as a foreign country, in all questions except citizenship. On that question, the West German Supreme Court ruled that all GDR citizens were to enjoy the protections of the Basic Law—a ruling heartily disputed by the GDR. By the mid-1980s, mutual contestation of regimes began to look more like mutual cooperation and assistance, and most citizens in both states seemed to have made accommodations with their regimes. As part of this mutual recognition phase, GDR state and party chairman Erich Honecker flew to Bonn to meet FRG chancellor Helmut Kohl in September 1987, the first-ever meeting between the heads of the two postwar states on West German soil. In a legal case concerning this visit, a former GDR citizen (Rolf Kulike), who had been imprisoned in the GDR and then bought by the FRG, went to court claiming that Honecker had been responsible for his illegal imprisonment. The Supreme Court dismissed the petition, asserting that Honecker could not be held responsible during his visit to the FRG because he was the head of a foreign state, thus contradicting the decisions cited above (Schroeder 1992: 13). Though the meeting did not entail full diplomatic recognition of the GDR by the FRG, at the time it was taken to signify an implicit acceptance of the legality of the East German state.

The GDR's domestic and international success in the mid-1980s was severely tested, initially only domestically, by Gorbachev's rise to power in the Soviet Union. Gorbachev's reforms emboldened a small group of critics in the GDR, who in 1987–88 were arrested, jailed, and either temporarily sent into exile or had their citizenship revoked. A Soviet Union that no longer maintained its legitimacy through Cold War confrontational tactics was warmly greeted by some of the other East bloc countries, specifically Poland and Hungary, who used this climate to claim more sovereignty for themselves. The opposite was true for the GDR, whose leaders saw their sovereignty dependent on Soviet strength and on a continuation of the Cold War's bipolar model. Hence in the area of criminal law, for example, the GDR increased the penalties and made tougher a 1979 law that had already expanded the activities of possible oppositional forces that it considered criminal (including collecting newspaper articles without a purpose, preparing to commit a criminal act).

After the opening of the Wall in November 1989, and continuing through formal state unification eleven months later, the question of the Rechtsstaatlichkeit of the GDR and its reformability became a central issue of debate. Often, West German politicians and scholars asserted that since the GDR was not a Rechtsstaat, it must be an *Unrechtsstaat* (illegal state), a nonsense word that was employed only because it represented the GDR as the opposite of the FRG. Alternative classifications of East German legal history, such as the *vor-rechtsstaatliche Vergangenheit* (the past before the Rechtsstaat) (Schulze-Fielitz 1991: 894–906), were seldom used. Such other concepts might have taken into account the asymmetries and overlaps, and not merely the oppositions, between the two legal systems, and the way in which the GDR did reform its legal structure in 1990. If the GDR was an Unrechtsstaat, then it was comparable to the Nazi regime (which prior to 1989 had often been called a criminal state but not an Unrechtsstaat), in which case nothing from the East German social order of the last forty years, including its laws, should be taken over into the enlarged FRG. According to this view, much as the Western Allied occupation after World War II had been necessary for West Germany, a form of West German oversight or occupation of the GDR would now be called for. After the March 1990 GDR elections made clear that unification would take place, the classification of East Germany as an Unrechtsstaat carried increased rhetorical weight and also, as we shall see, presented particular problems in criminal prosecutions after the GDR was dissolved.

Political unification occurred on October 3, 1990, achieved by means of article 23 of the West German Constitution, which required a negotiated treaty (Unity Treaty), a single parliamentary vote, and quick accession into the FRG. The alternative method that was rejected would have been through article 146, which would have required steady negotiation followed by citizen ratification and an incremental fusing of the two states. After October 3, 1990, the West German Rechtsstaat and liberal democracy became the single referent and arbiter of value for both East and West. According to the principles of Rechtsstaatlichkeit, members of the former ruling Politburo along with other state officials were not considered above the law but were to be prosecuted by the (new) Rechtsstaat itself acting as the sovereign to protect the people and bring about justice. This protection and search for justice was not the province of the parliament, but the Ministry of Justice, which soon was centrally involved in reasserting principles of accountability by prosecuting members of the old elite for violations of their own laws.

Unlike other East-Central European socialist states, the GDR was not transformed into a Rechtsstaat and liberal democracy but was formally eliminated and subsumed (as a *Beitrittsgebiet*) into the FRG. The precondition for the subsumption was the idea that while the GDR as a country was both Inland and Ausland, internal and foreign, to the FRG, the East Germans as a nation of peoples were fully native. Approximately one-seventh of the East German population (2.7 million people) had moved to West Germany between 1949 and 1961. An additional 250,000 moved between 1961 and 1989. Many of these people intended to initiate legal claims to recover former property or to receive indemnification for harms for which they held current East Germans accountable. Moreover, the FRG itself had asserted continuous historical ties and legal claims to the territory and people of the GDR, which it now intended to make good on. Anticipating these claims, the Unity Treaty compelled the FRG to apply different legal registers—for example, GDR law, Soviet occupation law—to crimes that were the result of actions after the defeat of the Third Reich and prior to October 3, 1990 (unless FRG law was milder). The next several chapters are devoted to an account of the first five years of this transition.

Part Two

ETHNOGRAPHY OF CRIMINALITY

The Invocation of the Rechtsstaat in East Germany: Governmental and Unification Criminality

THE INVOCATION

In the chaos that followed the opening of the Berlin Wall on November 9, 1989, illegal activities of an unprecedented scale proliferated to such an extent that police and public prosecutors in East and West Berlin felt overwhelmed. They immediately reestablished the contacts that had been destroyed with the division of Germany in 1949. Officials in the Ministries of Justice commiserated with the police and public prosecutors about difficulties they encountered in responding to the deluge of demands for justice. These demands involved investigating and prosecuting both old crimes committed by the GDR's elite and new crimes made possible by the disintegration of East German authority and, what at that time was not apparent, the impending unification of the two states.[1] This transformation was not an isolated event but part of a general collapse of Cold War controls. It made possible new movements of people and generated new activities and exchanges that had previously been difficult or even impossible.

Following the March 1990 elections, the East and West German governments agreed to a Unity Treaty that included provisions requiring the application of several different legal registers after formal unification. These registers included: GDR law; GDR law supplemented by FRG law; GDR law changed through the United Treaty; Soviet Occupation Law; and FRG law when the penalty was less severe than GDR law. In the months preceding the dissolution of the GDR, jural personnel at federal and local levels in East and West Germany began to meet to discuss how they would merge upon the day of unification. These discussions reached a special intensity in the divided Berlin, for it was clear that the duplication of formerly competing structures and institutions in the eastern half of the city would be superfluous, if not an actual obstacle to further unification.

Indeed, duplicate structures—government ministries, foreign embassies, industries, universities, research institutes—were dealt with on an ad hoc basis. All of those in the West were initially saved. Those in the East that symbolized Cold War differences, that were too costly, too competitive, or not competitive enough, or that posed ideological threats, were eliminated. On the day of unification, October 3, 1990, West Berlin police absorbed the East Berlin Volkspolizei (People's Police) and fired no one. By contrast, West Berlin's Ministry of Justice dismissed all of East Berlin's public prosecutors and judges. Although these East German civil servants were encouraged to reapply for their positions, in the following four years only 15 percent of the 281 new judges and public prosecutors who had worked in East Berlin were reappointed. Thirty percent retired or willingly left public service, with the remaining 55 percent actively rejected by the ministry. Outside of Berlin, judges and public prosecutors were not all initially dismissed, and the rates of reappointment were much higher: for example, Saxony, 65 percent; Brandenburg, 54 percent (Peschel-Gutzeit cited in *Der Tagesspiegel* 1994: 10).[2] In a sensitive account by someone who participated in the evaluations, Inga Markovits (1995: 197) concludes that the "wholesale rejection saves everyone the trouble of acknowledging and facing each individual's specific failures and achievements." Because of the centralized nature of the GDR's police and judicial units, the major archives and federal ministries had been located in or around Berlin. For this and a variety of other reasons, the task of investigating and prosecuting the old and new crime was left primarily to West Berlin officials.

Approximately eleven months following unity, on September 1, 1991, the German Bundestag, Chancellor Kohl, the Federal Ministry of Interior, and the Ministry of Justice followed a recommendation of a conference of interior ministers to create the Zentrale Ermittlungsstelle Regierungs- und Vereinigungskriminalität (ZERV) (Central Investigative Office for Governmental and Unification Criminality). On that date, ZERV began with a team of three men, working under the leadership of Manfred Kittlaus and the auspices of Berlin's president of the police, to coordinate the different ongoing investigations into governmental and unification crime. Public prosecutor Christoph Schaefgen became the leader of the division Regierungskriminalität in the Ministry of Justice. Since then, ZERV has become one of the "five pillars" of the Berlin police department.

ZERV was charged with investigating what has become known as the *strafrechtliche Bewältigung der Vergangenheit der DDR* (overcoming of/reckoning with the GDR's past through criminal law). Technically, its function is to gather and prepare the evidence for the state and, in cases involving the GDR, to prosecute. ZERV inherited 130 members for its investigative staff from various units of Berlin's police. Staff coordination proved exceptionally difficult, for not only was this staff spread out in seven different locations within the newly united Berlin, but also many different city and federal bureaucracies refused to cooperate in building the new unit. As ZERV head Manfred Kittlaus reported in his 1993 midterm report, "The fight to overcome the . . . problems and obstacles was in some respects extremely depressing; it often imparted a feeling of powerlessness against the administration" (ZERV 1993: 46).

For example, in December 1990, before the creation of ZERV, the police departments of other German *Länder* (provinces) had promised to support Berlin by sending two criminal investigative *Beamten* (civil servants) from each of the fifteen Länder—they sent only four. Six months later, in May 1991, the interior ministers promised to send thirty-four investigators to Berlin—instead, only eight arrived. Within Berlin, ZERV fought frequently with other governmental authorities for housing its office and staff, even in cases where buildings had already been assigned to it. In one case, Kittlaus reported that office space that had been employed by the United States army was allocated to ZERV, but the relevant federal authorities refused to acknowledge that the building even existed, much less that it was empty, until they were shown photographs of it (ZERV 1993: 46). By 1994 it appeared that ZERV had solved its space problems by renting buildings from the Berlin-Tempelhof Airport. The problems continued, however. In September 1994, ZERV was suddenly asked to pay rent for parking its vehicles near the airport, forcing employees to park forty of the vehicles a half-hour drive away. This move, in turn, increased transport costs and wasted time that could have been better used for investigations (Kittlaus 1994: 5). Conflicts between Berlin, the Länder, and the federal government over financing also contributed to delays in investigative work.

In December 1991, the new ZERV team completed a review and analysis of the work already accomplished and the tasks yet to be performed. It estimated that with a full staff of 345 investigative civil servants and 100 assistants (secretaries, accountants, economists), its work would last up to ten years (ZERV 1993: 8). In fact, a federal law passed in 1994 obligates the police and public prosecutors to complete all of their work, except for cases involving murder, by October 2 in the year 2000. In private interviews with public prosecutors and ZERV employees, I was told that while ZERV's investigations and prosecutions of governmental criminality will likely end by the year 2000, its investigations of economic crimes were growing in number and would continue well into the next century.

By mid-1993, ZERV employed a total of 331 investigators and administrative assistants, with 149 coming from Berlin, and 182 coming from the Länder and federal government (ZERV 1993: 9). Since its formation, about half of the initial staff (154) have returned to their home bases and have been replaced by new investigators (Kittlaus 1994: 6, pt. 3), with an average yearly fluctuation rate of 20 percent (ZERV 1995: 6).[3] Because most investigations take several years to complete, lack of staff continuity severely hampers the effectiveness of ZERV's work. Continuity in staffing suffered another blow in 1994, when the federal government decided to cut the salary subsidy for ZERV employees who have a home base outside Berlin and therefore must maintain two households.

ZERV is divided into two divisions: Referat 1 deals with unification criminality, Referat 2 with governmental criminality. Unification criminality refers to crime having to do with the economic background and consequences of unification—in other words, primarily with crime that took place after November 1989. About half of the suspects here come from the old Länder of the Federal Republic, half from the GDR. In fact, most of ZERV 1's investigations are of suspected criminal activities engaged in jointly by organized criminal gangs from the old Federal Republic of Germany, or other West bloc states, *and* by former members of the East German state security (Stasi) or former GDR functionaries in the political parties and mass organizations (ZERV 1993: 4).

Crime is a socially constructed category of wrong and unjust deeds; such acts are by definition both socially disapproved of and legally prohibited. Needless to say, definitions of crime vary by place and over time. In the remainder of this chapter, I will focus on the social process in which ZERV has tried to frame various actions as violations of justice, or "crime." This process is a fluid and interactive one. The public pressures the state to react to wrongness; the state, in turn, prosecutes wrongness, sometimes in response to public pressure, but always also according to its own dictates, to which the public is asked to respond. Often public pressure will be insufficient to prompt state action, and the perceived wrong will remain a "misfortune." Or, alternately, state action will find no resonance and support in the public, leading the state to avoid or truncate prosecution, and the designated wrong will go unpunished. In either case—of the action remaining a misfortune from the public's perspective or a designated wrong from the state's— the deed will not become a "crime." In short, crime is never merely what is written in penal codes. It is a result of a complex interaction between the public and the state. And it is an interpretive process, involving the selection of categories of "wrongness" for investigation, the construction of evidence, and a trial.

CREATION OF CRIMINAL CATEGORIES
AND INVESTIGATION OF CRIME:
ZERV 1—UNIFICATION CRIMINALITY

Shortly after its founding, ZERV 1 organized itself into roughly ten different investigative units, with much overlap between units in suspects and sources for evidence. The categories are: (1) Transferrubel fraud, (2) property of the former Socialist Unity Party (SED/PDS) and of mass organizations, (3) the Ministry of State Security (Stasi), (4) the Treuhandanstalt, (5) the currency union, (6) Kommerzielle Koordinierung (KoKo), a GDR agency set up to accumulate convertible (Western) currency, (7) extortion, (8) Western groups of the former Soviet army, (9) embargo violations, and (10) weapons sales. Taken together, these ten units are intended to account for an estimated total of DM 26.5 billion ($17.7 billion) in damages between October 1990 and the fall of 1993. By the end of 1995, ZERV investigations were underway for 13.5 billion of this total. Approximately DM 3 billion has already been recovered since work began in 1990.

The first and fifth categories of crime concern money laundering. The "convertible *rubel*" fraud (category 1) involves a currency, a special rubel, that had been valid only for trade among East bloc countries; it was not convertible into Western currencies. ZERV has been investigating seventy cases of fraud, with damages estimated at DM 8 billion, mostly at the expense of the Deutsche Bundesbank and the Deutsche Außenhandelsbank AG Berlin. By the end of 1995, DM 1.8 billion had been recovered from fraudulent transactions. After the unification of German currencies on July 1, 1990, the exchangeable rubels were converted through GDR currency into West German deutsche Marks. Deutsche Marks, for example, would be exchanged on the black market into Polish zlotys, which would then be legally exchanged into the special rubels, then into GDR Marks, and then into deutsche Marks. Through such exchanges, the value would increase by sevenfold. Many of these cases were settled with fines rather than trials. In an important case that has already made its way through the courts, the accused included a tax consultant and an exiled Russian who were accused of fraudulently accumulating DM 63 million. The district court (Landgericht) found them innocent. The prosecutor won the appeal to the Federal Supreme Court, which sent the decision back to the District Court, which, due to lack of capacity, has not yet reopened it (Kittlaus 1994: 15).

Twelve investigators are at work on 230 cases of other forms of fraud perpetrated in the currency union (category 5). On July 1, 1990, East

German Marks were converted into deutsche Marks at various official rates, pegged to give preference to small private accounts over large ones and to residents of the GDR over West Germans and foreigners. In addition to individuals, many institutions, including West German banks, manipulated their accounts to take advantage of this one-time exchange opportunity. Currently, 360,000 bank accounts are being reviewed, 60,000 of these subject to more thorough review. To date, one-third of all persons investigated have been accused of crimes. Damages are estimated in the billions, the highest estimate being DM 50 billion.

The second category (2) covers approximately 100 investigations into illegal disposal/conversion of property of the ruling political party (SED/PDS), of mass organizations (e.g., the state trade union, the youth organization [Free German Youth], and the Society for German-Soviet Friendship), and of the National People's Army. At stake is property worth an estimated DM 400 to 500 million. Much of this property was merely administered by the party or other proto-state organizations and then, following unity, was turned over to universities, parapublic organizations, private institutions, or private individuals. Also under investigation is the suspected laundering of money or property to the right-wing Russian politician Zhirinovsky, to members of the so-called Russian mafia, and to communist parties in other countries; some of this money now sits in banks in Liechtenstein and Spain. The largest sum to be recovered to date is DM 217 million, from the so-called Putnik Deal, where money was illegally hidden in Norway and the Netherlands.

Twenty investigators have been assigned to category 3, which involves large numbers of widely variant cases of transfers of property and money by the members of the former State Security (Stasi). The Stasi had at its disposal large amounts of cash, automobiles, and buildings, along with 90,000 bank accounts, each used for very different purposes; some, in fact, were used to pay West German agents.

By 1994, 69 investigators were working on illegal activities in the Treuhand's transformation of state into private property (category 4), so-called privatization. The Treuhand officially dissolved in December 1994. Investigations into its work are steadily growing in number, as many of the companies in the initial privatization were simply pillaged of their most valuable assets and must now be reprivatized. As ZERV investigators complete work in other areas, much of the staff is being transferred to this unit. The estimated damages total in the billions of deutsche Marks and are continually being revised upward. The majority of violations here concern either fraudulent representations of the worth of real estate and land, or breach of contract. ZERV uncovered one case, for example, where a firm was sold for one deutsche Mark when the worth was later calculated at DM 100 million (Kittlaus 1994: 23). This type of violation was frequent, as the Treuhand systematically ignored pricing mechanisms in sales on the condition that a certain percentage of workers be carried over into the new firm and that the new owner have a plan for future investment. Later, the buyer easily reneged on this agreement, given that no institution had been set up to control the conditions of the initial contract. In fact, some West German firms under investigation are suspected of having bought East German firms in the same branch with the intent not to make them profitable but to eliminate them as competitors, and to use the government renovation subsidies to prop up West German firms.

The investigation of Koko (category 6), involving three commissioners with 35 investigators under each, was already underway before unification. In the public mind following the opening of the Wall, this "criminality" is linked to the former head of Koko, Stasi employee and leading East German businessman in East-West trade, Alexander Schalck-Golodkowski. The media created him as the personification of all that was corrupt and wrong about the GDR and therefore as the number one object of public scorn. ZERV has had difficulty building an indictment against him, for reasons about which there is constant speculation: he knew too much about West German/European political corruption to risk putting him on trial; he was so smart that he successfully hid culpability for his own illegal dealings; over the years he had established a personal relationship with many of the most prominent Western politicians and businessmen, who now are trying to protect him; the financial dealings were so complex and extensive that it is taking prosecutors longer than in other cases. Under Schalck's leadership, Koko traded in goods of every sort on every continent, from weapons to antiques, with many bank accounts in West European countries. DM 9 million has already been recovered, and the amounts yet to be recovered are estimated in the billions of deutsche Marks.

Category 7 includes 122 cases of extortion of individuals, often prisoners, whose petitions to leave the GDR (*Ausreiseantrag*) were allegedly approved only in return for their agreement to sign away (or sell for a ridiculously low price) their property. Twenty-one of these cases involve Professor Dr. Wolfgang Vogel, the lawyer responsible for arranging not only 150 spy exchanges during the Cold War but also "the freedom" (meaning that the freedom was purchased by the FRG) of 350,000 East Germans by securing property from them and/or money from the West German government in return. The next chapter is devoted to the trial of Dr. Vogel.

Category 8 is an unintended result of the agreement signed by Helmut Kohl and Mikhail Gorbachev in October 1990 that sealed

German unification. In return for his support of German unification, Kohl promised Gorbachev a great deal of money, including some to resettle Soviet troops in Russia, to pay for their return, and to build them housing. He promised DM 3 billion immediately, DM 3 billion on a long-term credit basis, and another DM 1 billion to pay for the transport back. Much of this money has since disappeared, however, with ZERV suspecting deals between "Russian exiles" living in Germany and former Stasi agents. Damages are estimated at DM 500 million.

Twelve investigators are pursuing the violations of embargoes (category 9). Prosecutors have already taken 50 cases to court, mostly involving West German firms selling (through Koko; see category 6) high technology products and industrial secrets or plans, primarily to customers in Russia or other former Soviet countries. Damages are estimated to be in the hundred million deutsche Marks. Category 10 involves the very lucrative post-1989 business of smuggling Soviet and GDR military weaponry and goods to states officially under a weapons embargo (e.g., Yugoslavia, Iraq, Iran). This business has boomed since the opening of borders throughout East-Central Europe in 1990. And because high-ranking officials in several countries are suspected of involvement, it is extremely difficult to gather sufficient evidence.

In 1995, ZERV opened up two new investigative areas: crimes involved in the return to former owners of GDR property and crimes committed in transforming GDR's agricultural collectives into West German property forms. As of fall 1994, the public prosecutor had handed out 27 indictments in this entire area of unification crime. Ten cases resulted in sentences, with 6 of them final judgments.

CREATION OF CRIMINAL CATEGORIES AND INVESTIGATION OF CRIME: ZERV 2—GOVERNMENTAL CRIMINALITY

ZERV 2 investigates high-level representatives of the party and government as well as state functionaries who committed crimes while carrying out their offices. These crimes are acts of violence against people and often involve human rights violations. By the end of 1995, ZERV 2 had investigated 7,414 incidents. Moreover, 70 percent of all the investigations of ZERV 2, and over half of the overall total of ZERV investigations, have been for either attempted or completed homicides (Kittlaus 1993: 38). The acts investigated took place over the entire period of GDR history, from 1949 to 1989, and the people subject to investigation worked at all levels of the state hierarchy, from the post office to the Politburo. Of the 4,691 individual suspects, 213 held high-level posts (first lieutenant, major, major general, general, minister of state) (Kittlaus 1994: 29).

The first completed investigation that resulted in a trial and conviction was of election fraud, with a focus on the regional elections of May 7, 1989. It resulted in five trials, with five convictions, including those of two former party secretaries in Dresden. Prosecuting this case of election fraud was both a direct response to demands of the GDR's dissidents, who had thought they could delegitimate the GDR by getting voters to take their participation seriously in the 1989 election, and an attempt to establish the credibility of the new political system. It stands, however, as a singular case and does not fall into other categories of ZERV investigation.

The Public Prosecutor's Office lists three major areas of criminal prosecution, while ZERV 2 divides its criminal investigations into roughly nine categories. ZERV 2 is investigating (1) border violations, (2) contract murder by the Stasi, (3) kidnapping, (4) deaths on the Baltic Sea, (5) *Rechtsbeugung* (judicial illegality), (6) repression of the GDR worker rebellion on June 17, 1953, (7) doping of athletes, (8) forced relocation in 1952 and 1961, and (9) environmental crime. The Public Prosecutor's Office has made indictments in three general areas: "attempted and completed manslaughter on the inner-German border"; "Rechtsbeugung in acts involving imprisonment or manslaughter though the judicial organs of the GDR"; and "manslaughter, imprisonment, and violation of mail privacy by members of the Stasi" (Schaefgen 1994: 151).

Investigations of border violations (category 1) encompass all *Gewalttaten* (violent acts) that occurred over a period of forty years, from January 14, 1949, to February 5, 1989, on the German-German border and at the Berlin Wall. Over 4,000 border incidents were initially listed, resulting in 2,668 investigations, with 2,641 suspects, of whom 213 are of high rank (ZERV 1994: 8). In cases that occurred outside Berlin, the prosecutions are given over to the Länder within whose jurisdiction they fall. By mid-1994, over 300 indictments had been made, limited by the public prosecutor to cases of manslaughter or attempted homicide by border guards, police, and their superiors. Following a Bundesgerichtshof (Supreme Court) decision on June 8, 1993, in which a soldier was found not guilty of attempted homicide for shooting at someone's legs, the prosecutor stopped indicting soldiers when shooting did not result in death (Schaefgen 1994: 154).

By February 1995, forty border guards and their superiors had been indicted (the so-called Mauerschützenprozesse) on charges ranging from manslaughter to assisting homicide, and twenty of the trials have been completed. Of the border guards and their officers already tried, judgments range from acquittals to several years of imprisonment. The first case resolved was that of the shooting of twenty-year-old Chris Gueffroy in early 1989, the last victim at the Wall. The trial resulted in the conviction of two guards of manslaughter, one sentenced to three and one-half years imprisonment, the other to two years on probation. Two others accused in this case were acquitted. In another case, one former leader of the border guards was sentenced to six years imprisonment in 1992, for shooting a man who was defenselessly cowering in a ravine at the border in 1965. A third trial, completed in July 1994, sentenced a thirty-two-year-old guard to two years on probation for killing a refugee, having shot him in the head after he had already stopped (whereas GDR law specified to try to stop the flight by shooting at the feet).

The most famous trial in this domain completed to date was that of members of the National Defense Committee. It took place between November 12, 1992, and September 16, 1993, and resulted in the sentencing of the three senior officers—Heinz Keßler, Fritz Streletz, and Hans Albrecht—to seven and one-half, five and one-half, and four and one-half years imprisonment for 74 cases of "attempted and completed manslaughter." The case was appealed because the accusers wanted a more severe charge and a higher penalty, which they got from the Federal Supreme Court in July 1994. In November 1994, the Federal Constitutional Court issued a temporary stay on the imprisonment. However, when the Constitutional Court finally decided the case, in November 1996, it upheld the convictions and penalties. Other members of the GDR officers corps at different levels have also been indicted.

The longest running and most complicated ZERV investigation was completed in January 1995. State prosecutors indicted seven members of the Politburo, including Egon Krenz, the successor to Honecker, for their responsibility in "manslaughter and attempted manslaughter" on the border. The judge received a 1,600 page indictment, with the major charge being that these men did nothing to stop the human rights violations (homicide on the border) though they held the positions on the National Defense Board responsible for them. An earlier indictment against Erich Honecker on similar grounds was stopped because he fled or was allowed to flee to Chile. Trials of two other members of the Politburo, Willi Stoph and Günter Mittag, were stopped because of Stoph's incompetency and Mittag's illness. Erich Mielke was sentenced to six years imprisonment for a 1931 murder, and while imprisoned awaited a second trial on six manslaughter charges for deaths on the border. On August 1, 1995, the eighty-seven-year-old Mielke was released after having served two-thirds of his sentence. At the time, he was the only man accused of governmental criminality while he was still sitting behind bars. Through the fall of 1994, this entire complex of border crimes had resulted in 52 trials, with 16 convictions, of which 7 are final judgments (Schaefgen 1994: 158).

Contract murders (category 2) and kidnapping (category 3) are crimes involving the same category of victim (former West Berliners/ Germans) and the same group of suspects (members of the Stasi). To date, ZERV has uncovered 21 cases of attempted or completed "elimination" of what the GDR called *Staatsfeinden* (enemies of the state). Kidnapping was officially called an act of *Rückführung* (return), and it was followed by a trial with a certain death sentence or long-term imprisonment. Three groups of persons were kidnapped: political opponents (e.g., journalists, emigrants), *Abtrünnige* (disloyal former members of the Stasi, army, or police), or people of interest to the KGB (Soviet secret police). By fall 1994, public prosecutors were investigating 550 incidents concerning 580 victims, ten of whom had been executed in the GDR. They had made two indictments (ZERV 1994: 8). By fall 1994, 30 of the 54 investigations of attempted and successful homicides of people fleeing the GDR on the Baltic Sea (category 4) had been completed, with the rest to be completed by the end of 1995.

Rechtsbeugung (judicial illegality) (category 5) is a term without an equivalent in the Anglo-Saxon legal tradition, where there are many checks on or corrections of the judge's power. In the German tradition judges and public prosecutors enjoy a great deal of autonomy. This autonomy, coupled with the (on-the-surface-contradictory) fact that GDR judges and prosecutors tended to be selected (or self-selected) for their loyalty to state doctrine and the political leadership, led at times to two kinds of abuses of power: of state prosecutors purposefully misconstruing evidence to construct a crime (in the interests of the state), and of judges giving sentences disproportional (in excess of) to the crimes. The police are investigating 1,068 sentences where the judiciary apparently failed to guarantee its independence and functioned as an arm of the executive. Suspects include both jural personnel (judges, state prosecutors) and the party functionaries responsible for subverting the judiciary. By the end of 1994, ZERV had investigated 346 cases, with several thousand more to be examined; it had identified 532 victims, of whom 16 had been executed. Outside of Berlin, the other Länder are investigating their own cases. Most of the indictments have been for failure to protect the rights of citizens who had petitioned to leave the GDR since the mid-1970s. Most of these petitioners had been systematically discriminated against, even after the GDR agreed in 1975 to the Helsinki provisions supposedly guaranteeing freedom of movement. By fall 1994, 17 indictments had been made against judges and public prosecutors, 40 against other jural officials; four of the completed trials resulted in sentences that were overturned on appeal. Thus far, courts of appeal have refused to penalize East German jural personnel for enforcing policies that were held to be "normal" in the GDR; they have sentenced people only for "clearly arbitrary application of GDR law" or for the application of excessive penalties that resulted in a clear violation of human rights (ZERV 1995: 20).

Another ZERV team is taking statements from witnesses and searching archives for information on those in the leadership of the party responsible for criminal activities during or suppression of the GDR worker rebellion of June 17, 1953 (category 6). A total of 125 people died in and following the riot, of whom 48 were immediately shot after its suppression. Twenty-three Soviet soldiers were executed for refusing to shoot at the Germans.

Thirty-two GDR doctors and sports officials in gymnastics, swimming, canoeing, track and field, weight lifting, and rowing are charged with systematically doping (category 7) at least eight hundred athletes without their consent in order to improve their performances. ZERV investigators have focused on a series of hormone experiments performed on juvenile athletes between 1985 and 1990, and on the use of dangerous and perhaps illegal vitamin concentrates during the Olympic games. Seventeen of these athletes are known to suffer from resultant health problems; several deaths are being investigated.

Two waves of forced resettlement in 1952 and in 1961 (category 8) are part of another investigation. In both periods, the GDR attempted to create a secure border through a *Säuberungsaktion* (cleansing action) in the border regions along the German-German border. In 1952, 8,422 persons were relocated; in 1961, 3,640 persons were resettled. In the 1952 action, the state singled out certain categories of people for resettlement: foreigners and stateless people, owners of large farms, prostitutes, criminals, economic criminals, border crossers, agents, and the politically unreliable (Kittlaus 1994: 50).

Finally, ZERV is investigating environmental damage (category 9) that violated GDR environmental regulations. The violations were caused either by overzealous fulfillment of economic plans or purposeful dumping of military wastes by Soviet military units. Most of damage was to nature, but some individuals who worked in specific industries or lived in certain areas also suffer lasting effects such as bronchitis and cancer.

By the end of 1994, over 700 criminal investigations had either been completed or stopped. Other investigations have been stopped because ZERV gathered insufficient evidence, the trials were not clearly in the "public interest" (which I discuss in more detail below), the suspect died, ZERV was unsuccessful at either the indictment or the trial stage, or because higher courts overturned initial convictions. Calculating and responding to "public interest" has been a decisive issue for ZERV, since prosecuting without public interest would have little immediate effect on either the incidence of crime or the establishment of the principle of accountability. Prosecuting against the wishes of the public would in most cases create the image of persecution of a surrogate victim. Hence, for ZERV the issue has been not only choosing actual perpetrators of crime, but also of choosing the "right" ones for prosecution. For example, loss of public interest was one of the major reasons public prosecutors dropped further investigations into mail fraud. A probe into the violation of citizen rights by wiretapping telephones and violating mail privacy (even stealing money or other valuables from the post) initially found wide-scale abuse. But when the Supreme Court ruled out wiretapping as a crime in a decision on December 9, 1993, all investigations in that area were dropped. And in cases involving violations of mail privacy, both lower and higher courts issued contradictory opinions. The most famous case of this kind, in which postal employees stole 32 million (GDR) Marks in cash, and over DM 10 million worth of objects from packages, resulted in a not-guilty finding in February 1994 by a Berlin district court (reaffirmed on appeal) because the employees (working for the post and the Stasi) had not personally enriched themselves. On March 7, 1995, the Fifth Senate of the Federal Supreme Court overruled the decision of the Fourth Senate (which had reaffirmed the decision) and found the employees guilty. The public prosecutor then decided to make further investigations contingent on the interest of the victims (Schaefgen 1994: 154). With no interest group or other public organization showing interest in this area, all further action by ZERV has been stopped.

THE INVESTIGATION

Many of ZERV's investigations began in response to citizen complaints or tipoffs. During all the probes, the *Staatsanwalt* (public prosecutor) is expected to remain neutral and is bound by law to investigate on behalf of both the defendant and the state. Prosecutors are called *Köpfe ohne Hände* (heads without hands), because they have no investigators of their own and instead have to rely on the police. Police investigators follow up an initial tip or complaint by interrogating suspects or questioning witnesses to determine whether the act (*Tat*) constitutes a crime (*Verbrechen*). An *Ermittlungsrichter* (judge who deals with investigations) may be asked to issue search warrants or authorize arrests.

If the police gather sufficient evidence to warrant a trial, then the prosecutor is compelled to proceed only if the case is in the public interest (*das öffentliche Interesse*). Considered "guardians of the law," prosecutors are not independent, as are judges, but act in the public interest as *Beamten* (civil servants), supervised by the Ministries of Justice of the different provinces. Prosecutors need not proceed if they consider the matter insignificant or something that can be resolved personally by the parties involved. Alternatively, if they deem the evidence insufficient, they may suspend an investigation temporarily until more evidence or sources turn up. Though a suspect is presumed innocent until proven guilty, the suspicion of wrongdoing remains until the crime is publicly accounted for. Prosecutors retain the right to reopen closed cases if new evidence is found, provided the applicable statute of limitations has not expired. Except for homicide cases, which can be reopened indefinitely, the statute of limitations for most of the crimes investigated by ZERV, already extended twice, will expire at the end of 1996. As mentioned earlier, lawmakers specified October 2, 2000, as the date by which ZERV must have completed all investigations.

TRANSFORMING MISFORTUNE INTO INJUSTICE: THE ROLE OF ARCHIVES AND EVIDENCE

The evidential base of ZERV investigations has been one of the most controversial aspects of its work. Without corroborating and believable sources outside of the victim's own account, prosecutors would not have the kind of evidence needed to make an indictment in most cases. Yet most of the corroborating sources on governmental and unification crime are documents written by the suspected perpetrators or their accomplices, not by putatively independent or impartial witnesses. If the GDR was an *Unrechtsstaat* (an illegal state), as many claim, a criminal band unconcerned with truth or justice, then its own data banks and archives are of questionable reliability. Without reliable corroborative sources of evidence, a deed cannot be linked to a crime, and the courts have no obligation to remedy the suffering caused by acts of GDR functionaries. The experience of the victim remains merely a misfortune and not an injustice.

ZERV must find, in addition to evidence that links the deed to the crime, an agent to hold accountable for the crime. If both conditions are not met, then the misfortune does not become an injustice, and the deed is relevant to criminal law. Natural catastrophes such as earthquakes and floods, for example, can be proven to have occurred, but rarely can they be said to be caused by human agency. With nobody

responsible for the deed, there is no crime and therefore can be no prosecution. What prevents a full account of injustice and the clarification of
"crime" is obscurity about how and when this transformation from
misfortune to injustice occurs. Contrary to what Judith Shklar claims
(1990: 8–9), it is not the "groundless belief [in] a stable and rigid distinction between the unjust and the unfortunate" that prevents us from
giving a full account of injustice. Perhaps it is true that jurists and legal
scholars represent legal systems *as if* they hold to a firm distinction
between misfortune and injustice. But this distinction is nowhere "stable and rigid." It is fluid and changing, and frequently subject to political respecification. With sufficient evidence linking a deed to a formal
"crime," and with a suspect to hold accountable for the deed, one can
turn any misfortune into an injustice.

ZERV's investigations are precisely about performing such a transformation from misfortune to injustice. Together with public prosecutors, ZERV creates the possibility to claim "injustice" by constructing a
narrative that sequentially links crime, deed, and suspect (agent of the
crime). The legal name for this narrative is indictment (*Anklage*). A
judge need not accept the grounds for this indictment, but can either
reject it altogether or reconstruct its legal reasoning. In any case, this
narrative is to be constructed from the evidence, which, in turn, must
be uncovered and gathered.

Most of ZERV 2's initial investigations were of deaths, in particular,
manslaughter on one of the GDR's borders. For this work its most important source was the *Zentrale Erfassungssstelle der Landesjustizver-
waltungen* (Central Register of the Country's Judicial Administration)
in Salzgitter. In 1961, shortly after the first person was shot at the Berlin
Wall, Willy Brandt, the ruling mayor of Berlin, called for the opening of
an archive to document *SED-Unrecht* (crimes of the Socialist Unity
Party). The response was to establish the center in Salzgitter, near the
German-German border in Niedersachsen, to investigate GDR crimes,
particularly those having to do with shooting at the border or the Berlin Wall, mistreatment of prisoners, kidnapping or political persecution, and judicial illegalities (Grasemann 1992: 55–63). This archive was
not tainted by GDR functionaries and therefore was considered to con-
tain reliable, if insufficient, evidence. It became relevant for the judicial
system only following the resignation of Erich Honecker in October
1989, after which the East German Ministry of Justice began revising
certain laws and reforming the judicial system. Soon thereafter it became possible to use West German or reformed East German criminal
courts to hold accountable those who had ordered and carried out the
shootings during the GDR's history. Within weeks of the opening of
the Wall, parents of young men who had been shot trying to cross the

border appealed to West Berlin's Ministry of Justice for remedy. They wanted to transform what was once an accident or even a "heroic act" of the perpetrator, according to GDR law, and a misfortune (if not even a "shameful act") for the deceased and his relatives, into a crime or injustice, with an identifiable victim and with particular individuals held accountable.

The number of potential victims of injustice, and, in turn, the potential number of criminals, has steadily increased with the opening of new archives. In 1989, for example, the Salzgitter register listed 199 deaths and 700 wounded on the border (Grasemann 1992: 58). By 1992, the number of deaths had risen to 372. By December 1992, ZERV noted that "with certainty the dead number more than 400" (Kittlaus 1993: 2). By 1994, information in other archives had increased the number to 538, with 369 intentionally shot, and 40 killed by mines (ZERV 1994: 8). The roles of victim (or hero) and criminal (or villain) have reversed: the former GDR criminal engaged in *Republikflucht*, "flight from the republic," has become a hero for his flight to the West, commemorated in the Wall Museum in Berlin on Friedrichstraße, while the border guard and his commanding officers, the former heroes, have become criminals.

The Salzgitter register is no longer the sole source of evidence used by police. In September 1992, the Militärisches Zwischenarchiv Potsdam (Military Interim-Archive Potsdam) also opened. This former GDR archive near Berlin includes daily records of all incidents involving the border guards of the National People's Army, a kind of "insider log" unavailable in Salzgitter. After ZERV investigators (category 9, environmental crime) compared Salzgitter records with those in Potsdam, they increased the number of border incidents they were investigating, depending on the year, from two- to sevenfold. For example, in 1961, Salzgitter had recorded 56 border incidents, Potsdam 141; in 1963, Salzgitter 38, Potsdam 191; in 1971, Salzgitter 11, Potsdam 87 (ZERV 1993: 28). Since accounting for deaths on the German-German border is considered important for the greater public good, ZERV is investigating these incidents for illegalities, and above all for cases of attempted homicide.

Two further sources of information for the above cases first became available to ZERV in early 1992: the 2,400 volumes of documents of GDR's Ministry of Interior and the records of the Ministry of State Security (Stasi), the latter now administered by the Gauck-Authority (more on this below). In the Stasi archive, ZERV found two hundred papers and documents that describe acts taken to "secure the border-system of the GDR" (Kittlaus 1993: 48). Stasi film, radio, and television archives, in particular, have been important sources in prosecutions of manslaughter.

In a similar manner, the team investigating deaths on the Baltic Sea (category 4) was formed in response to information in the Potsdam archive, which, as mentioned, first became available in September 1992. Since then, however, this team has gained access to other information (e.g., death certificates, autopsies) in the Institutes for Forensic Medicine in Bad Saarow, Greifswald, and Rostock, as well as details from Danish police authorities, who also witnessed some of these events. The new information has both increased the number of probable victims of official criminality and strengthened the case of ZERV investigators against those suspected of Baltic Sea crimes. With additional evidence on the nature of deaths, the new archives are literally making possible the transformation of misfortune into homicide.

Other new evidential sources include such widely disparate collections as the archive of GDR's Ministry of Health (especially useful for environmental crime); documents of the former State Bank of the GDR and of the Savings Bank of the State Security (revealing double identities, double residences, illegal securing of property belonging to the Treuhand, spying activities of West German agents for the Stasi); and the Zentrales Einwohnerregister der DDR (ZER) (Central Register of Residences of the GDR). This last register was closed in August 1992, with the documents turned over to the 239 different registration offices in the five new Länder. The office in East Berlin was given over to West Berlin shortly after unification. The physical and administrative dispersal of formerly centralized residency files has made it extremely cumbersome for ZERV to gain access to this information. Another register containing information on GDR residency was held by the Stasi and is now controlled by the Gauck-Authority, but it remained closed until February 1994. ZERV began working with this register during the last half of 1994.

RECKONING WITH THE CRIMINAL PAST:
ZERV AND THE GAUCK-AUTHORITY

The fate of ZERV is closely intertwined with that of the Gauck-Authority. In 1991, the German Bundestag passed a law, the Stasiunter-lagengesetz, which established the Stasi Document Center, colloquially known as the Gauck-Authority. For ZERV the archives of the Gauck-Authority have been by far the most important source in the investigation of economic crimes, which is primarily the domain of unification criminality covered by ZERV 2. To a much lesser extent, ZERV 1 has used these archives to prosecute governmental criminality. Beyond the judicial use of the files, their primary function has been for private citizens and historians to uncover those parts of their past involving Stasi activities.

Both before and after the regime change, "the Stasi" invoked a mythical authority: it was both an object containing knowledge (unknown details about the pasts of approximately one-third of all citizens) and an object producing knowledge (a mysterious force to which many people imputed all-knowing omnipotence). Given the actual power of the former State Security to influence if not control the lives of East Germans, access and control over the Stasi archives has been central to the German imaginary since the opening of the Wall.

During the demonstrations in October 1989 leading to this opening, demonstrators feared that the Stasi would brutally repress them in order to save the regime. Citizen fear turned to resentment once the Stasi proved unable to keep the people from organizing and demonstrating. In early December 1989, local civil rights committees in the GDR decided to occupy Stasi regional centers. It took another six weeks before they managed to occupy the main office in Berlin-Lichtenberg. Three thousand sacks of shredded documents and damaged dossiers awaited the citizen committees. The electronic databases that linked files to names had been destroyed as well. Following the March 1990 elections, the minister of interior set up a committee under the direction of civil rights activist and minister Joachim Gauck to supervise the breakup of the security forces. In 1990, the East German Volkskammer passed a law regulating access and use, which was later slightly modified and written into the Unity Treaty. Gauck was then appointed to administer the documents. In October 1990, the West German public prosecutor and judge Hansjörg Geiger joined Gauck to build the administration. Thereafter Gauck represented the public face of the Stasi Document Center, emphasizing independence from the political parties, loyalty to ordinary East Germans, to the civil rights movement, and to democracy. Geiger worked behind the scenes as a *Beamte* (civil servant), loyal above all to the Federal Republic.[4]

Both the Gauck-Authority and ZERV were set up to perform a uniquely German postwar function: *Bewältigung der Vergangenheit* (reckoning with the past). In this case, the past was that of the GDR. The Gauck-Authority was charged with a general enlightenment about this past through personal and historical research; ZERV with a reckoning through the mechanisms of criminal justice. Bewältigung is a highly disputed practice in Germany. Up to 1989 among West Germans, *Bewältigung der Vergangenheit* has been taken to mean "overcoming/reckoning with the Nazi past." The meaning of *Bewältigung* in conjunction with a "past" has proven impossible to fix. Both terms are continually redefined, especially among historians (who tend to focus on reckoning with the everyday and the political) and legal experts (who focus on reckoning with the political and the criminal). Given this specific West German history of the phrase, its use today implicitly sets up a comparison of the GDR with the Third Reich.

In East Germany, the term *Bewältigung* was less frequently used. There the state had represented itself as officially antifascist, and the judicial system had dealt harshly with suspected Nazi crime. For many East Germans, this new reckoning with GDR's past tends to equate their personal histories with those of Nazis and, by comparison, makes West German personal histories look untainted and clean, or, in short, morally superior. They also suspect that this reckoning is intended to make up for the West German judicial system's avoidance of or failure to reckon with Nazi crime following the Third Reich. Consequently, some East Germans, most vehemently those under suspicion for crime, have denounced ZERV's work, calling it: *Siegerjustiz* (victor's justice), *Hexenjagd* (witch-hunt), *Kriminalisierung weiterer Teile der DDR-Bevölkerung* (a criminalization of more portions of the GDR population), and *politische Strafverfolgung im Auftrage der gerade Herrschenden* (political persecution through criminal law commissioned by the present ruling class).

The Gauck-Authority employs more than 3,000 staff members and administers almost 120 miles of shelves of documents. Its relative significance in the political arena is apparent when its large staff is compared to the 345 investigators with ZERV. Controversy surrounds all three of its functions (judicial, historical, and personal), but the archive has been most problematic when used to vet political figures or civil servants for Stasi collaboration, either as full-time or as *Inoffizielle Mitarbeiter* (IM), undercover collaborators. Someone found to have worked for the Stasi is subject to immediate disqualification from public service.[5] Failure to distinguish between degrees of culpability has discredited the archives as a source and Gauck as the public representative of a moral authority. In fact, perceived injustice in the treatment of IMs has consistently led to calls for a general amnesty or a closing of the Stasi files (cf. Heitmann 1993; Schätzler 1995). Such calls for a stop to IM review and disqualification are, then, often extended to argue for a stop to ZERV investigations also. ZERV, in turn, has tried to distance itself from the issue of the treatment of IMs. In fact, not a single IM has been investigated for his/her undercover activity by ZERV, for only the actions of full-time Stasi agents fall under criminal categories.[6]

Without public support, the kind of reckoning with the past engaged in by both the Gauck-Authority and ZERV would end. Hence, both Gauck and Kittlaus (for ZERV) must convince the public, over an increasingly vocal opposition, of the need for the continued existence of their offices. To this end, they are frequent contributors to newspapers and appear often on radio and television. The public prosecutor's office has followed traditional German legal practice of not publicizing its own work directly in the press except for reports on indictments and trials made by the Ministry of Justice itself. Closing the Stasi files altogether, which is possible but unlikely, would severely hamper ZERV investigations.

PRELIMINARY PROCEEDINGS (ZWISCHENVERFAHREN)

Unlike prosecutors, who are civil servants and bound to represent the interests of the state, the approximately twenty-thousand judges in Germany enjoy radical autonomy. They are appointed for life and cannot be dismissed except under extraordinary circumstances, and they are bound only to the Basic Law. Even precedent does not bind judges, as it does in the common law tradition. Appeals to higher courts result in decisions binding only for the individual cases at hand. Hence the decisions of the Federal Constitutional Court (Bundesverfassungsgericht) or the Federal Supreme Court (Bundesgerichtshof) need never be reconciled with various federal court opinions, though national legal norms do develop over time.

Before a case goes to trial, the public prosecutor, as noted above, must first decide if there is sufficient evidence for an indictment (*Anklage*). He then presents his case to a court, presided over by a judge. Which court receives any particular indictment is a matter of accident. Usually cases are assigned to a court alphabetically for the year. For example, a court might receive for consideration cases where indictments are of persons whose last names begin with *U* and *W*. A second evaluation of the evidence, called a preliminary proceeding (*Zwischenverfahren*), takes place in the lowest court for the type of case under consideration. If that court concurs with the prosecutor, the case is assigned to a trial judge.

THE TRIAL (HAUPTVERFAHREN)

Even if the judge in the preliminary proceedings decides positively, the trial judge may still reject the case (*Ablehnung*) on the grounds that there is insufficient evidence or that the case is not in the public interest.

If the judge tries the case, s/he takes an active part in the process, directly questioning witnesses and discussing evidence. The prosecutor and the defense counsel (*Rechtsanwalt*) also pose direct questions, but the partial and rapacious cross-examination typical of Anglo-American trials is absent. This is so partly because the crime, and not the defendant, is the object of a criminal proceeding. Hence clarification of "the crime"—what actually happened that potentially violated a law—is, at least theoretically, the focus of inquiry. Also, the defendant frequently engages in cross-examining witnesses.

At this point, before moving on to a more general account of the the results of the trials and the evaluations of these results, I will offer an ethnographic description of a trial. Most media, literary, and social scientific accounts focus solely on the actual trial and tend to neglect the aspects that I have been describing: the investigation of evidence, interpretation of crime, construction of categories of victims and criminals, and, to follow, the vindication of victims and the legitimation of the Rechtsstaat. My focus is intended partially to rectify omissions in other accounts. In addition, I suspect that the actual trial proceedings are only of minor significance in terms of invoking and legitimating the principles of Rechtsstaatlichkeit today. Trials are not well attended, and most of what the public learns about them comes either from print media or television. Moreover, in a Rechtsstaat the sequence of events in a trial follows regular procedures that have changed little over the last century. In Germany the unusual and rapid installation of the Rechtsstaat form in the East after the revolution in November 1989 did not require any radical changes in the procedural aspects of criminal justice. However, the nature of evidence, the (inter-national) framework, and the interpretation of accountability changed dramatically. In particular, this legal reckoning with the past illustrates the conservative uses to which both a hermeneutical and a system theoretical approach lent themselves in postunity debates about justice.[7] Theorists working within both traditions clearly lacked a critical perspective with respect to the relation of truth to power, and with respect to the principle of state sovereignty, a point to which I return in the following chapters.

CHAPTER 5

Accountability on Trial

WHAT HAPPENS when former government officials of East bloc states are put on trial? How is accountability framed? Do such trials legitimate the new Rechtsstaat? Do such trials contribute to the control of violence? I have selected a single prosecution for ethnographic description before I move on to a more general evaluation of this and other trial results. It is by no means typical of justice in either East Germany or other former socialist states; each political community has concerned itself with different domains of accountability. This case does illustrate, however, the challenges of bringing about justice and establishing principles of accountability in East-Central Europe in several ways: the difficulty of making clear distinctions between criminal and victim, the difficulty of locating criminality in the center, the difficulties inherent in an originary invocation of the principles of the rule of law, and the difficulty in establishing a fair evaluative position given the intertwining of socialist and Western European legal regimes during the Cold War. The trial is of Professor Dr. Wolfgang Vogel, who was charged with extortion in the German Democratic Republic.[1] Two major issues framed his trial, one empirical and one theoretical. The empirical question posed is whether Professor Vogel functioned as a typical lawyer in his relations with clients or whether his behavior was in some way exceptional. What does "normal behavior" consist of in a lawyer's interactions with clients in the GDR, or, in more general terms, in a former socialist state? If his behavior was normal, then it might seem unfair and arbitrary to single him out for accountability. The theoretical question concerns whether Vogel was a "substitute sacrifice" (in which case his prosecution would delegitimate the rule of law) or the "actual perpetrator" guilty of committing wrongs (in which case his prosecution would legitimate the rule of law).

The following description is based primarily on my own intermittent witnessing of parts of the trial from December 1994 through July 1995 and on legal transcripts. The trial lasted approximately fourteen months, with a verdict reached on January 9, 1996. I have also drawn freely on the following sources: a summary of this trial by the legal historian Uwe Wesel (1995: 2); a transcribed interview with the head public prosecutor in this case, Dr. Bernhard Brocher; an interview with two of the plaintiffs, Waldemar and Vera Zapff; discussions with others whom Professor Vogel had represented when he practiced law in the former East Germany; and primary source written documents, in particular a report by an investigative commission of the German Parliament (Bundestag 1994b: 1–548).

EXTORTION: PROFESSOR DR. VOGEL

In November 1994, the public prosecutor's office in Berlin indicted the seventy-year-old Professor Dr. Wolfgang Vogel for extortion. The trial took place in the Sixth Senior Criminal Court of the District Court of Berlin, in the criminal courthouse in Berlin-Moabit, a mammoth building with an attached prison first completed as part of a wave of new courthouses following the German unification of 1871. This District Court meets alternately in one of several small rooms made entirely of wood, with old wooden chairs and benches that squeak loudly with the slightest movement. The rooms have horrible acoustics, which made it extremely difficult for me to hear the judge, lawyers, and witnesses, seated as I was in the back on one of the spectator pews that could seat around twenty to thirty people but most frequently included only five or six others. The only regular visitor was a television crew that usually came to catch Dr. Vogel as he arrived, on days when the court called an unusual witness or when the court was expected to make a significant decision. The television crew often brought the cameras into the courtroom but had to leave before the judge opened the proceedings. Early on in the trial, most of the other spectators were witnesses with a particular interest in the case, for they hoped that a conviction of Professor Vogel would increase their chances to reobtain the houses they had sold with the help of the accused before they left the GDR.

The presiding judge in the case, Dr. Heinz Holzinger, led the questioning of the defendants and witnesses in a friendly, neutral, and careful manner. Sitting next to the judge were two other professional judges and two lay judges (*Schöffen*), who together with Dr. Holzinger eventually reached a verdict in a complex voting procedure. Theoretically, all five judges have equal voting rights. In practice, the lay judges nearly always follow the presiding judge. Flanking these four men and one woman were a stenographer, a substitute professional judge, and two substitute lay judges. Also at the bench sat one or two state prosecutors. Perpendicular to and beneath the bench where the judges, prosecutors, and stenographer sat are two tables where the accused sat with their attorneys. There were two accused in this trial: Professor Vogel and Erika Dörrfeld, a former employee in Dr. Vogel's law office. At one table sat Professor Vogel, flanked by his three attorneys; at the table facing them sat Erika Dörrfeld with her two attorneys. In between the two tables and facing the judge was a chair where witnesses sat when they testified.

The public prosecutors said very little during the trial, and attorneys for both sides only occasionally asked questions of the witnesses or the judge. Professor Vogel himself appeared to know the material and the law extremely well, and he conducted much of his own questioning of witnesses, as did Erika Dörrfeld. To an American visitor such as myself, it was often striking that neither the judge nor the public prosecutors came to the aid of witnesses when Professor Vogel and his attorneys appeared to have led them to a specific response that contradicted their general testimony. Before the trial began, the defense attorneys and public prosecutors drew up a list of witnesses, from which the judge selected those he thought necessary to call. Professor Vogel's major indictment was for twenty-one cases of extortion. Erika Dörrfeld was indicted as an accessory.[2]

To coerce someone with force or threat is intimidation (*Nötigung*). When intimidation involves property, the act becomes extortion (*Erpressung*). Although Professor Vogel's violations involved actual harm done to persons, the significance of his case lies not in the degree of harm suffered by the victims (issues of corrective justice) but in the nature of the moral wrongness of his actions (issues of restitutive justice). In other words, intimidation and not loss of property is the central issue to be explained in this case. As we shall see, however, moral wrongs and harms are very difficult to separate clearly in legal cases.

Decisions about whether to return property to the people from whom Professor Vogel and Frau Dörrfeld putatively extorted it rest not with this criminal court, but with a special administrative court responsible for settling "open property questions," as they are called—ownership disputes since unification. Many of the people who had sold their houses through Professor Vogel had gotten them back already in 1990. Others, however, are still waiting for decisions from this court. In preparation of their administrative cases, they have access to documents from Professor Vogel's office or from the Gauck-Authority, but the can do so only if they can claim to be "harmed" as the term is defined in criminal law. Because of the trial against Professor Vogel, most of the putatively extorted individuals are able to obtain documents from state-controlled archives that will strengthen their administrative cases involving corrective justice. Decisions of the administrative court concerning their property will likely be influenced by the result of this criminal trial, but the administrative court is not required to take into consideration the decision of the criminal court regarding Professor

Vogel's guilt or innocence. Furthermore, at issue in Vogel's trial was not the property itself but the context in which he committed extortion: was he acting as a "normal" private lawyer in the interests of his clients or as an agent for the state?

At stake in this case was real estate such as property on Wandlitz Lake, an hour's drive north of Berlin (where the former GDR Politburo had built its residential quarter), a two-family home in Berlin-Köpenick, a weekend house on the island of Rügen, and a small apartment in Berlin-Kaulsdorf. These pieces of real estate were passionately valued in the former GDR. Although there were many potential buyers for such private property, the market was small because owners had little incentive to sell. Given limited and cheap consumer goods and limited opportunities to travel, what would they do with the money?

When people applied to leave the GDR, they wrote a petition, *Ausreiseantrag*. This petition took time to process—a couple of years in most cases, a full six years in one case that I know of; some petitions were never approved. The people who applied to leave usually suffered immediate employment discrimination. They either were demoted, or they were forced out of their jobs; subsequently, many had to live off friends until their petitions were approved. Or, if they held high-level or politically sensitive posts, or if they were identified as *Staatsfeinden* (enemies of the state), they were often accused falsely of crimes, given sentences disproportional to these crimes (which they usually had not committed), and eventually released from prison directly into the Federal Republic under what, at the time, were thought to be secret arrangements between East and West Germany. For some of these trumped-up charges and severe sentences, some former GDR judges and public prosecutors now sit on trial in Berlin.

If any of the people who wanted to leave had valuable real estate, it would frequently be sold before they left to officers of the Ministry for State Security, the Stasi, or to politicians, artists, doctors, and other important persons who, according to today's terminology, were *Staatsnah* (close to the state). These buyers would put their wishes for real estate on a list for Professor Vogel. Stasi officers might, for example, "reserve" one apartment for their daughter and son-in-law or a villa for the parents of their son-in-law. In one case concerning real estate on Wandlitz Lake, the Ministry for State Security bought a piece for its own use, for secret meetings when members planned particularly sensitive actions.

It was common knowledge in the GDR that if one wanted to leave for the West, the best way to expedite that exit was to own a piece of real estate. Everyone knew that if you could offer a piece of property for sale, especially something that state and party functionaries in Berlin might covet, you had a good chance of getting your petition approved quickly. The central factual issue of the trial is whether people freely "offered" this property or whether Professor Vogel coerced them into selling. How did Professor Vogel, as the official East German lawyer for "humanitarian questions," arrange the sale of two to three thousand pieces of real estate? In return for his work in selling their property and arranging their exit, most of Professor Vogel's clients also paid his law office a standard legal fee.

THE INDICTMENT

In preparation for the trial, ZERV and public prosecutors sifted through 168 cartons containing 1,700 files from Professor Vogel's office. During the course of the trial Professor Vogel and Frau Dörrfeld both admitted to having doctored some of these documents after 1990. Professor Vogel testified that he did this only where "clarity" was at stake, in which case he added notes in the margin or even "corrected" what he took to be errors. Only in some of the documents did he date his corrections. When asked about written comments that directly contradicted the typed content of a letter, Professor Vogel replied, "I don't remember." In addition to Vogel's own files, ZERV made extensive use of documents obtained from the Stasi archives in the Gauck-Authority.

The trial judge's indictment focused the case neither around "the act"—the evidence that Professor Vogel did indeed meet with these people and arrange the sale of their property is not contested; nor "the crime"—West German and East German law give nearly identical descriptions of extortion. All of the major questions were directed to an interpretation of what went on in Professor Vogel's office: when and under what conditions did extortion occur?

The "legal theory" from which Judge Holzinger conducted the trial differed considerably, if not radically, from that proposed by the public prosecutor in the initial indictment. Legal theories are those sets of assertions that, if proven true, will establish the validity of a claim. Of the 283 cases concerning petitions to leave examined by the public prosecutor and ZERV, the prosecutor found sufficient evidence for indictment in 53 of them. From an alternative legal perspective, however, Judge Holzinger found only 21 of the original 53 worthy of indictment. The public prosecutor appealed Judge Holzinger's decision to the next highest court the Kammergericht, which insisted (*zwangseröffnet*) that 31 of the 32 cases that Judge Holzinger had discarded also be tried. But Judge Holzinger had already decided to go ahead with the trial of Vogel and Dörrfeld based on the 21 indictments from his own legal theory. Following this trial, he would begin another one as directed by the Kammergericht. If the court found Vogel not guilty of the narrow charges brought against him in this trial, it still could not acquit him, for under West German law (and on orders of the Kammergericht) acquittal is possible only after one considers the evidence from the other legal theories developed in the initial indictment. Therefore, immediately upon completion of this trial, Judge Holzinger's court was obligated to begin another one that combined the old and new grounds for indictment.

In the original indictment that was rejected by Judge Holzinger, the prosecutor accused Professor Vogel along with Major General Gerhard Niebling, the person who had exercised final authority in the Ministry for State Security (Stasi) to approve petitions to leave, of 53 cases of extortion. (Niebling became head of this Stasi division after the death of Dr. Heinz Volpert in 1986. Volpert, who stood directly under the command of Stasi chief Erich Mielke, had been Vogel's personal friend and official Stasi contact for these exchanges since 1960.) It also proposed a second trial, of Frau Dörrfeld, who would be indicted separately for only 20 of the 53 acts of extortion. Judge Holzinger, however, dismissed the indictment of Major General Niebling, and he opted to try Professor Vogel and Frau Dörrfeld together, using an alternative legal theory. Instead of Vogel sitting across from the Stasi boss, he instead sat across from his own secretary.

It follows that the kinds of questions asked and evidence permitted in this trial differed substantially from what the initial indictment intended. The West Berlin court is concerned with whether Professor Vogel, together with the aid of his secretary, committed extortion as defined under East German law. Excluded were all of the questions that have political and historicizing implications: Was the GDR an *Unrechtsstaat,* and who might be responsible for its state-sponsored Unrecht? Was Vogel was just another lawyer (in the West German sense of *Rechtsanwalt*), or was he an exceptional one employed by the Stasi and thereby the state? Who had the authority and thus could be held accountable for arbitrarily denying people the right to leave the GDR? Did Professor Vogel's "threat" consist less in what went on in his office than in other repressive measures and forms of subjugation, such as demotions in the workplace and the threat of prosecution for "fleeing the republic" if one wanted to leave? Were the deals in his office a mere completion or culmination of a series of threats originating elsewhere?

The second trial, then (which first began on May 5, 1996 and was completed November 29, 1996), according to the directions of the Kammergericht, also considered, first, which party was responsible in each individual case for the decision to approve or reject petitions to leave. And second, who made the decision to approve a petition to leave contingent on exchange for property? The question of the "threat to extort" was in all cases posed in terms of GDR laws, which, at least since 1967, had guaranteed freedom of movement except under special conditions. In other words, every "normal" citizen was generally entitled to leave and only in exceptional circumstances did the state have the right to prevent it. Therefore, according this legal theory, the GDR had an obligation to approve citizen petitions to leave, except in exceptional circumstances, and Professor Vogel and Major General Niebling were the ones ultimately responsible for the arbitrariness in rejecting or approving specific petitions in exchange for property.

THE RIGHT TO LEAVE AND COLD WAR ORDER

According to the legal theory employed by Judge Holzinger, the only significant issue in this first trial, on which I will focus, was extortion. If he granted that illegal coercion in (during) the sale of property of *Ausreisende* (those who petitioned to leave) occurred (and some administrative courts have indeed made this ruling), then his first interpretive problem was to determine the wrongdoer. If the 21 former property owners in this case were the victims of extortion, who victimized them? Who was responsible for putting them in a position where they had to give up their property in order to exercise "the right to leave"? Even if Professor Vogel was guilty, culpability for this threat did not rest solely with him, for he did not act alone in these "sales." Nor did it rest solely with Erika Dörrfeld, who was neither his only nor his major assistant. Certainly Major General Niebling of the Stasi (and his predecessor, Dr. Volpert) also took part in the approval of the sales. A case could have been made—though the pertinent evidence was not discussed in this trial—that many West German church and government officials facilitated, or even initiated, these sales.

The first such exchange was of fifteen imprisoned church employees for goods. It occurred in 1962 and was arranged by the Catholic and Protestant churches, not by the West German government. By the end of 1963, West German churches had bought approximately a hundred prisoners from the GDR, including, on request by the FRG, an employee of the West German Office of Constitutional Protection. At that point in time the Federal Republic, still holding to its own Hallstein Doctrine, which forbade commerce with the GDR, itself played no active role in the sales. But as the churches soon ran out of money, they appealed to the government to take over further financing and organization, which it did at the end of 1963. Its first purchase of eight political prisoners at a price of DM 320,000 became the average price (DM

40,000 per prisoner, more for a doctor, less for an unskilled laborer) until 1977, when, for unexplained reasons, it was raised to DM 95,847 without regard for the qualities of the person exchanged.

Thereafter, the West German government in Bonn had a list of people, mostly those considered "political prisoners," whom it was willing to *freikaufen* (buy the freedom of). The exchanges soon became regularized, and the East German partners in these deals were the Stasi agent Volpert and the lawyer Vogel. In November 1953 Vogel had begun writing reports for the Stasi (without pay) as a "secret coconspirator" (GM: *Geheimer Mitarbeiter*), initially under the self-chosen code name "Eva." In 1955, his code name was changed to "Georg," and he was systematically retrained to enable him to work simultaneously as a lawyer in West Berlin. In order to protect him from suspicion of working with the Stasi, they "broke off" contact in 1957 and wrote a report accusing him of "working in his own interest" and "dishonesty." In 1960, his reports reappeared in Stasi documents, where he was listed again as a GM (code name "Georg"), with Volpert as his contact. The head of GDR's secret foreign trade division, Alexander Schalck-Golodkowski, who had close contacts with both Volpert and Vogel, testified in court that the two men had a *Seelengemeinschaft* (were soul brothers). And, after Volpert's death in 1986, Vogel employed Volpert's wife, Inge, in his law office (Bundestag 1994b: 319). Except for a single report from 1968, Stasi documents mentioning Vogel's work after 1966 have disappeared. Because both the East German Stasi and the West German churches and government tried to keep these exchanges away from public scrutiny, Vogel's role as the mediator between the two Cold War sides was also hedged in secrecy and invested with unspoken, perhaps ambiguous expectations. In this manner, Vogel maintained a fictive neutrality that enabled him to become the trusted contact person for both East and West German governments. However, the evidence seems conclusive that Vogel's two roles, as private lawyer for prisoners who wanted to be "bought free"and as attorney for the GDR (*Bevollmächtigte der DDR-Regime*) placed him in frequent conflicts of interest. When accused of such a conflict by an investigative committee of the German Parliament, Vogel denied the charge, claiming that he worked only for individual clients, although the Federal Republic then often paid for his legal fees (Bundestag 1994b: 322).

In any case, Professor Vogel had to balance different interests. He was always working with two lists: one from Stasi officers (and other prominent persons, artists, and intellectuals) listing preferences for types of real estate they wanted to buy, and one from various officials in the Federal Republic listing preferences for people, primarily political prisoners, they wanted to buy. For this work, the Federal Republic paid Professor Vogel a yearly sum of DM 360,000 from 1984 to 1989; from 1963 to 1984, it paid him a fee for each client. The GDR, in turn, offered him tax breaks (some illegal) but no cash. If people had no property, and if the FRG was unwilling to buy them, sometimes private West German citizens provided cash (up to DM 150,000) in exchange for their East German relatives or friends. Twenty such cases have come to light. This cash was given directly and secretly to Volpert/Niebling, was accompanied by Professor Vogel, and from there went to a secret account of the Ministry for State Security. The major issue in this trial, however, concerns not the cash exchanged but the property.

Those who had petitioned to leave were usually eager to get on one of the two lists. Those who managed to get on either list received priority in their petitions to leave. Wherein, then, lay the coercion of Professor Vogel when people eagerly and willingly entered his office to get on one of the lists? Did not the West German list quite consciously exclude people who could afford to buy their own way out? Even if the answer is no, it is clear that members of the West German government knew about Professor Vogel's practice, tolerated and worked around or even with it for many years. This fact of West German complicity did not, of course, exculpate Vogel and Dörrfeld for their roles in the so-called extortion, but then, given the formal agreement of the petitioners and the inter-national cooperation in this exchange, was Professor Vogel in fact committing extortion according to GDR law? Or was he instead simply expediting the petitioners' requests for exit visas? In other words, was he violating the law or carrying it out? Or did Professor Vogel perform many roles, alternately and simultaneously: mediating between East and West German desires and laws, representing East German clients to the two states, representing the East German's state's interests, and fulfilling his own needs at the expense of his clients and both German states simultaneously?

Another problem in this case, as in all of the trials against GDR border guards and others having to do with border violations, is how precisely to interpret the relation of national law to human rights law. For international law to become legal practice, it is generally assumed that it must first be ratified at the national level. But the right to leave one's own country is neither part of the core of human rights nor has it been ratified in a similar form by most states. The right to leave one's country is part of the 1948 General Accord on Human Rights (art. 13, sec. Abs. 2), and part of the Fourth Protocol of European Human Rights. However, only half of the states approved this latter protocol, which had not guaranteed this right at the initial convention, but only later, in an additional protocol in 1967/68, which was then ratified by only sixteen of the twenty-three states that had signed the original agreement. In 1989, for instance, approximately thirty states had guaranteed a right to leave only after a visa was issued (Ott 1993: 339–41). Even the Federal Republic of Germany limited "freedom of movement," or the conditions under which people could leave, for example, in cases of juvenile delinquents, suspected criminals, or fathers behind on their alimony payments. The point is: no automatic right to leave one's country existed; thus, to have to buy one's exit is not a violation of anyone's rights. The deals in Professor Vogel's office therefore were not necessarily extortion.

The response to this general argument was twofold: First, the GDR was one of the signers of the 1967/68 Protocol and therefore had indeed agreed to a general right to travel. But it interpreted this right to move as valid only within one's own land of citizenship, not as a right to leave the GDR and travel outside its border. Such an interpretation became challengeable, however, with the signing of the Helsinki Accord in 1975, where the GDR agreed to a mutual obligation to monitor national restrictions on freedom to travel. Second, rather than assuming that anyone could travel except under exceptional circumstances, the GDR consistently assumed that no one could travel except under exceptional circumstances. To be sure, it did liberalize this practice in the mid 1980s, enlarging the categories of people who could obtain an exit visa to travel in Western countries. Nonetheless, within the category of people wanting to travel, the GDR singled out and handled arbitrarily those who wanted to leave permanently, that is, those who wrote a petition to leave, *Ausreiseantrag*. Professor Vogel represented this category of people, and, according to the indictment, subjected them to extortion.

The prosecution of Wolfgang Vogel was difficult for other reasons as well. His engagement in the Cold War had been as peacemaker and as international mediator. He had arranged the exchange of 150 spies on the Glienicke Bridge connecting Potsdam with Berlin, including the exchange of Abel and Powers in 1962. As the GDR's commissioner for humanitarian questions," he had been arranging the release of people who took refuge in foreign embassies, which, since the first case in 1974, included negotiations with sixteen countries. In 1973, he arranged a meeting of Erich Honecker and Herbert Wehner, the first meeting of an East German head of state with a representative of the West German government, and in 1981 of Honecker with Helmut Schmidt. He gave an interview to *Playboy* in the 1970s, and had been celebrated internationally as a human rights activist. In 1983, the GDR honored him with the award of Great Star of Friendship among Peoples. Even as late as 1990, shortly after German unification, a West

German commission considered recommending him for a *Bundesver-dienstkreuz*, an honor to Germans for service to the society.

For twenty years (1969–89), Dr. Vogel was the only person "commissioned," with direct access to the Politburo and Stasi, to deal with those who petitioned to leave. In other words, if one did not want to rely on the discretion of some unnamed, unseen Stasi functionaries (*Die Mächtige*, "the powerful," as Vogel called them during the trial), one was forced to turn to Vogel for help. Permission to leave the GDR was ultimately up to Dr. Volpert until 1986 and thereafter to General Major Niebling, who headed the division of State Security that approved petitions. A very few petitions of prominent people even went to the Politburo and Erich Honecker for approval. Vogel helped 350,000 citizens leave the GDR, among them 34,000 political prisoners whom the Federal Republic bought between 1963 and 1989 for an average price of DM 95,000 (Grasemann 1992: 59).[3] Another way of leaving the GDR, to get on that West German list of preferred persons to be bought, was to argue that you were "uniting your family" (*Familienzusammenführung*), and many of the people who had left through this category appreciated, at least at the time of their exit, Vogel's intervention.

Some of these former petitioners testified at his trial. In court, their stories varied little in descriptions of the sequence of events in Professor Vogel's office. Some former property owners were able to reclaim their homes because Dr. Vogel had made an error in their sales contract. These people said that they knew their only chance to leave the GDR without a long delay was to sell their houses. They said that they did not feel themselves to be under pressure while they were in his office. Many were still thankful to Professor Vogel, and in court adamantly repeated the statement, "Professor Vogel did not subject me to extortion." When questioned further by the judge, they often said that it was "the state" or "the State Security" that had subjected them to extortion. Many of those who could not recover their homes went to the administrative court to recover their property. When called as witnesses in this criminal trial, they claimed that they had felt blackmailed when they signed away their property, that when Professor Vogel told them that someone wanted their real estate, they immediately felt threatened.

ZAPFF'S COTTAGE

For Vogel perhaps the most damaging of the twenty-one sales concerned a cottage on the island of Rügen, the premier vacation spot in the Baltic Sea. The problem here was that Vogel bought the house himself, or, more precisely, his wife, Helga, bought it just as she was moving from the Federal Republic to East Berlin, in 1980. The house was owned by Waldemar and Vera Zapff, whose case was listed as number five of the indictments against Vogel. Mr. and Mrs. Zapff had been unable to get their petition to leave approved, so they asked a friend, Peter Pragal, a West German journalist who worked in East Berlin, for help. Pragal visited Dr. Vogel, who made clear that he wanted the cottage on Rügen. Zapff's petition was approved and the house was sold, under value, of course, to Vogel's wife. Shortly thereafter, Pragal's newspaper sent him to Bonn, where Zapff later visited him. Zapff told Pragal's wife the history of his cottage on Rügen.

Mrs. Pragal found it shameful that an attorney might coerce his client by asking from him a piece of real estate in return for permission to leave the country. She demanded that her husband complain to Vogel directly, which he refused to do. In court she found the opportunity to do that herself. She appeared as a prime witness in the Berlin-Moabit courthouse, and she used every opportunity to address Vogel directly and to inform the court of her opinion of him. Whether her emotional testimony influenced Judge Holtzinger and his team of professional and lay judges is doubtful, yet the state's attorneys appeared very pleased as she spoke.

Professor Vogel was guilty of extortion, said the witnesses, because he pressured his clients through his silent demeanor as he bought or arranged to sell their property. One witness described him as "ice cold." He certainly had to know that he placed his clients under incredible pressure, and in particular Mr. Zapff, when Zapff was informed that Dr. Vogel would help him leave the GDR—after however, he secured Zapff's house, not for himself but for his wife. Yet every witness who testified went to Vogel voluntarily; he did not seek them out. In fact, Vogel had claimed in an interview that some of these witnesses threatened him if he refused to help them. The coercion, he insisted, had been exerted on him by those wanting to leave, not vice versa. Such coercion, *Nötigung*, is also a crime for which he could seek legal remedy. In his office, Professor Vogel offered his clients a deal. In this deal, he insisted that he had represented their interests in an attorney-client relationship; they insisted that as an agent of the state he had threatened them, violating the attorney-client relationship.

According to West German criminal law, extortion is a "threat resulting in a grievous wrong." For Waldemar Zapff was it a grievous wrong when his attorney, Professor Vogel, indicated, in a conversation with Mr. Pragel, that he would not help Zapff and his wife to leave the GDR unless Zapff agreed to sell him his cottage first? Paragraph 127 of the GDR Criminal Law book defines extortion in nearly identical terms, as a "threat resulting in a serious disadvantage." The Unity Treaty of 1990 obligated the court to apply GDR law to all crimes committed before the day of unification, October 3, 1990, unless the West German law was milder. Here it seems as if there is no danger of violating the principle of the rule of law known as *nonretroactivity* (*nulla poena sine lex praevia*: "no penalty without a prior law"), which the prosecution would have violated had the two definitions of extortion differed.

From a hermeneutic perspective, however, the two seemingly identical laws are marked by a crucial difference of intent because they are part of different legal systems (cf. Wesel 1995: 2). From the West German perspective, constantly reiterated in practice over forty years by its refusal to recognize the GDR as a legal state, to remain in the GDR meant suffering a grievous wrong. That is why the West German government "bought the freedom" of East Germans. But the question before the court was whether the law of the GDR possibly envisioned living there as a grievous wrong. From Professor Vogel's perspective, his putative threat not to help Waldemar and Vera Zapff to leave the GDR could not possibly have resulted, according to GDR law, in "a serious disadvantage," for living in the GDR was considered a privilege, not a disadvantage. In fact, to leave the GDR was to enter *feindliche* (enemy) territory, the reason for the border guards and the other means used to keep people from leaving. According to this hermeneutic- and systems-based theory, one must respect the different logic of the East German state system; from this perspective the German legal theorist Michael Pawlik has argued that "Vogel's demand was not extortion, but an element of a comprehensive 'deal' between the state and those who wanted to leave" (1994: 116). This "deal" was also part of a larger deal involving the receiving country, the Federal Republic, which, as I have indicated, was complicitous by giving Dr. Vogel lists of preferred persons. Therefore, Uwe Wesel, a leading German legal historian, concluded, "The court must find Wolfgang Vogel not guilty of the charge of extortion, for we have to judge according to the law of the GDR and not that of our own. Even when it's not easy for us" (1995: 2). The question remains, however, whether "the law of the GDR" is so unambiguous that it precludes other interpretations of extortion.

There is another side to GDR legal practice that West German legal analysts, eager to respect the separate intent and integrity of East German law, ignored (brought to my attention by Professor Ilona Stolpe). While GDR law objectively recognized no *Nachteil* (disadvantage/ harm) for its citizens to remain, it did in fact recognize subjective grounds for leaving. Based on subjective arguments that established individual disadvantage if one were to remain in the GDR, such as the necessity to care for one's sick parents who lived in the West, or the possibility of inheriting a company, real estate, or fortune only if one lived in the West, East German state authorities consistently approved petitions to leave. Therefore, it can be argued that because GDR criminal law acknowledged subjective disadvantages of living there as grounds to leave, it also implicitly recognized the possibility of extortion in such cases. One common response by West German legal experts has been to insist that GDR citizens lacked status as "legal subjects," that the state was an *Obrigkeitsstaat* (authoritarian state) that granted its citizens privileges but guaranteed no rights. Following this logic, the East German elite, including Dr. Vogel, could not possibly have extorted GDR citizens because they had no such rights as legal subjects to begin with.

In November 1995, Erika Dörrfeld was judged unfit to stand trial further due to psychological stress. Her trial was suspended and never reopened. Despite the publicly stated intention of the presiding judge and public prosecutor to have ended Dr. Vogel's trial before the summer of 1995, it sputtered on through the fall of 1995. First Judge Holzinger went on vacation; then the court agreed to call additional witnesses.

On January 9, 1996, Judge Holzinger and his court announced their verdict: Wolfgang Vogel was guilty of extorting five clients out of money and property, committing perjury in another unrelated case, and abusing his privilege as lawyer by falsifying contracts in five cases. Judge Holzinger took an hour to read the verdict. He sentenced Dr. Vogel to a two-year suspended prison term—the public prosecutor had asked for three and a half years—and ordered him to pay DM 92,000 ($65,700) in fines for the last charge, falsely swearing notarized statements for five other former clients. Included within this sentence was a prison term of one year and one month specifically for Vogel's role in the sale of Waldemar Zapff's property on Rügen. The court concluded that Vogel had succumbed to the temptation to misuse his power in only some of the twenty-one cases brought by the prosecution. The judges rejected arguments by Vogel and his lawyers that the Zapffs and other former clients had turned against him because the properties they had been forced to leave behind had acquired enormous value.

Judge Holzinger emphasized that the judgment was not for Vogel's entire service over four decades but for violations in individual cases. In those cases, Vogel misused his position of power, said the judge, for he had it in his personal power to approve or reject petitions of those who wanted to leave the GDR. He abused his position both for his own interests and for the interests of others. The decision states that Vogel acted "above all and with the intention of enriching himself. His wife served occasionally as a strawman [*Strohfrau*]." The court reasoned that

Vogel chose this "irregular way to obtain the property on Rügen" because otherwise he would have had to pay a higher price for a comparable piece of property. The sales contract was made possible only through a threat to the seller. In the cases of extortion, the court's decision cited specifically both Vogel's use of "icy, silent demeanor" and Vogel's statements to his clients that there could be no exit from the GDR except through a sale of property arranged by himself. I did not attend the second trial, of Wolfgang Vogel together with Gerhard Niebling, for the thirty-one indictments initially dismissed along with eight new ones. It lasted six months. Judge Holzinger acquitted both of the accused on all charges. In this trial, the court gave much consideration to witnesses who claimed they did not feel intimidated or extorted by Vogel but merely took up his offer to sell their houses after having exhausted other possibilities of expediting their petitions to leave. And even though Vogel could place his clients on the preferential list for approval to leave the GDR, he did not promise and was not able to secure their release. The court also concluded that Vogel was "no employee of the Ministry for State Security in the technical sense." Although the Stasi did pay him from DM 100,000 to DM 150,000 yearly, it was not for work as an agent but as "honoraria" for services rendered, including exchange of agents and the sale of prisoners. At the same time, the court emphasized that the "exchange of humans" practiced by the GDR was a violation of "basic human rights." But Vogel himself was not responsible for approving the petitions to leaving, said the court (Averesch 1997: 7). The verdicts of both trials are now under appeal to the Federal Supreme Court (Bundesgerichtshof).

Whatever the outcome of the appeals, these verdicts will not be a final judgment about the value of ZERV's work or the reckoning with the criminal past. In this attempt to "reckon with the GDR's past through criminal law," the victim's legitimate claim for justice and retribution is being acknowledged, and former government officials are being held publicly accountable for the wrongs they perpetrated on the people they were to serve.

POSTSCRIPT

The other aspect of the Zapff case concerns corrective justice: his attempt to get his property back. As I have indicated, this decision rests not with a criminal but an administrative court that is independent of all criminal proceedings. In most of the property disputes, the administrative court tries to get the parties to agree among themselves to a

ACCOUNTABILITY ON TRIAL 95

settlement without itself making a final judgment. Here, however, an out-of-court settlement has proved impossible, for, as is apparent from his courtroom demeanor, Vogel clearly resents Zapff's accusations of extortion and detests the man. Zapff had in fact two property claims for the administrative court. For one, he had sold a two-family house in Berlin-Köpenick for $16,500 less than the $52,000 for which it had been officially assessed. For this house, Zapff reached agreement with the new owners and recovered the house. The other case involves the property on Rügen described above.

The Rügen property has a complicated history. Zapff had received the house from his mother-in-law, who had received it as a gift in 1958 from Frau Brecht-Schall, Bertold Brecht's daughter, who, in turn, had received it from the municipal authority in exchange for another piece of property that she had inherited from her father. The municipal authority had initially expropriated the property from the family of Frau Ursula Wesch. Frau Wesch, as legal heir to this expropriation, also wants the property back. Immediately after the end of the war, in 1945, as the island of Rügen was part of the Soviet occupation zone, many residents abandoned their homes and fled to the West. The local municipal authority on the island hence expropriated a great deal of land from these people. Frau Wesch's family had received 130 hectares of land elsewhere through a decision of an administrative court—but she wanted the original land back.

Zapff had listed his daughter, Annette Beck, as the owner of the property. Acting in her name, he sold this prime piece of vacation property to Dr. Vogel's wife, Helga, for $10,000, in order to obtain an exit visa from the GDR. The settlement is further complicated by changes Vogel made in value to the real estate. Zapff's house on this property was a shabby cottage that Vogel subsequently tore down and replaced with what is considered the most expensive house built in the GDR, estimated at around a half million deutsche Marks. If Zapff were to get the land back, he would also have to buy Vogel's house from him—which he cannot afford. Zapff argued in court that the original prewar owner, now represented by Frau Wesch, had a claim against the municipal authority for the expropriation but not against himself. He had had a proper legal contract recognizing his ownership of the house before Vogel's putative extortion.

Professor Vogel indicated before the court that he was willing to give the land back to Frau Wesch, the old property owner, but only on the condition that Zapff receive absolutely nothing. The administrative court reached a decision before the conclusion of Vogel's criminal trial for extortion. On June 23, 1995, it decided that the property should be returned to Frau Ursula Wesch, as she was the the first who had been expropriated. Herr Zapff has appealed the judgment and is still awaiting a decision.

In a letter to me dated September 3, 1996, Waldemar Zapff wrote: "We hope to have been helpful with this complicated material. In case there should be incorrect representations in your book due to linguistic misunderstandings, which we have not been presented to correct in advance, we reject any possible responsibility in a legal process with Herr Professor Vogel. Since Professor Vogel has already sued publications several times, you should not neglect the possibility of a trial." I thank him for the warning. All errors are of course mine.

Part Three

ETHNOGRAPHY OF VINDICATION

CHAPTER 6

Democratic Accountability:
Results, Evaluations, Ramifications

EFFECTIVE criminal law establishes the state as a moral agent representing the entire community. It does this by reiterating the principles of accountability for injustices as part of an attempt to reestablish the dignity of victims. Have the criminal investigations and trials in Germany been effective in reckoning with a past? In the context of the other trials for governmental and unification criminality, an acquittal of Wolfgang Vogel for extortion, as in his second trial, was not an exceptional verdict. Much to my surprise, however, Vogel was indeed found guilty in his first trial. On January 9, 1996, the court found him guilty of extortion, aiding extortion, and perjury. He was sentenced to two years imprisonment, released on good behavior, and assessed a fine of DM 92,000. He was then tried and acquitted on the remaining charges of the public prosecutor that were omitted from the first trial. The fact that the court convicted Vogel and sentenced him is only one effect of the ritual purification performed by the trial. The performative aspects of state investigation, public defense, and, perhaps most important, the historical record left for future generations by the prosecution are also part of its efficacy.

A complete list of the results of investigations, indictments, and verdicts is nowhere to be found. But even a partial list indicates that the results cannot be inferred from the numbers alone, which in any case are changing. In the fall of 1994, the head state prosecutor in Berlin, Christoph Schaefgen, drew up an initial list. At that time he concluded that on the basis of the numbers alone, the results "look meager" (1994: 159). From October 3, 1990, through the fall of 1994, ZERV 2, charged with investigating governmental criminality, had opened 3,000 cases, of which 100 had resulted in indictments. In only 30 cases were suspects convicted, making a 1 percent conviction rate, or 30 convictions out of 3,000 cases opened; or, if one measures convictions per indictment, the success rate is 30 percent (*Der Tagesspiegel*, October 1, 1994: 10). After this release, the press along with most intellectual commentators widely criticized the work of ZERV and the public prosecutor.

TABLE 1
Case Resolutions of ZERV 1 and ZERV 2, March 31, 1996

	ZERV 1	ZERV 2
Cases opened	19,264	5,807
Cases closed	11,873	4,074
Indictments	300	167
Uncompleted cases	7,391	1,733

Source: Senatsverwaltung für Justiz 1996: apps. 1–6.

TABLE 2
Indictments and Convictions of ZERV 2 (Governmental Criminality),
March 31, 1996

	Indictments	Convictions
Border violations	69	45
Judicial illegality	38	7
Stasi illegality	14	2
Economic illegality	38	19

Source: Senatsverwaltung für Justiz 1996: apps. 1–6.

A new evaluation by Berlin's Ministry of Justice that considers events through March 31, 1966, indicates a changing picture. Consider again for a moment merely the more controversial work of ZERV 2. It had opened 5,807 cases, out of which 167 resulted in an indictment. With 159 trials completed, in 73 cases suspects were convicted (some verdicts are on appeal), making a 2.5 percent conviction rate, or 73 out of 5,807 cases opened; or, if one measures convictions per indictment, the success rate is 46 percent (Senatsverwaltung 1996: sec. 1). Depending on how the numbers are tabulated, the rate of conviction has increased slightly, from 1 to 2.5 percent, or from 30 to 46 percent. ZERV 1, charged largely with economic crime, has engaged in even more investigations (19,264) and issued more indictments (300), though no numbers are available on convictions. These findings are summarized in tables 1 and 2.

In sum, there have been tens of thousands of investigations, there have been hundreds of indictments, there have been some convictions holding both minor and major figures accountable, and there has been a great deal of money recovered from economic crime. By and large, however, these successes have been too few in number and too costly in time and attention to convince a large number of people, especially legal experts and politicians in the new Germany, of the necessity and appropriateness of the criminal investigations and prosecutions.

The head Berlin prosecutor, Christoph Schaefgen, responds to public reservations by arguing that "justice is obligated to the principle of legitimacy and not that of public or political opinion." He suggests that the task of justice here lies in "enlightenment and in the prosecution of criminality and criminals who in exercising political power violated the law of their own states, not in reparations *Wiedergutmachung* for wrong that originated in the former GDR" (1994: 159). Clearly, a full account of the results of reckoning with GDR's past through criminal law means more than listing trial results. To focus on trial results alone, that is, on the conviction or acquittal of suspects, places jural work in an economistic frame of reference. Efficiency of justice becomes the primary criterion by which results, or the "rationality" of jural process, are evaluated. Such a framework may be useful in the domain of distributive justice, where outcomes most frequently involve material goods whose value can be clearly measured. But it is the wrong framework for retributive and corrective justice. Employing this logic for all types of justice claims, the political scientist Jon Elster (1992a: 15–16) went so far as to argue that since "essentially everybody suffered under Communism," and "because it is impossible to reach everybody, nobody should be punished and nobody compensated."[1] Surely, comprehensiveness and outcomes that correspond to rational actor logic are not what criminal justice is about. Justice is about morality and the principle of legitimacy, which in turn rest not on efficiency but on various cultural standards. The question is not whether criminal justice is efficient but whether it is effective in reckoning with a past. It is important not to impose a single efficiency standard on justice systems, for the particular means by which effectiveness is measured varies. I would think that most justice systems have never been particularly efficient, since in most places of the world most crimes are never solved, most suspected criminals go free, and most harmed individuals do not find remedies. Effectiveness, on the other hand, is a culturally and temporally variable standard, and a matter for not speculative but empirical research. In the German case, have the criminal investigations and trials been effective?

The head of ZERV, Manfred Kittlaus, justifies the criminal investigations in terms of three desired effects: (1) *Rechtsgefühl*, defined as "the direct effect on the people's respect for legality," (2) trust in the *soziale Marktwirtschaft* (social market economy) generated by ZERV's ability to deal with "organized economic crime," and (3) the improvement of the "appearance of Germany abroad." Respect for the legality (Rechtsgefühl) can be obtained, writes Kittlaus, only by the fulfillment of the *Verpflichtung* (obligation and commitment) to the "10,000 victims and the 100,000 GDR citizens who in 1989 worked to bring about the collapse of the morally, politically, and economically bankrupt GDR-system" (Kittlaus 1994: 1). The primary groups to whom criminal reckoning is obligated, then, he argues, are the victims and the citizens who worked to bring about the collapse of the GDR.

Public reaction to the first Vogel verdict, especially of Western commentators, who control most of the editorial positions in media in the new Germany, tended to follow a different logic. Many prominent Germans had always shown solidarity with Vogel. Former chancellor Helmut Schmidt even visited Vogel while he sat in prison during the initial investigation. Following the trial, the voices of West German public figures reached near unanimity in support of Dr. Vogel. In a front page editorial in *Die Zeit*, for example, Robert Leicht (1996: 1) argued that the majority of those who claimed they had been extorted by Vogel were motivated by the desire for profit, by the chance to get their property back cheaply—and that because many had given false testimony, they would now in turn be charged by the public prosecutor. "The great extortionist had been actually the GDR-State itself. . . . [Vogel] was neither a resister nor a good Samaritan. He was a tool, not responsible for making the decisions. . . . Is justice served," concluded Leicht rhetorically, "by punishing the hammer while the smith goes free?" In an editorial written for the German public, Donald Koblitz (1996: 5), former legal adviser for the U.S. State Department in Berlin, accused the "inexperienced and poorly counselled" public prosecutors of making "pseudo-legalistic and completely ahistorical accusations." He characterized the Vogel trial as a "comical episode" in the pursuit of justice, but he then dismissed this characterization, since Vogel was a "decent man" who had to sit six months in prison awaiting a trial for charges that were based on a "silly and mean-spirited version of history." In my own discussions with East Germans, I found that most either had no opinions or were very conflicted about what they actually thought of the verdict in Vogel's trial. Only those who, as petitioners to leave, had personally experienced Vogel's abuse of power, adamantly insisted on his guilt.

Even those who have long opposed this reckoning through criminal justice, such as the senior editor and owner of *Die Zeit*, Marion Gräfin Dönhoff (1995: 1), the political scientist Egon Bahr (1993), and the legal historian Uwe Wesel (1995), for example, had reservations about ignoring the feelings of the victims. But on the whole, they concluded, as did the political scientist Claus Leggewie and legal scholar Horst Meier (1992: 71), in an otherwise extremely insightful article, "that the balance of GDR things must be in the first instance a societal business—meaning free of the state. . . . Public discussion . . . is always more valuable than all of the paltry results of criminal justice taken together."

In pleading for an end to the criminal reckoning and a general amnesty, Wesel wrote, "The single serious argument against an amnesty is the feeling of the victims. But everyone must make a contribution to the new beginning. Also the victims." Instead, he proposed a law of restitution "for which the sentencing of perpetrators is no substitute." He also insisted that the actual "reckoning with the past . . . is the task of historians anyway, who are already at work. . . . The Honecker trial has brought nothing new to light that was not already well-known" (1995: 3). Finally, he argued for an end to criminalization through an amnesty, drawing a parallel to the West German amnesty of Nazis in the 1950s, which, he claimed, was instrumental in the West German success story. The question he addresses but did not ask is: Whose trust in the new West German law is he most concerned with, that of the perpetrators or of the victims? Both groups are actually small in number. Regardless of with whom one identifies, it is unlikely that an amnesty of suspects before they are brought to trial, before there is any finding of innocence or admission of guilt, will contribute to a society's ability to come to terms with the past.

What Wesel seems to confuse is the task of the historian—to bring something new to light, to make the known unknown; and the task of the justice system—to reestablish the dignity of the victim and to prevent further wrongdoing. The latter task cannot be readily accomplished by historians whose (idealized) function is diligent research, the uncovering of new evidence, the construction of events and the interpretation of them in new frameworks. Rather, reestablishing dignity would seem to require a process more similar to a criminal trial than to historical research, namely, a public participatory process, like that of Dr. Vogel's trial, where following an open hearing one draws a thick line between the victim and those accountable for the injustice. Moreover, laws of restitution, like those Wesel proposes, invariably rely on monetary dispensations, so that again an economistic framework is imposed on a jural solution. Jewish victims of the Holocaust who received monetary sums from the West German government in its Wiedergutmachung policy have by no means renounced the use of criminal justice to hold individuals accountable for criminal actions. A law of monetary restitution is desirable (and indeed, has already been passed) but not in itself sufficient for settling accounts. Individuals must also be held accountable for wrongdoing, and the state, I have been arguing, as the only institutional moral representative of the entire community, has an obligation here. The state's obligation is not only a hermeneutic one but also a performative one. Its primary concern is with the consequences of what it does for legitimating the principles of its rule.

A brief comparison of states that did not take this obligation to engage in retributive justice seriously suggests some commonalities. In those states that did not hold anyone accountable, where it was assumed that the system was at fault and that changing "the system," whatever that is, would in itself be sufficient, there has been a form of sacrifice or ritual purification in reckoning with the past, but in each case the earmarked victim for sacrifice has been different. In Czechoslovakia no serious internal criminalization took place; rather the Czechs criminalized the Slovaks, who in turn criminalized the Czechs.[2] Such practices of "ethnic cleansing" are expressions of a drive for revenge and retaliation, in which perpetrators and victims of the past strike at each other in ever new coalitions. Responsibility for past problems was exteriorized, projected onto an "outside" that had at one time been part of oneself. As soon as this split between Slovaks and Czechs was finalized, debate turned to the old question of the grounds for the sacrifice immediately after World War II of almost three million Germans, or individuals identified as such, who were driven from their homes. These *Sudetendeutsche* living in Germany, or young people who want to identify themselves that way and who had never personally suffered this harm, in turn called for retaliation.

In Romania, the Ceausescu couple and the Politburo on top served as the objects for internal purification, though in the first moments of euphoria most European observers did not even notice that this ritual was accompanied by a scapegoating of two marginalized groups, Romanian Gypsies and Hungarians. Partly through these substitute sacrifices the old power structure was actually preserved. In Russia, Chechnya was sacrificed in a similar way, though the Russian leaders still want to control what they identify as external to them. In Yugoslavia, archenemies Croatia and Serbia united to sacrifice Bosnia— and they nearly succeeded. These regimes "secured" their rule not through the legitimate domination of the rule of law but in genocidal acts of exclusion and abjection of an internal other. Moreover, an active, nonelected clique of former perpetrators and victims directly incited and manipulated the violence. To be sure, the Croats and Serbs did not act alone but with the complicity of the international community, including the aid of irredentist populations in Europe and the United States. But if we focus solely on the role of the jural "transitions," inasmuch as the word applies to this situation, they were most frequently subordinated to strategic political operatives, which in turn were directed by former perpetrators who readily identified new scapegoats—the Bosnian Muslims, interethnic couples—on whom the ethnonationalists could project their feelings of guilt.

In none of these states did former victims receive much recognition; there was little or no retributive justice and internal cleansing; accountability was shifted from the political center to some posited exterior, which was then sacrificed. My emphasis here on the lack of retributive justice and on jural process is not meant to deny the significance of other variables in producing the violence of different transitions. In Hungary, Slovenia, and to a large extent in Poland, some people claim no sacrifice was necessary since state form was already a "rule of law" and therefore the transformation was not from one type of regime to another but within the regime. This may be true. And, indeed, the relative inclusiveness of these regimes is to be applauded. But one should not overlook the reappearance of anti-Semitism in Poland, especially given its history of dealing with internal divisions through demarcation from its minorities, including a history of recurrent pogroms. And in Slovenia, state functionaries have had it easy escaping personal accountability and responsibility for their own errors by pointing the finger at their "dangerous and barbarian" neighbors and former federal comrades in Serbia, Croatia, and Bosnia.

The political transformation in Germany since 1989 is a part of this political and psychological dynamic in the former East bloc. For this reason, reestablishing the dignity of victims required a prosecution of perpetrators among the old elite for their moral-legal wrongs. But since the state's legitimacy is now tied to the principles of the rule of law, it must also, especially in the hours of the initial invocation of the principles, avoid criminalizing politically expedient substitutes. It must prosecute and punish actual wrongdoers, with the understanding that for a variety of political and procedural reasons it will not be able to punish them all. The old East German political elites, Professor Vogel included, do not fall into the category of substitute victims, for they are being held accountable for what they actually did—nothing more, nothing less. That Professor Vogel also did good in his role as mediator between East and West did not erase the state's responsibility to seek retributive justice for those injured by Vogel in his work for the East German state. And when, as has most frequently been the case, it is impossible to convict following the procedural protections of the principles of the rule of law, the new state has not thereby failed, for each trial must be viewed alongside other prosecutions. The major significance and efficacy of Vogel's trials, then, were not the verdicts. Rather, the trials demonstrated through their performance the ongoing necessity of reiterating the state's moral principles. Effective criminal law, as I have argued, is not to be equated with efficient justice. Effective criminal law establishes the state as a moral agent representing the entire community by reiterating the principles of responsibility and accountability for injustices as part of an attempt to reestablish the dignity of victims.

That the justice system has been effective is attested to by another kind of evidence: steadily increasing public trust in the judiciary, indicated in public opinion polls. Of all the institutions in the united Germany, eastern and western Germans trust the Constitutional Court the most, followed closely by the other courts and the police. Least trusted are the press and the political parties. In the middle and far below the judicial branch are the legislative branch and the military (Gabriel 1993: 3–12).

Is it possible to go beyond the enclosed scenario of the trial and the jural system at work, and beyond the reactions of victims with whom I will deal in the next chapter, to describe ethnographically everyday reactions to and ramifications of retributive justice? I am, after all, claiming that a strong relationship exists between the use of retributive justice and a lack of violence. Where, exactly, does one locate the situations in which retributive justice is received? Finding this location is a formidable task, given that the primary descriptive evidence to which I am appealing is to the lack of violent demonstrations directed against one's neighbors, the willingness to defer in social conflicts to the state's courts and administrative bodies.

On the surface, the major contrary evidence to be explained would be the significant increase in violence perpetrated against foreigners in both 1991 and 1992: more than two thousand acts, including the bombing and burning of homes of asylum seekers and seventeen murders by right-wing groups, of which eight of the victims were foreigners. At that time, the Office of Constitutional Protection estimated that political parties of the radical right in eastern and western Germany had about forty thousand members, of whom six thousand were ready to use violence.[3] Equally if not more disturbing than these specific acts of murder was the acceptance, often extending to support, of this brutality by a large number of German bystanders.

This violence quickly subsided, however, largely in response to a concerted effort by the state to investigate and isolate these perpetrators, and by large numbers of individual citizens to identify with the victims and the groups to which they belonged. In the fall of 1992, several million East and West Germans demonstrated publicly their opposition, organizing peaceful marches and demanding that politicians and police take resolute action. Following these demonstrations, politicians and significant numbers of relatively apolitical citizens were spurred into action against this new wave of right-wing violence. To be sure, this action alone did not stop the violence, for at the same time the police and other governmental institutions began taking it seriously. One may criticize the kinds of responses, but they are clear indications of a successful refusal to exteriorize a part of the social group. And they were in fact effective in preventing the violence from escalating. I am not arguing here that the use of retributive justice contributed directly to the lessening of attacks on foreigners. My argument is that the state's engagement in retributive justice in this same period helped instill trust in legality, and therefore established the space in which that part of the public opposed to other-directed violence could mobilize the larger public for social peace.

There are of course many other factors which have contributed to a peaceful transformation of state form in Germany. Above all, there is the well-developed German social welfare system, which cushioned the difficult economic transitions. Hence despite the displacement of more than half of the workforce in the East and unemployment of from 12 to 40 percent, depending on how it is calculated, the standard of living of the vast majority of people in the East has actually improved. German democratic political institutions and the political party system also play an important role. The Party of Democratic Socialism, the renamed Socialist Unity Party, has channeled the voices of those who have felt disenfranchised into the institutional structures of the West German state. Finally, there are the nonjural institutions that have taken up the task of reckoning with the GDR's past, especially historians through the investigations of the parliamentary Enquete-Kommission,[4] private citizens who have read Stasi documents about their own pasts made available through the Gauck-Authority, and a proliferation of newspaper, television, and public forums for the discussion of discontents. Beyond these institutional contexts, how has retributive justice been taken up in everyday life?

During the last six years, I have attended many public forums in Berlin and I have watched many of the televised discussions. These staged events serve as catalysts for reactions in homes or among small circles of friends in bars and restaurants. When opinion pollsters or political scientists remark on the silence concerning these issues, they are merely registering the final effects of intensive social involvements: watching, listening, and sometimes talking. "Silence" in this context is not passivity or disinterest but a measured response to a public and private working-through of present injuries and past wounds. To explain this response in terms of the old culturalist clichés—that Germans historically just follow orders, that they are a prototype of subaltern peoples—does not adequately explain the remarkable changes in postwar domestic arrangements and public culture (Borneman 1992). Admittedly, these changes are more extensive in the metropolis Berlin than in smaller provincial settings. Yet the cultural processes and events in Berlin exert a disproportionate influence on national developments, disproportionate in numbers, in the setting of cultural trends, and in media coverage.

Perhaps a good illustration of the audience reception to retributive justice is the changing reaction to the fate of particular perpetrators and victims in the public imagination. Two of the most prominent public figures identified in 1989 as perpetrators, Erich Honecker and Alexander Schalck-Golodkowski, have by 1996 disappeared from public attention. In the public mind, both figures served as synecdoches for the entire regime. By contrast, the person most identified with the victims, Bärbel Bohley, who lost much of her public following within a year of the revolution, is currently enjoying a renaissance. Both trends are direct indexes of the effects of successful retributive justice.

Take, for example, the cases of Honecker and Schalck-Golodkowski After Honecker voted himself out of office in October 1990, he was forced to leave his home in Wandlitz, the Politburo residential compound he had built in an isolated forest an hour north of Berlin. Threatened by public scorn and with nowhere safe to stay, he and his wife took refuge in the home of a Lutheran minister outside Berlin. The newly reformed East German television and print media directed public anger and resentment to the governmental abuse of power, focusing on Honecker's Wandlitz compound and on the illegal trading activities of Schaslck-Golodkowski for the regime. During this same period, Bohley, the moral dissident who helped bring about the regime collapse, was considered increasingly out of touch as she criticized people for the very materialism that led them to be discontented with the GDR.

Fearing arrest, Honecker fled to Moscow, but then the Federal Republic pressured Russia to send him back to Germany for trial. Hence he was denied refuge in the Chilean embassy in Moscow and returned to Berlin. He arrived only to discover that he had terminal cancer and would not likely live long enough for the prosecutors to be able to complete the case against him. After a brief stay in prison, he was allowed to join his daughter, who was living in Chile. He died in May 1994, but his death received little notice in the media, and no discussion among the people I know. When in the summer of 1996 I asked people what they thought of Honecker, those in the East always mentioned embarrassment at having submitted to his petty rule, along with allowing themselves to be subjects of his political repression, a factor those in the West foregrounded in their comments. Nobody mentioned the base motives of hate, resentment, or revenge. By 1996, people who had expressed so much anger at Schalck-Golodkowski (who was acquitted in his first trial but awaits others) were now satisfied that he was still under a kind of house arrest and they were relatively unconcerned about his eventual fate. As to the voices of victims, in 1995 and 1996 the public esteem of Bärbel Bohley and other former dissidents grew, acclaimed by people across the political spectrum, as they were acknowledged to be speaking from a position of dignity based on past moral actions on the side of "the good." In other words, an actual closing of the books is occurring, a thick line is being drawn, but only through a ritual purification of the center.

This closing of the books does not imply that memory of the past will be accurate and continuous but merely increases the likelihood that future generations will be skeptical about attempts to use these memories to mobilize retaliations against other persons or groups. It therefore decreases the likelihood of retributive violence much as it affirms the principles of the rule of law. In the meantime, many reminders of this past will be erased. Not every memory of harm can or should be permanently memorialized. Honecker's house in the Wandlitz compound north of Berlin, for example, which I visited in the summer of 1996, is surrounded by a barbed wire fence falling quickly in disrepair. The small petit-bourgeois-looking single-family houses of the former Politburo members have been renovated and integrated into a large state-run health spa. All that remains that reminded me of its former use is the seven-foot-high metal entrance gate, the result of a union between security needs and *Kleinbürger* garden-style taste. During the summer, a small van is parked outside and someone sells maps of the former government compound, a few books, and GDR memorabilia. Large numbers of private condominiums are under construction, but the settlement is now centered around an already completed six-story health spa, complete with fountain, swimming pool, café, and well-kept strolling paths in the forest. People on crutches recovering from accidents or needing long-term physical therapy wander the grounds with their entire families in tow. When I asked where Honecker's house was, people directed me to it, but it is totally unmarked. I engaged a couple leaving the house in a brief conversation; they expressed no anger, no resentment. The complex is theirs to recover in from an automobile accident. The historical kindling used to ignite future fires is gone.

When I told a friend who had always been skeptical about a judicial reckoning with the past about ZERV's most recent report, she remarked, "That is pleasing to hear, John. It gives one faith that the justice system is working after all." Her noneventful deference to the state's legitimacy is in stark contrast to the eventful turn to violence by those who reject state legitimacy to settle accounts. Her reaction resembles that of others: there is no reference to the technical categories I have employed, but there is an appreciation of what Kittlaus called Rechtsgefühl, a respect for legality. Another woman commented on the reaction of her two children, ages sixteen and nineteen: "They are uninterested in that. They only want to have fun. Fully depoliticized. And they are not worried about the future, they take things in stride." For the moment, the young heirs to the transformations are not directing their energies against or in critique of anything in particular but instead toward their own projects in self-fulfillment. Even if one does not subscribe to this attitude toward life, one must recognize that these young people have an implicit trust in the Rechtsstaat as providing the framework in which to experience their freedoms.

In November 1994, ZERV published a small, slick, green bulletin of eleven pages. It is meant both to inform the public about the work ZERV is already doing and to involve citizens in the criminal justice process by asking for their help in investigating criminal activity. It lists a telephone number to call to obtain or provide information, which in the first twelve months following publication drew 150 callers (ZERV 1996: 8). For the bulletin's cover ZERV (1994) chose the slogan: "When victims are silent, everything always begins again from the start" (Wenn die Opfer schweigen, beginnt alles immer wieder von vorn). Coming from the police, this reminder of the past repeating itself serves as a kind of self-critique (cf. Buruma 1994). It suggest that the current German reckoning with the injustices of a particular past through criminal law is a counterexperiment to the silence-induced terror that engulfed Germany, Japan, and Italy in the 1970s—a terrorism that can be understood as retaliation for the crimes committed by the Axis powers in World War II. In other words, to avoid a cycle of retributive violence, it may be wise to go through a longer phase of painful historical reckoning with the past—that is, of retributive justice in the present.

CHAPTER 7

Justice and Dignity:
Victims, Vindication, and Accountability

DIGNITY AND RESTITUTIVE JUSTICE

Dignity is a concept that has become nearly universally translatable. Yet it is not to be found in every state's constitution, and where it is employed, it is subject to different interpretations. Tzvetan Todorov (1996: 139) identifies it, along with caring, as one of the two "ordinary virtues: those moral acts that each of us can perform without having to be a hero or a saint." Dignity is preserved by transforming a situation of constraint into one of freedom. It is always a quality of individuals and cannot be derived from any group or collective character. One of the most common assertions of dignity is an act of refusal to obey a command, an assertion of self against a group norm. Acts asserting dignity can be found in every culture and in any era; dignity never belongs to any particular cultural group or time. During the Cold War, dignity was an essentially contested term. Theorists of socialist legality derived their definition of rights from group identities and assertions of positive rights such as the right to work, whereas theorists of liberal democracy premised their system of rights on individual identities and negative rights such as freedom from forms of coercion. Arguments between the two Superpowers about justice during the Cold War inevitably turned around these differences. With the collapse of socialist legality, the liberal democratic definition of dignity has now been extended to redress perceived injustices suffered in socialist states during the Cold War.

This chapter presents an ethnography of the work of an East German Commission of Vindication/Rehabilitation (Rehabilitierungskommission). Set up in the workplace of certain firms, such commissions, analogues of which were also established in other East-Central European states, took it upon themselves from late 1989 through 1994 to restore the dignity of victims of the old regime through acts of vindication or rehabilitation.[1] This restoration becomes particularly interesting in the German case, since article 1 of the West German Basic Law of 1949, which provided the framework for the invocation of the rule of law in

East Germany, boldly posits a fundamental, inviolable "human dignity" out of which human rights and many basic property rights were subsequently derived.[2] Though interrelated, the socio-logic and history of property and nonproperty rights, as well as the logic of distributive, corrective, and retributive justice, are not identical. Unfortunately, a discussion of these differences will take us too far away from the major set of problems addressed here. I will focus my analysis on nonmaterial wrongs, on moral injuries and retributive justice.

Vindication/rehabilitation is a relatively minor concern of justice systems, and public or media discussion of the status of victims of the former socialist regimes has been largely displaced throughout the East bloc by a discussion of present harms resulting from privatization and global market pressures. Yet the process of vindication offers a revealing example of how postsocialist states and societies have dealt with the usually neglected aspect of retributive justice: rewarding the good. The particular case that I have chosen to examine, the Commission of Vindication/Rehabilitation for Radio and Television of the GDR, resembles superficially what is often called *popular justice*. Sally Merry (1993: 35) defines popular justice as "a legal institution located on the boundary between state law and indigenous or local law, 'culturally' conceptualized as similar to indigenous law and opposite to state law." While these commissions were generated by indigenous nonjural groups, their goals throughout were to achieve legal recognition for their findings. Hence their workings shed very little light on issues of popular justice (indigenous assertions of sovereignty against the state). Instead they reveal particular problems involved in the invocation of the rule of law: how some practices came under the penumbra of state law following unification. The people who appeared before the commissions claimed to be victims of a criminality that was, if not state sponsored, then at least supported or benignly tolerated by the state. In response, the commissions engaged in a particular form of justice that combined both corrective and retributive aspects. Often this entailed both compensating the victim for harms (corrective justice) and compensating the victim for moral injuries (retributive justice). Their work was the flip side of punishing wrongdoers: the issue of governmental criminality dealt with in previous chapters. In that domain I focused on attempts to hold the wrongdoer accountable for a moral wrong, defined by the wrongness of the act itself and not by the concrete damage inflicted on a victim. By contrast, vindication directs us primarily to redressing the victim and only secondarily is it concerned with the perpetrator.

The relation of the victim to the perpetrator is, as we shall see, often the core issue in vindication, for in order to confirm the victim's importance through a procedure of vindication, it is often necessary to lower the unjustly elevated status of the wrongdoer. To reestablish the self-worth and value—the dignity—of the victim requires that an event be staged whereby there is a public repudiation of the message of superiority that initially caused the diminishment in the victim's worth. This public event seeks, as Jean Hampton argues, both to "repair the damage done to the victim's ability to realize her value" and to defeat the wrongdoer's claim to mastery over the victim. It does not thereby compromise the wrongdoer's value as a person, but it "confirms them as equal by virtue of their humanity" (Hampton 1992: 1686–87). They are affirmed as equal in the sense that both are recognized as agents exercising free will—the minimal condition of humanity.

If free will, or, paraphrasing Kant, "the capacity of the individual to remain a subject with a will" (Todorov 1996: 16), is a necessary condition for dignity, it is not the only one. Todorov elaborates on a second. In his examination of moral life in the extreme situation of concentration camps, the gulags of the Soviet Union, and the *Lager* of Nazi Germany, he argues that the other ingredient of dignity is to demonstrate "that it is possible to establish an adequation between the internal and the external: purely internal decisions . . . do not lead to dignity" (65). By this he rejects a purely subjective definition of dignity: "It is not enough simply to decide to acquire dignity; that decision must give rise to an act that is visible to others (even if they are not actually there to see it)" (61). In my analysis of the Commission of Vindication, I wish to stress the public recognition of acts that were by nature already public, and to examine how that public recognition contributed to the restoration of dignity.

HISTORY OF VINDICATION AFTER 1989

Following the opening of the Wall, media accounts proliferated documenting a plethora of innocent victims from 1945 to the present. The victims had suffered as a result of numerous state-sponsored activities: the scandalous reuse of Nazi concentration camps by Soviet/East German authorities to imprison critical social democrats and communists, Stalinist show trials, government kidnappings, extortion in return for freedom to emigrate, and many other less sensational acts. Thousands of self-identified victims came forth, many of them now living in West Germany, to demand vindication, or rehabilitation by their former work units or by the new government, or financial remedy for their suffering. Public discussion about such injustices had already began before the opening of the Wall, in October 1989, with the publication of

Walter Janka's *Schwierigkeiten mit der Wahrheit* (Difficulty with the truth), a documentary account of Janka's persecution and imprisonment in the 1950s as head of the leading East German publishing house, Aufbau Verlag. Before the end of the year, the self-reforming East German justice system had rehabilitated Janka, though he himself had not applied for any restitution.

Many of these injustices began with the Soviet occupation in 1945 and continued with the implantation of the former Soviet-Stalinist system onto East Germany. Hermann Weber estimates that Stalin's "cleansings" resulted in 20 million Soviet victims alone, of whom about 10 million died or were killed. After 1945, the Soviets interned 123,000 Germans, of whom 43,000 disappeared or were killed (1991: 41, 43, 45). Schwanitz estimates that between 1945 and 1990, 340,000 Germans had been given prison sentences for political reasons, and hundreds of thousands had been deported, among whom 90,000 had either died or been killed (1991: 33). Göhler writes that approximately 150,000 "political" sentences had been handed out. By the end of February 1991, 40,000 petitions for rehabilitation had been made, with 20,000 in Thuringia, 11,000 in Sachsen, 7,000 in Brandenburg (1991: 29, 30).

From November 1989 through March 1990, the East German Roundtable discussed possible remedies for victims of three regimes: Nazi crimes from 1933 to 1945, Soviet authorities from 1944 to 1989, the GDR from 1949 to 1989. On September 6, 1990, the freely elected GDR parliament passed a rehabilitation/vindication law, the SED-Unrechtsbereinigungsgesetzes, dealing with rectification for nonproperty related harms. (*Bereinigung* means literally "settling," "clearing-up," "removal.") The preamble to this law, which was subsequently stricken from the Unity Treaty, articulated the following philosophy: "Rehabilitation/vindication is an essential element of the politics of democratic renewal of a society, a state, of the law" (cited by Däubler-Gmelin 1991: 24; see Heitmann 1991; Schwanitz 1991). Here, the idea of rehabilitation and justice to the victims was tied to a theory of democratic state legitimacy. Promulgators of this law defended it as more than a goodwill measure to former victims; they claimed it was also necessary to establish the legitimacy of the reformed state.

Article 17 of Unity Treaty called on the united German parliament to write a new rehabilitation law that would regulate these claims. But the dissolution of the GDR was followed by a paper war in the federal and provincial ministries, and passage was delayed for more than two years. The official reasons they gave for rejecting the law passed by the GDR parliament were that "parts of the law were too indefinite" and other parts concerning illegalities of Soviet military tribunals violated international law (Göhler 1991: 30). It is also clear that many in the government hesitated because of fears of the large costs entailed in rectifying victims. Herta Däubler-Gmelin, who worked with the Social Democratic Party opposition toward passage of such a law, reported that in the fall of 1990, shortly after unification, "there was a proposal for a law that had been prepared, that spies and conspirational workers of the State Security should be amnestied. That we prevented. But the group in the Ministry of Justice that concerns itself with revisions of the rehabilitation law was put together much later. That is a scandal!" (1991: 25). In other words, the postunity ruling coalition government (Christian Democrat and Free Democratic) was initially more united about amnestying certain categories of suspected criminals than with rehabilitating victims of state-organized criminality.

Following the decision to unify the two Germanys, various kinds of meetings between East and West German interest groups took place from March to October 3, 1990. In one such meeting, Klaus Kinkel, then (West German) federal minister of justice in the Christian Democratic–Free Democratic coalition government, invited leaders of the Prisoners and Victims Unions, Häftlings- und Opfervereinen, to Bonn to discuss a new version of rehabilitation/vindication law. Members of the Prisoners and Victims Unions report that they were ultimately disappointed because "none of their criticisms, and above all, none of their suggestions, were recognizable in the new law" (Faust 1994: 172). Without a powerful lobby, these victims groups have been unable to attract the same media attention—and therefore receive some priority—as obtained by those accused of crime or wrongdoing.

When the government did get around to planning the rehabilitation law, it was done without consulting the actual work of the commissions already engaged in such work. Even when the commissions themselves inquired as to the legal status of their work and the stage in which the proposed law stood, they rarely received responses. Several times Herr Grollmitz, the second chairperson of the Commission for Radio and Television (the first left after less than a year), asked me to write to Bonn. He thought that I, as a foreign scientist, could pressure or perhaps even shame Bonn into expediting passage of the law. I did once write to the Ministry of Justice, but I received no response. Grollmitz informed me that his only source of information about legal redress possibilities and the legal proposals by the government was the daily press.

Although the victims' voices and those of the commissions were never directly heard, their concerns were eventually addressed. On October 29, 1992, legislators passed the First Law for Settling SED-Illegality. On June 23, 1994, they passed a Second Law for Settling SED-Illegality. Article 1 of the First Law clarified the scope of the law as concerned with "rehabilitation and restitution of victims of illegal measures of criminal prosecution in the *Beitrittsgebiet* [the legal euphemism for the GDR]." This First Law established a list of GDR laws that should be considered illegal (therefore sentences were to be nullified) and identified the victims who were to be rehabilitated "insofar as the laws are irreconcilable with the essential principles of a free legal order [Rechtsstaat]." It uniformized the grounds for rehabilitation and set amounts for the financial restitution of victim categories. In a review of four interpretations and applications of this law by different courts, Schröder (1993: 350) found that in some cases those who had been prosecuted for refusal to do military service were rehabilitated while those who were prosecuted for fleeing the republic were not—in other words, definitions of what constituted illegality were arbitrary. Schröder (355) found that rehabilitation or restitution was often denied unless exceptional injuries could be documented, dependent on criteria such as forms of political persecution, violation of due process, or excessive sentences.

The Second Law corrected some of these problems. Primarily, however, it simply broadened the group of victims to include those who were harmed through administrative illegalities or through political prosecution, and it increased the amounts of restitution for some categories. For example, the category "bureaucratic illegalities" was broadened to include redress to those individuals who had been forced to give up their homes on the border regions of the GDR in 1952 and 1961, the times when the GDR established these borders. Taken together, both laws seem to operate with a spirit of inclusiveness in recognizing a broad range of victims and victimization, including harms suffered to one's health, property, or occupational career, and they propose corresponding remedies.

This law also specifies the need for corrective justice concerning both measures (acts, fiats, laws) not reconcilable with "the foundations of the Rechtsstaat, [including] the principles of justice, legal security, or the principle of proportionality," and acts of "political persecution or [laws] that are arbitrarily applied." Costs for legal proceedings are waived. If a petition is found warranted, the corresponding remedies are to be taken from laws of the Federal Republic. If the harmed party has died, his/her survivors can claim the remedy. The law directed the different eastern German provinces each to construct its own rehabilitation bureaus. These bureaus are directed to address an extremely detailed list of harms and to propose possible remedies for them. In article 1, paragraph 17 of the First Law, those individuals who had been unjustly imprisoned would be provided with DM 300 for each month. If the person still was a resident of the GDR through November 9, 1989, they received an additional DM 250 per month. Another example: article 2, paragraph 7 of the Second Law proposes preferential treatment in occupational advancement and education for those who suffered occupational discrimination; victims are provided with money for the necessary institutional fees and instructional costs for reschooling—up to DM four per hour of instruction, and DM 60 per month per child if childcare is necessary.

As this history illustrates, the governmental response to the victim's fight for the restoration of dignity has been characterized primarily by disinterest and neglect. This is partly due to a general public understanding of retributive justice as entailing only the punishment of evil without the rewarding of good. For many, redressing victims has little to do with bringing about justice in postsocialist states. Most scholars—criminologists, legal theorists, political analysts—wish to separate the fate, or even the voice, of victims from decisions about prosecution of wrongdoing, political accountability, and the rule of law. Their reasoning is that adding the victim's voice would create a situation of partiality, making it impossible to construct a dispassionate account of events, or to reach an objective decision on the relation of suspected criminals to the law. Former East German government officials now on trial appeal to these more scholarly opinions. They, in particular, have a personal stake in excluding the voice of victims. Accordingly, these former officials have sought to deflect attention from their own complicity in wrongdoing by reinventing themselves as the victims of overzealous judicial reformers. Here we have the unusual situation in which those accused of wrongdoing are in agreement with most legal experts that the voices of victims should remain irrelevant to considerations of their innocence or guilt; at the same time, those accused of wrongdoing have tried to re-create themselves as victims of the new regime. The overall effect has been to obscure the line between criminal and victim, and to turn public attention away from a consideration of the conditions under which the society and state are recognizing some misfortunes as injustices—hence subject to law—while not recognizing others.

While the change of regimes in 1989–90 in Germany has been relatively free of violence against members of former ruling elites, it has created new classes of dispossessed and new categories of victims. Also, it is likely that new cores of criminality have taken shape within, or at least with the complicity of, the reformed government itself (cf. Bisky, Heuer, and Schumann 1993). The necessary task of reckoning with new injustices, however, does not alleviate the need to settle accounts with old ones. In the remainder of this chapter I present the voice of these victims of the old regime and their role in the present restructuring of justice in eastern Germany.

THE COMMISSION OF VINDICATION
FOR RADIO AND TELEVISION

During the period of jural restructuring in 1990, the courts alone could not handle the number of claims made concerning past injustices, so some people in work units established their own Commissions of Vindication/Rehabilitation.[3] They were inspired by suggestions made at Roundtable discussions in the fall of 1989 but were also responding to demands made by former victims within companies themselves. Their deliberations were not adversarial but took the form of an open yet limited inquiry into the nature of the wrong, the plausibility and veracity of the claim, and the possibility of procuring remedies. The primary need expressed in their work was for the restoration of a lost dignity, for public recognition of two kinds of injustice: harms suffered either directly at the hands of fellow workers or from political instrumentalization of the workplace bureaucracy ("bureaucratic illegalities"). The types of injustices for which victims wanted vindication/rehabilitation included criminalization and imprisonment for *Westflucht* or *Republikflucht* (attempting to flee the republic), "removal and forced adoption of children," "repression, persecution, and judicial illegalities," and "defamation because of a critical position." Petitioners rarely made claims in the domain of corrective justice: to reclaim property, reassert status, obtain retribution—all material harms that the legal system would have felt compelled to address immediately. Instead most claims concerned moral injuries: harms that did not result in readily quantifiable injuries but were nonetheless wrong. The most common remedies proposed by the commission were either formal apologies, adjustment of the pensions lost, or "economic compensation" for particular losses.

According to Herr Grollmitz, chair of the Commission for Radio and Television, the function of the these commissions was "to work through the old political burdens of the SED period" (politische Altlasten aus der SED-Zeit aufarbeiten). Since the Unity Treaty nullified the former GDR law that would have regulated the activities of the commissions, the commissions had to wait until the fall of 1993 for notification of the legal status of their findings, and even this law did not take effect until April 1994. Hence for the first four years of operation, the commissions operated in a legal no-man's-land, neither inside nor outside the law, but as nonlaw.

The commissions were to determine the validity of the claims and to issue an honorary declaration: a letter of apology (*Ehrenerklärung*). In these letters, the Commission for Radio and Television repeatedly used the expression: we "reaffirm the political and moral integrity" of the victim. The letters expressed "regret for the repressions and discriminations," for "the destruction of meaningful career development," and for "the severe psychological stress"; they offered sympathy for the suffering caused; and they "condemned the arbitrary measures employed" to isolate and persecute critical voices.

These apologies were then made public so that either the findings could be challenged or the righting of the wrong acknowledged by the larger social community. Herr Grollmitz offered lists of people vindicated to the newspapers and other forms of media, though they rarely made use of these. Grollmitz stressed that these commissions were not primarily bodies to rectify injuries to victims, although they did actively engage in finding remedies for harm suffered. Nor did they have investigative powers that would enable them to go to court on behalf of petitioners. Their primary function was to right a wrong and in so doing to reestablish the dignity of the victim.

If a petitioner's claims were found warranted, the commission took it upon itself to offer an official apology on behalf of the company. If a particular individual was responsible for the violation, the commission would often ask him or her also to apologize.[4] Since most of those responsible for violations had already left the company through voluntary retirement, such apologies were rare. A second aspect of the commission's work was to help the victim overcome losses suffered from discrimination, and to raise his or her status to a level comparable to what it would have been had he or she not been victimized. As Grollmitz stated, they helped former employees "to find their way back into normality." This work often entailed securing employment for former victims or pressuring social security boards to adjust pensions.

I began observing commission proceedings in December 1990. The commission met for the last time in November 1993, after which its documents were given to the Gauck-Authority. Throughout his three years of commission work, Grollmitz, who became head of the commission six months into its existence, complained that there was "too little interest on the part of the public," perhaps because, after years of shortages of information, the media was saturating people with information about the past. Grollmitz thought, "It doesn't interest anyone any longer because it is already considered a part of the past." In 1992, an Enquete-Kommission had been established as a lay commission by the united German parliament to inquire into a "political reckoning with the repressions of the Soviet Occupation Zone/GDR." It concluded its investigation and issued a final report in 1994. However, as some politicians and members of the commission criticized the report for dealing only with the negative aspects of GDR history, parliament set up another investigatory commission in 1995. The Enquete-Kommission, Grollmitz claimed, was interested more in "historical abstractions of what went on and in the historical evaluation of this period . . . than in the fate of individual histories." It, as well as the general public, complained Grollmitz, showed "only limited interest" in the Rehabilitation/Vindication Commission's goal of "reestablishing the honor and standing of former radio and television workers."

In the majority of cases where a positive determination was made, the Rehabilitation/Vindication Commission offered the remedy of adding compensatory years to retirement pensions, for those years when workers were coerced into quitting or were fired for political reasons. The Neue Fünf Länder Gesellschaft (New Five State Society), the reconstructed holding firm for GDR radio and television, which was then dissolved in May 1995, had a special fund set aside for such remedies. As well, it paid commission members DM 35 per sitting for their work. Acutely aware of the limitations of commission work, Grollmitz insisted that above all he regretted that victims could not recover the lost years where "the family suffered actual misery, where it was damaged." He wanted to give victims "a sign of restitution, something to make the new beginning easier." The other frequent remedy, as mentioned, was to secure employment for workers not of retirement age.

Of the one hundred petitions received by the commission through 1993, 75 percent were decided in favor of the petitioners. In most of the successful cases the worker had been fired illegally according to GDR law, but the means used to terminate the labor contract varied. In the radio division people were fired directly; in the television division workers were manipulated into a situation where they usually were forced to quit. About half of the petitioners who came before the commission had written an *Ausreiseantrag*, petition to leave the GDR. In most cases, such people then suffered a occupational ban, *Beschäftigungsverbot*, which was carried out by members of the party and state security who were also coemployees at the radio and television company. These people were then classified as "political opponents" and regularly observed. Most often the Stasi formulated a plan to discredit them among their colleagues and neighbors. Sometimes such measures resulted in altercations with authorities, after which some people were taken to court and sentenced to prison terms. Many of these individuals had already been rehabilitated by the courts and therefore did not come before the commission.

In the television division, it took an average of eight years before petitions to leave were approved, though this period of waiting was substantially shortened during the fall of 1989. If petitioners owned real estate, they usually approached Professor Vogel to "buy their own freedom," as they called it.

Of those who had not applied to leave, most were fired because they expressed opinions contrary to official policy. The commission also considered petitions of former members of the Socialist Unity Party or of party functionaries. But Grollmitz asserted that although these people also suffered political difficulties, their petitions were not given the "same benefit of doubt as the others."

If individuals appealed their dismissals or demotions to GDR labor courts, their cases were nearly always decided in favor of the functionaries of the company, especially if the worker had written a petition to leave. Only one case had come to light before the commission where the worker's appeal was affirmed by the court. A law passed in the late 1960s tightened work and disciplinary measures within state-owned companies, but GDR radio and television went even further and formulated their own work and disciplinary procedures. Thereafter, "absolute obedience" was demanded of workers. A critical opinion against a decision of the party could be considered a criminal offense, and evidence of such opinions was used to dismiss workers from their jobs.

CASE STUDY OF VINDICATION
COMMISSION PROCEEDINGS

From 1991 through 1993, I regularly talked with two members of the Commission of Vindication in December and during the summer, and the commission agreed to permit me to attend their meetings provided that the petitioners also agreed to my presence. The following description of one such meeting on June 28, 1993, might be typical of the format of these sittings but it is exceptional as to the content of cases discussed. For one thing, the second case dealt with in this meeting is one of the 25 percent that did not result in a vindication. I have chosen it precisely because of its exceptional character, for it indicates some of the limits of the use of vindication and the difficulties in classifying victims. It also raises intriguing questions about the relation of criminality, accountability, and victimhood to the use of a "surrogate victim," which I discussed earlier.

Two women and three men attended, seated around a square table. A secretary, who was also a woman, served coffee and cakes. She remained in the room to take notes. One of the men had been adviser to the head of personnel for GDR television, another had played in the orchestra for GDR radio; one woman had been chair of the drama division of GDR radio, the other woman had herself been a victim of the state radio/television, and had been fired in the late 1970s for a series of suspicious activities, including having friends who were dissidents and voicing critical opinions herself. The third man was chair of the commission; he had worked in an administrative function for television. All of the members had been elected to their positions by a vote of workers in the company.

Each time I attended a meeting, the committee members were asked if they had any objections to my presence, and the people who came for a hearing were also asked the same question. On this day the committee was to decide on one case (which they had heard in the previous sitting) and they were to hear a second. In the first case, members were unanimous in wanting to vindicate Dorothea, but they had not yet agreed on what to put in the letter (*Ehrenerklärung*). To protect the anonymity of the participants of these meetings, I am changing names and a few details in this description.

Dorothea's history was constructed in a general question-and-answer session. She had been persecuted in the late 1970s for speaking her mind and for defending other employees against actions by their superiors. She quit her job under pressure. A discussion followed concerning the differences between state persecution in the 1950s and that of the 1970s. One woman suggested that the letter emphasize Dorothea's civil courage. The others nodded agreement. One man commented that this might appeal to the moral conscience of those who now would be asked to (re)employ Dorothea, who in the interim had never found work in the field of radio and television. Another woman added that Dorothea had been victimized for being an individualist, someone who fought alone, whereas some others had been persecuted after a single event as part of a campaign against like-minded people in order to frighten them into being silent. Such campaigns took place after events like the worker uprising in 1953 or during the rise of the Polish Solidarity movement in 1980. Members of the commission expressed frustration about not being able to do more for Dorothea. Several agreed it was unlikely that their letter of support would mean much either to potential employers or to legal authorities should Dorothea pursue her appeal in court. A draft of a vindication letter was passed around for comments. Some minor details were changed.

After a short pause, Christina, who had worked with GDR radio since 1968, was invited into the room. This was the start of the second case. She had already appeared before the commission, the first time on

July 5, 1990, when the GDR still existed, to ask for the rehabilitation of her husband—I will call him Jan-Peter. Since then, the commission had lost several members and gained several new ones, but at no time had it been able to make a decision. They could not agree on the facts of the case.

Jan-Peter committed suicide in 1985, under circumstances never adequately explained to Christina or to their three children. Christina was convinced that the Stasi had something to do with her husband's mysterious suicide, that they had blackmailed him. After the opening of the Wall in November 1989, the Stasi became a focus of public resentment and hope—resentment as a symbol of a repressive state, hope because the Stasi could be used as an explanation for what had gone wrong in individual lives. Many people thought that Stasi documents could help them come to terms with their own pasts, locate the specific dates and persons involved in their personal failures or tragedies. Christina explained that already in early 1990 she had sought access to Stasi documents but the files were then still not open. She therefore went to the commission and asked them to petition the GDR parliament—this parliament was first dissolved on October 3, 1990—for her to see her files and those of her husband.

The point was, she argued, that she had assumed the entire responsibility for the suicide of her husband. That suicide had destroyed her family, for after Jan-Peter's death she became estranged from her children. She had also developed cancer—who knows, perhaps from the stress? Only in the second half of 1992, after a five-year battle, had she begun to recover. By March 1993 she felt healthy enough to pursue the case further but, getting nowhere on her own, she formally appealed to the commission again, on June 17, 1993, to petition for access to her own husband's files.

She was thanked for her presence and asked to leave. Members of the commission began discussing the case. The chairman of the commission explained what he knew of the facts: Her husband had hung himself, and Christina had found him. She unfortunately seemed to carry a sense of guilt for this suicide.

One member, who had known her and her husband fairly well, explained cautiously that at the time of the suicide some of her colleagues suspected that she had driven him to it. Jan-Peter was known to have drinking problems, and his coworkers often attributed these problems to his inability to adequately handle his work. Christina was acknowledged as a very capable worker, greatly respected by her coworkers. But Jan-Peter had difficulty fulfilling the requirements of his jobs. He had been steadily promoted because he was one of the few members of the working class employed in the bourgeois profession of radio and television work. Many of his coworkers thought that his drinking was a result of his inability to withstand the pressure of job expectations, and the more he drank, the more his work performance deteriorated.

Since the first sitting in 1990, commission members had come across some internal documents of the radio and television that included several reports written by unofficial co-conspirators (Stasi IM, *inoffizielle Mitarbeiter*) for the Stasi. In one report, it seemed to indicate that the Stasi had indeed tried to recruit Jan-Peter to work for them. This report stated, "He is not suited [for] unofficial cooperation [because he is] not truthful." Other documents seemed to indicate that Jan-Peter had indeed worked, at least a short time, as a Stasi "contact person," not as an "unofficial coworker." A contact person was considered only a *Geheimnisträger*, a carrier of secrets, and not an informer. Unlike informers, they were rarely paid anything and contact was irregular.

One member of the commission who was doing research on the structure of the Stasi in radio and television explained to the other members how to read these designations in terms of careers within the Stasi organization. She distinguished between *Opferakte* (victim files) and *Täterakte* (perpetrator files), and explained that some of the designations could only be found listed in the perpetrator files. Since Christina had access only to her own victim files, she had seen no reference to her husband, since victim files listed only "unofficial coworkers" and not "contact persons."

Further discussion of the case focused on why Christina wanted her husband vindicated. He had in fact committed no crime. Some commission members felt that Christina wanted to be released from the suspicion that she had driven her husband to suicide. It was pointed out that both of her brothers had left the GDR, the first one already in the 1950s. The second brother had to petition to leave the GDR, and eventually received permission, along with his wife, in the 1980s. At that time Christina admitted having discussed with her husband leaving the GDR, but that he had rejected the idea. Left undiscussed in the commission was why Jan-Peter himself rejected the idea. It seemed to me that his relation with the Stasi was the primary motive, for people with relations to the Stasi or relatives working for the Stasi had even greater difficulty than others getting petitions to leave approved.

The commission member who knew the family well claimed that Jan-Peter was "a failure, a typical fraud. He had everything but journalistic talent. He claimed he could do anything." He added that Jan-Peter's alcoholism did not start later in life; he had this tendency even when he started working for radio and television. Ultimately, he concluded, "Jan-Peter couldn't hold out under the pressure. And the suicide is something that Christina couldn't deal with." Much like her husband, Christina had enjoyed a stellar career, eventually holding the position of television producer. But all of her colleagues seemed to agree that she was talented. Jan-Peter, on the other hand, "was clearly the one who had to play second fiddle in every decision they made." Still, the company files greatly praised the quality of his work. He had even served as head of the local Kampfgruppe, a paramilitary unit organized in the workplace to be ready in case there was an attack on the GDR by the West.

During a previous sitting, Christina had told commission members that she and her husband "had had a good marriage," that she "loved him." As one member pointed out, after Jan-Peter's death, her career did not suffer. She worked on, seemingly unaffected by his death.

"What can the Rehabilitierungskommission do?" the chair of the commission asked bluntly.

One member commented, "She wants to use us as an alibi function."

The others took turns responding. "We don't hand out papers for people's wishes."

"I don't think we can do anything for her."

"Why should we rehabilitate him?"

"She wants to know what happened to her husband. Perhaps we can help explain the circumstances if she opens up all of her Stasi files to us."

"Something else. She needs a psychiatrist. Are her children accusing her of his suicide?"

"She has suffered from the uncertainty. And through her work she has been compensated for this uncertainty. It seems as if the activities of the Stasi have created the situation where the family has been hurt. They suffered psychological pain and harm."

"Yes, but someone who has not worked for the Stasi also suffers from psychological damage. We don't vindicate him. The ministry for state security was not the cause of all these problems."

The commission ended the discussion, agreeing that although the case needed more research, they should compose a letter for her. This letter would not rehabilitate her husband, but it might help her understand the connections between her husband's death, the Stasi, and the radio and television. The commission felt obligated to give her information and make the example public.

Someone concluded, "We could have dismissed this case easily. She should be happy that we have taken her seriously."

Christina's appeal for vindication illustrates several of the facets in a process of reestablishing the dignity of victims. Although the "facts" are what seem confusing to the commission, it is their narrative ordering and neither their facticity nor chronology that is in doubt. Any account of the suicide must include a determination of who was responsible, a position toward Christina's status as self-perceived victim, a justification of the moral consequences for the position taken. Four narrative versions appear to me plausible accounts.

Version one. Jan-Peter commits suicide. Following his death, the relations between his wife and children deteriorate. Christina, his innocent wife, suspects that the malicious Stasi, for whom her husband had worked conspiratorially, is the cause of his suicide. She seeks to rehabilitate her husband by showing his death to have been caused by an outside agent and not an act of free will. She asked a Commission of Vindication to confirm this interpretation.

Version two. Jan-Peter commits suicide. Following his death, the relations between his wife and children deteriorate. But unlike the events in version one, both the evil Stasi and Christina, his careerist wife, are assumed to have contributed to his death. They had both placed great pressures on him, primarily to transcend his working-class background, driving him to drink and eventually to suicide. Christina feels guilty. She wants to be exculpated from responsibility for his death and comes up with the scheme of attributing his death to the Stasi, a convenient surrogate victim after the GDR's dissolution. She asked a Commission of Vindication to confirm this interpretation.

Version three. Jan-Peter commits suicide. He had been a heavy drinker, which contributed greatly to the deterioration of relations with his wife and children. Despite her innocence, Christina, his wife, feels responsible for the suicide. Therefore she sought to have a Commission of Vindication alleviate her of her guilt by placing the blame for the suicide on the Stasi.

Version four. Several years before Jan-Peter committed suicide, his relations with his wife and children deteriorated, driving him to drink. Christina, his wife, imagines that the Stasi is the cause of his suicide and seeks to rehabilitate her husband by showing his death to have been caused by an outside agent and not an act of free will. She asked a Commission of Vindication to confirm this interpretation.

Each of these versions lists a different narrative ordering and hence cause for the suicide: the Stasi, the Stasi and the wife, a drinking habit, deteriorating relations with the wife and children. To any of these versions, the commission as a moral body had several options to respond: In version one, it agrees, holds the Stasi guilty, and vindicates Christina; in version two, it disagrees and finds her and the Stasi guilty; in version three, it disagrees and finds his drinking to be causal; in version four, it disagrees and sees deteriorating relations within the family as causing the suicide. Or, the commission takes no stand other than sympathy for Christina's grief and clarifies the possibilities of explanation—in fact, this was the commission's response.

Each of the four versions forces the commission to act as a positivist historical or juridical body. Members were asked to determine a set of "facts" and their narrative order independent from Christina's own present problems of self-worth. But her self-worth was the primary reason why she and all the other "victims" of the past had petitioned for vindication. Christina's self-worth is in turn intricately linked to the political community in which she has lived, the structure of work, her and her husband's class positions, and the nature of hierarchies. A historical investigation such as that performed by the Enquete-Kommission (parliamentary investigative committee) would leave the facts in the past and seek their true meaning in that past; above all, for them Christina's own present needs should not be allowed to influence the narrative ordering of these facts. A juridical investigation would look at the law and match these facts to the law; if no law covered them, then it would have no responsibility to take up the case and prioritize any specific causal sequence. The commission rejected both approaches and instead acted as an ethical body. It struggled to balance Christina's needs with its own mission, "to work through the old political burdens of the SED period." I do not mean to say that historians and jurists do not act morally, but that if they act within the constraints of (and devotion to) their professional guidelines, the ethical aspects of their work will remain secondary to obligations to either truth or law, and therefore they will often be left unattended.

Christina clearly feels responsible for the suicide of her husband, Jan-Peter, and for the breakup of her family. She wants to be absolved of this sense of guilt. Her need is only human, and a moral community will understand its primary goal is neither truth nor legality but to help her recover her sense of moral worth so that she can resume acting as a full member of that community. In her confusion, she displaces her guilt onto the Stasi, a potential and convenient surrogate victim for all sorts of evils in the former East Germany. That reaction is also human, but unfortunately wrong and potentially harmful to others. She goes to a Commission of Vindication to have this view of reality confirmed. The commission, a paralegal, quasihistorical body, is aware of the ambivalences in Christina's story but also of its own responsibilities. Since Christina herself was never accused of a crime, however, and since there is no evidence that the Stasi had forced her husband into doing anything against his will that might lead to his suicide, the commission is at a loss as to whom to vindicate.

Alternatively, most members of the commission see their function not in rigid historical terms as determining truth nor in the rigid juridical terms of determining who can claim victim status legally, but as a moral one of confirming the victim's, any victim's, importance. One need violate neither the commitment to truth nor to the principles of legality in order to perform this job. It is accomplished by fulfilling an ethical demand that both the search for knowledge and the law presuppose: acknowledgment of the subject's worth. For the commission, this demand entails repairing the damage done to the victim, and reestablishing his or her dignity. Since the Stasi as part of the state apparatus was engaged systematically and arbitrarily in lowering the worth of people, in damaging them, Christina's thesis that her husband's suicide was caused by the Stasi (version one) is plausible. And the commission would have no problem apologizing for Stasi crimes or moral injuries if those injuries could be inferred from the doings of the Stasi working within state radio and television, which the commission now represents. Yet it is difficult to get around the fact that it has no evidence linking the pressure of the Stasi, or acts of any other member of radio and television, to the suicide of Jan-Peter. Lacking sufficient evidence to link the suicide to any particular narrative order that might indict a particular perpetrator, the commission nonetheless does not shirk its obligation to help Christina work through the burdens of their collective past. It does refuse to hold the Stasi accountable, and it feels able neither to rehabilitate Jan-Peter nor to vindicate Christina. The commission concludes uneasily by agreeing both to investigate further the kind of narrative linkages Christina has used to make sense of her personal chronology and to write a letter evaluating the relative plausibility of these linkages.

EVALUATIONS OF THE VINDICATION COMMISSION

In September 1993, in a project funded by the American Council of Learned Scholars, I, together with my German partners, Michael Weck and Ilona Stolpe, sent a questionnaire to each person who had gone before the commission. Herr Grollmitz had provided us with the addresses of all those who had appealed for vindication. In response to our open-ended questionaire, twenty-one petitioners (out of one hundred polled) returned either letters or comments before the end of 1993. People were all identified by name and we asked them if they would be willing to correspond with us further. Only one person indicated that he did not want to discuss his situation further, writing that his vindication had been completed to his satisfaction; moreover, his "situation was not so serious." Nearly half of the respondents wrote a special note either thanking or praising us for researching their cases scientifically.[5] These responses, along with my own observations at some of the proceedings of the commission, interviews with several members of the commission, and written statements by the commission summarizing findings in particular cases, are different kinds of evidence I have used to evaluate the work of vindication. To give the reader a sense of the range of responses to the work of this Vindication Commission and its relation to the rule of law in the minds of the victims, I will present four examples in some detail.

Example One

Rita Maria Bartoszweski had worked for the state radio station and had written a petition to leave, which resulted in her being released from her job. After several years, her citizenship was revoked and she was released to the Federal Republic. She now lives in Göppingen, West Germany, where she has been unsuccessful in securing employment in the field of radio. The efforts of the commission to find her a job for her in the East, using as pressure its protocol of her years of discrimination, have also met with no success.

In a letter dated November 18, 1993, Rita explains the meaning of vindication as "reestablishing social respect/appearance, reinstalling earlier (honorable) legal relationships, return to former activities, repayment of lost wages, active participation in the 'Abwicklung' (bringing to completion, closure) of the television and radio, release from work contract with a sufficient [departure] payment as is the case with active workers today." She complains that the commission did not perform this task because it was never given a "concrete task," and it has no "formal-legal competence."

When she appeared before the commission, she felt in the same situation as during her "disciplinary procedure" before she was fired: she sat "alone at the head of a long table," had to "talk and answer questions, was questioned, felt interrogated, they are sitting again like a court, are not able (or want?) to understand me and my arguments, although these people had lived in the same reality as I had."

She criticizes the commission members for being "totally unknown" to her, although they had worked for the same company. It apparently "was not possible to find a handful of workers with integrity to come together" and handle the petitions. She knew only two of the members and then, "only fleetingly." They had their own picture of her, "as always from secondhand sources," from protocols of meetings, from women's commissions, from reports about her from party meetings, and evaluations from colleagues. "They had their 'picture of me,' and it was plain to see that they wanted to have it confirmed," she complained. On the other hand, she praised the reaction of the chair, Herr Grollmitz, and said that only his personal intervention convinced her not to break the sitting and leave.

At that point in her response, Rita turns around and criticizes her own thoughts. "But really, who would I have accepted in a Vindication Commission out of the old coworkers and clique of appointed people? Honestly, I can think of no one." She doubts whether a fair handling would have even been possible. Her self-criticism is not that her standards are false but that her expectations about the possibilities for justice are unrealistic. She continues along these lines, describing the "West German reality" as also dominated by "old elites" who have a monopoly on authority, as lacking in "democracy, justice, or tolerance." She writes that "good contacts, elastic assimilation, and the recognition of existing hierarchies without contradicting them" are qualities also "sought in the media" and are "desired criteria" for employees.

These realizations have not, however, made her "bitter, insulted, or disappointed," she adamantly insists. "No," she writes, I am still "obsessed with the idea that one must reaffirm individual freedom, human dignity, and socially responsible behavior each day anew, and of course also be responsible for the consequences for such behavior."

Example Two

Hans Wachholz had protested the use of GDR troops in support of the Soviet invasion of Czechoslovakia in 1968, was arrested, imprisoned, and eventually released to the Federal Republic. He now works with in Stockholm with a Swedish radio station. After the commission had vindicated him, he attempted to recover the private property that the Stasi had taken from him in 1968. His requests resulted in a letter from the Senate in Rostock, responsible for such appeals. This letter first offered a "quasi-justification for the GDR practice" and submitted to Hans a bill for debts he owed to his former employer (the state's radio station). The bill had been concocted by the former State Security, but the Senate insisted it had been found in his files. Even though the Vindication

Commission had explicitly rejected this bill as a falsified document, the Senate in Rostock refused to respond to his further inquiries.

He concludes his letter ironically by contending that he "doubts whether the 'Rechtsstaat' is yet realized (in Rostock)."

Example Three

Ursula Prochnow, who was fired from the state radio in September 1961, praised the commission's handling of her case. It "filled her with pleasure," she writes, when she received the invitation to appear before the commission on October 10, 1990. The final protocol confirmed that hers was a clear "case of political persecution," and it recommended corresponding adjustments in her pension. Although, according to the GDR vindication law, her pension should have been adjusted, her situation was not covered by the laws of the Federal Republic. Therefore her appeals to the Federal Minister of Labor and to the Minister of Justice have been rejected.

Nonetheless, she praises the contribution of the commission to the Rechtsstaat, for it "analyzes and documents crimes and is able to make public old and possibly new illegalities." In this way, it protects "the norms of legality." She would like to pursue her case in court, but fears she will sink into a "sea of paragraphs." Further, she doubts whether she could afford a legal process.

Example Four

In early 1991, Wolfgang Preßler learned of the existence of the Vindication Commission. His first reaction was "irritation. Who had behaved erroneously? And hence who could rehabilitate whom?" His former employer could accuse him of nothing, but to the contrary, he could accuse his former employers, "the bosses who worked in contract with the party and the State Security," of much wrong. "If there is anyone at all to rehabilitate, then eventually I, as the one discriminated against, could acquit my former accusers of their certain guilt. . . . [I could] forgive them and thereby rehabilitate them."

Wolfgang went to his appointment before the commission "out of pure curiosity." He was astounded by the composition of members, for he knew one of them personally as someone whose position at the company would have compelled him to "devote himself to the state." Nonetheless, he explicitly praised "all of the other persons" on the commission for their "good intentions." Unfortunately, the assistance proposed was "inadequately realized." Wolfgang concludes sarcastically, accusing "our 'Rechtsstaat'"—referring to the new Federal Republic—of "total failure in the reckoning and judgment of forty years of injustice."

Following the apologies and other actions of the commission, individuals were divided about whether they felt that their dignity had been restored. The majority of those who responded to us were critical. Among the reasons for continued dissatisfaction, they listed (1) the further employment of individuals who were responsible for the initial injustice; (2) the failure to hold accountable those responsible for injustices; (3) the refusal of perpetrators to apologize for their deeds; and (4) inadequate compensation for discrimination (e.g., DM 4,500 restituted from lost wages instead of the DM 24,000 appealed for); (5) the inability to afford the costs of a legal process to obtain retribution (e.g., DM 10,000 to start a proceeding, DM 4,300 for the first instance, another DM 4,000 for an appeal); (6) the lack of juridical validity of the *Ehrenerklärung* issued by the commission; (7) the disinterest among the public in helping victims ("Who in this 'free time park' is interested in my problems?"). These criticisms explicitly link the status of victims to that of the perpetrators of wrong. A satisfactory resolution of the conflict, they seem to argue, entails both raising the status of the victim to that s/he had before having been wronged *and* not allowing the wrongdoer to retain the gain accrued from his/her offensive conduct.

Some individuals did go out of their way not to blame the commission for their frustrations with its inability to right the wrongs suffered in the past. Though the commission's apology may be insufficient, nearly all of the people who appeared before it still find its work an essential aspect of justice, of righting wrongs. Werner Meschkank, for example, writes that a "material restitution did not lie in the competence of the commission and I actually did not expect that." He emphasized that "suffered injustice cannot be undone or calculated in monetary terms. [. . .] Feelings of revenge are foreign to me. We should draw a thick line, but our conscience should remain alert."

He praised the commission for its concrete work, done "honestly and without cries of sensation. It was emotionally stimulating, without bringing forth hate or feelings of revenge." He also complained that "with the exception of one person, none of my former colleagues [who were] guilty in my case have excused themselves to me; instead most of them have long since repressed their complicity."

Barbara Große, who had been unjustly sentenced to prison in 1983 and whose children had been adopted into other families, was invited before the commission in February 1992. In the commission's apology, they not only asked the court in Leipzig to rescind its earlier decision and vindicate Barbara, but also responded to her wish "to thank her colleagues and announce her respect for those who stood by her with help during the time of difficult political and social incriminations." In response to our questions, Barbara argued that while the work of the commission was not in itself able to realize the goals of the Rechtsstaat, it was nonetheless extremely important for "the psyche of the affected persons." To the extent that the apparatus of the state responds to and gives legal force to the work of vindication, it contributes to establishing the accountability of the state and hence the state's legitimacy as an impartial moral agent (cf. Rautenberg 1994: 300–303).

This ambivalent sentiment was echoed by members of the commission with whom I spoke approximately a year and a half after their final meeting. One commission member told me that she thought most of the perpetrators had found jobs working for the radio station Mitte Deutschland Rundfunk (MDR), while the victims who suffered most have not been able to resume their careers. Perpetrators *haben sich reingewaschen*, "have washed themselves clean," and thus they have not suffered the lowering of status necessary to rectify injuries to the victims for the moral injuries inflicted upon them. Despite dissatisfaction with the limitations of the commission's work, members felt that the official apologies, restitutions, and rehabilitations were held to be important by the victims, and explained for them why not a single victim who had asked for vindication either returned to the commission for additional redress or resorted to formal legal or extralegal remedies.

CONCLUSION

My effort in this chapter is in part directed to a reorientation and a reclamation of law for anthropology, specifically the principles of the *rule of law*. These principles have developed historically as forms of protections from the arbitrariness of the rule of men. Although the rule of a law has a critical history, it has been abandoned by the critical left to the forces of order and reaction who cynically invoke it to justify the use of coercion by the state. Some of our most critical voices within anthropology have tended to view state law as purely coercive, as enforcing social norms against "society" (Clastres 1974) or ensuring their reproduction (Bourdieu 1977), rather than as a Kantian regulative ideal against which actual laws themselves are measured. To the extent recent critical voices have argued for the law, they have neglected criminal justice and the issues surrounding retribution in favor of arguments about equality and distributive justice.

My second goal is to affirm the importance of suffering and to point to the process of its reincorporation into the identity of the national subject. With the rise of the welfare state in Western Europe, the national subject has been increasingly defined in terms of consumption, as a wide range of theoretical and empirical research has shown. As subjects increasingly defined themselves in terms of consumptive ideals, of enjoyment and pleasure, a postwar generation of nationals has distanced itself from the nineteenth-century national narratives of heroic individuals who sacrificed and suffered for the group, for progress, and for some future version of communal bliss. This largely generational narrative became part of a Cold War regime of pleasure, distributed unequally in the colloquial divisions of First, Second, and Third World parts. Violence, or at least its acknowledgment, was also distributed, more or less banned from the center of the First World, but enacted in and projected onto marginalized others in the form of proxy wars and forms of economic exploitation, often in the Third World. Today this distributive regime is disintegrating; violence is returning in many forms to the First World, as is the guilt and ethical debates about violence that were absent during the Cold War. It is unlikely that most First World nationals will again be able to ignore the trope of suffering, the need to account and to assign responsibility for it. This means that issues of retributive justice will come to the fore: rewarding good, punishing evil. This does not mean that all suffering is equal, nor that only the good suffer. But it does mean that some forms of suffering will be given legal recognition and those victims will have legal redress, while others will be classified as "misfortunes" and remain in the nonlegal domain.

Since 1990 and formal unification, there is a renewed debate about filling in the empty sign of the German nation, with the debate put mostly in East/West identity terms—the West afraid of theft of their enjoyment, the East wanting to occupy that very site of pleasure. Frequently lost in this macronarrative are the efforts made to reestablish the state as a moral authority through retributive justice: holding accountable wrongdoers and rewarding the good by recognizing vicims of the old regime in the East. I have attributed the loss of empathy for these victims to the displacement of shared suffering by a pleasure model of national identification. Yet it is unlikely that the abjection of suffering, the placing of harmed or wounded individuals outside of one's own identification, will ever be fully successful, for with the likely return of violence to the center, the rationalist pleasure-seeking identity is at risk. The current moment that I am analyzing, which follows the collapse of socialist projects in East-Central Europe, might be characterized as one of ensuing psychic conflict between multiple identifications, a struggle with the return and reincorporation of that which was once repudiated during the Cold War.

The final chapter will suggest some of the differences between several of the former socialist states with regard to criminalization and vindication processes within the first four years following regime changes. It will also attempt a comparison of regime transformations with respect to political accountability and the position of victims among the new states. The reader should keep in mind that the failure to address victims in this short period is no sure indicator that states will avoid taking up the issue in the future. One need look only at the behavior of different political communities following World War II to see that nowhere are all groups of victims granted equal recognition and that the speed determining the extent of recognition depends on a number of complex and highly variable political factors. These factors include relation to external powers (e.g., the presence of occupation powers or competition with other states for the moral high ground), internal political party dynamics, organization and power of victim groups, the changing nature of local prejudices (e.g., some of World War II's victim groups—for example, Gypsies and homosexuals—received delayed recognition for their suffering in some countries, no recognition to date in others).

Part Four

LEGITIMACY

CHAPTER 8

The Rule of Law and the State:
Violence, Justice, and Legitimacy

THIS FINAL CHAPTER will make preliminary comparisons of the effects of the invocation of the principles of the rule of law on violence and state legitimacy in different postsocialist states. In the comparison I bring together four activities: invocation of the principles of the rule of law, prosecution and criminalization of the old elite for past crimes, vindication of victims, and state legitimacy and the control of violence.

Before going into this comparison, I will make a few final reflections on the dominant frameworks used to understand the transitions in East-Central Europe. The major American project documenting and analyzing the legal transitions has been run out of the Center for the Study of Constitutionalism in Eastern Europe at the University of Chicago Law School in partnership with the Central European University, with the political scientists Stephen Holmes and Jon Elster cofounders. This project has done extremely valuable work, and I have relied on their high-quality reports for much information in this book. Their explicit purpose, wrote Holmes (1992: 13) in the first issue of the *East European Constitutional Review*, was "to promote clearer thinking about the design of liberal-democratic institutions." Elster (1992a: 16) further clarified their logic: "Democracy, to be stable, needs a constitutional framework; constitutionalism, to be legitimate, needs a democratic pedigree." Hence the initial focus was on the design of constitutions and the institutional arrangements of the government apparatus—a single design and plan for its installation, irrespective of place and time. Although the center listed retribution as one of its the eleven basic research categories, subsequent country-by-country reports and analytical frameworks, operating theoretically within a liberal model, have tended to dismiss efforts at retribution as politically motivated justice.

Within a year and a half of the first publication, Holmes (1993: 21–25), to his credit, began questioning the limits of this liberal framework, specifically the focus on constitutionalism as a framework in which to measure the success or failure of the transitions. He asked whether "current-day Western advice" and "Western political and economic models [work] as an impediment to reform." He continued, "The most difficult problem facing the countries of Eastern Europe today is the creation of a government that can pursue effective reforms while re-taining public confidence and remaining democratically accountable." This position is very similar to the one I have taken in this study—except for one dimension: I foreground temporality. In his moment of self-criticism, Holmes never abandons the atemporal assumptions embedded in his framework. He reduces present problems to "painful legacies of the past—including ethnic tensions, personal habits of de-pendency, low tolerance for economic inequality, and the absence of a middle class." He calls these problems "crippling residua." Crippling, indeed, but what does it mean for problems to be "residua"? This term is reminiscent of the discredited anthropological term *survivals*—the label for what remained undesirable in periods of intense change, cul-ture traits from the past. Needless to say, present problems need to be analyzed as both caused by and potentially resolvable in terms of con-temporary processes. Not only is constitutionalism a temporal solution to institutional authority, requiring readjustments over time, but other problems in the jural transitions, to the extent they are crippling, are very much in the present, not to be attributed to survivals of the past.

While I have not taken it as a goal of this book to refute other theories and explanations of jural reform, it is worth entertaining alternative *explanations for differences* among East-Central European regimes. The two most commonly heard explanatory frameworks for variations in jural restructurings are of political expediency and power, and of cul-ture. The political expediency explanation dismisses moral and legal considerations and instead accounts for differences among states by the relative strengths and weaknesses of different social groups and their ties to political parties. The culturalist explanation attributes dif-ferences in moral and legal factors to local differences in historical and cultural traditions. These two frameworks are by no means mutually exclusive, for the first often unconsciously presupposes the assump-tions of the second, something I will demonstrate below in the work of Samuel Huntington, perhaps the leading political analyst of demo-cratic reform. Moreover, these frameworks are not only descriptive but also prescriptive. They work much like powerful myths, so firmly an-chored in the zeitgeist of contemporary intellectuals that they tend to share the self-perpetuating power of rumor—once repeated by enough pundits as an explanation, they obtain a mantra-effect. Thereafter, used by actors and observers alike to account for the past and to frame fu-ture choices, they effectively exclude from consideration a whole range of local facts and options.

Huntington (1991: 211–31) has consistently put forth a strong version of the "political expediency" explanation. Variance among regimes as to prosecution of the old elite is based on policy choices made by successor regimes and the relative power of different groups (e.g., government and opposition, reformers and hardliners) in the posttransitional period. Moral and legal considerations are irrelevant, for transition policy is determined by the "distribution of political power during and after the transition" (215).

In accounting for democratization and regime change in Spain and South America, Huntington argues that the nature of the transition from authoritarian to democratic rule determines how former officials are treated by a successor regime.[1] Prosecution of the old elite did not occur where reformist elements within the former regime had initiated or negotiated the transition. Only in those states where political authority radically collapsed and was replaced by an opposition did the possibility of prosecution present itself. In the short run, Huntington's thesis holds for much of Latin America and East-Central Europe. However, even in his primary examples of Latin American regimes, the possibility for retributive justice presented itself in Chile and Argentina only in the long run, more than a decade after the initial change in regime.

For the former socialist regimes examined in this book, Poland and Hungary present the clearest illustration of part of Huntington's thesis—where reformist elements negotiated the transition—though in both cases the extent of wrongdoing did not compare with that in Latin America, and both regimes had already engaged in periodic ritual purification before the 1988 democratic reforms. East Germany presents a strong counterexample, since the ruling Socialist Unity Party reformed itself out of power within a single year, 1989–90, in large part through an internal purification of the center. But in all three cases of Poland, Hungary, and Germany, if one did not consider the duration of the "transition," the framework of politics as assertion of rational interests would elide a consideration of long-term legitimacy. Within the classical framework of relatively stable, clearly demarcated states that Huntington employs, he necessarily omits consideration of the temporality of the international state system in general, and of the temporal relation of the resolution of justice claims to state legitimacy specifically.

The second framework is that of a culturalist explanation, to which Huntington (1993: 22–49) has more recently turned in his claim that future violence and world conflict will likely come from a "clash" between ancient "civilizations." This particular form of accounting reflects the widely shared Herderian view of the world as composed of discrete cultures, making it seductive for anthropologists and nonanthropologists alike. Much as peoples have their own invariant cultures, each culture has its own invariant jural norms and practices. From this perspective, all differences are assumed to be inherited from the weighty past—tradition, residua—instead of explained as products of the present. It is easy to parody this kind of thinking: We are doomed to live in a time warp. Hence Hungarian self-irony undermines any serious attempt at radical change: Hungary has enjoyed the rule of law since the twelfth century—communism, schmonumism; the more things change, the more they stay the same. Hence the Polish turn to reconciliation without much retributive justice is a predictably Catholic move: We are all sinners, aren't we? Hence the Czechs enact a Kafkaesque drama of political inversion, schizophrenia, and cynical play with appearances: A dissident who speaks the language of morality becomes head of a regime that stands only for the private pursuit of wealth. Hence Albania inevitably returns to its anarchic, tribal patterns of political organization. And as Germany courts its repressed Lutheran and Prussian past, its state becomes the authoritative, disciplinary, if not vengeful, father. Sound convincing?

What is the problem with these pictures? For one, they do not explain change. By taking culture as a constant that resists historical time, one cannot explain why the differences between regimes after 1989 are not the same differences as those between regimes after 1945. Albania is the single example where a culturalist explanation seems adequate, and it does so there because the Albanian state is the only place that more or less prevented its people from engaging in exchange with other peoples during the Cold War. Yet even Albania has now entered the historical dynamics of international markets and regimes, including an interaction with the principles of the rule of law. In many ways, today it is the most dependent of the East-Central European states on international agencies and foreign organizations. The Albanian state, too, is already taking new directions, largely due to pressures from the European Union and competitions from nongovernmental organizations.

One of the most dramatic changes in regime dynamics following the Second World War has been in the nature of and balance between internal and external legitimacy. Since 1945, international law has had such dramatic effects on national law that it can no longer be seen as purely external to it. In the last several decades, one can also witness the introduction of alternative definitions of legal agency within international law, with shifts from the individual as part of a territory or peoples to a principle grounded in the dignity of the individual independent of citizenship. Especially following the signing of the Helsinki accord by East bloc states, the dignity principle of recognition had major internal effects on the legitimation dynamics within socialist states. These states became increasingly sensitive to their own citizens as well as to world opinion, and to world political, legal, and economic regimes. This new density of interpenetration of global and local norms calls for an analysis—which has been absent in a culturalist account—that foregrounds not cultural spatialization but the temporality of legal regimes and the legitimation of states.

As to the culturalist explanation, I might again offer Germany as an example that counters this logic. Even before the revolution in November 1989, the East German regime had begun to behave less as a self-contained unit or in a "bloc" mode with other Soviet satellite states, and to pay more attention to international legal norms. The peaceful transfer of power within the regime can at least partly be attributed to a growing respect for the principles of the rule of law. And after the dissolution of the state in October 1990, jural reform, while occurring in fully chaotic circumstances, went nonetheless relatively peacefully. Contrary to the myth of the vengeful German judiciary, German judges, both those from the West and retrained Eastern ones, have been extremely reluctant to agree with public prosecutors' charges of regime criminality. The most successful prosecutions have not been for typical or "normal" forms of wrongdoing but for excesses in the performance of public duties. In the trials of border guards, for example, even though shooting was nominally justified under GDR law, those whose action was so intrinsically heinous that no positive law could be invoked to vindicate it were nonetheless convicted. In those cases, judges appeared to rely on the famous Radbruch formula, that positive law must yield to a higher law when the contradiction between positive law and justice reaches an "unbearable proportion." This justified a prosecution for excess without violating the principle against retroactive application of the law. While proving excess happened to be easier for clearly defined and identifiable crimes, like embezzlement, than for political oppression, or spying, or restricting the freedom of movement of citizens, the postunity judiciary was extremely wary of sentencing "substitute victims," or of holding "small fish" accountable while letting the "big ones" go free. In this, by contrast to the judiciaries in both German states following World War II, I think they have been successful.

Although the German reckoning with the past has happened under the singular condition of unity with another state and has been of an unusually large scale, it still must be situated within both East-Central European invocation of the rule of law and the global movement for retributive justice. What the eastern German transformation shares with the other East-Central European ones is a dominant concern with the invocation of principles of accountability, which socialist regimes had rejected. For eastern Germany this invocation is necessary to establish the state as a moral authority with a monopoly on the legitimate use of violence. What it shares with the global movement—and therefore with West Germany, Western Europe, and the United States—is a need to reaffirm these principles through a kind of ritual purification intrinsic to democratic regimes.

I have made two theoretical assumptions that, due to the short period of transformation examined here—approximately five years—cannot be demonstrated. First, invocation of the principles will never be completed, for these principles must be continually reiterated as part of a process where accountability is made central to the sphere of the political. This "political," in turn, is culturally and historically variable. Because human memory of injustice is selective and has no natural end, the invocation must be seen as a temporal process that also will never end. Consequently, the invocation of the rule of law in each of the East-Central European states has its own timeline and trajectory (depending on, e.g., institutional arrangements, the role of historical memory in social processes, the perceived extent of wrongdoing). At the same time, these states are also very much interconnected as part of a global system of nation-states; each is striving to invoke the same set of jural principles to obtain internal and external legitimation. This means that any analysis must balance a universalism about the process of invocation with a relativism about the specific cultural details of installation. Whereas the process of invocation is universal, the chronology, institutional arrangements, and practices involved are case-specific.

Second, although both criminals and victims are culturally and historically variable categories (and much of this book has sought to demonstrate just how this variability is being constituted today), who in periods of intensive change can easily switch places, it will nonetheless be necessary in a legal regime of the rule of law type to reaffirm the distinction between the two. This is necessary both to reaffirm the possibility of the community to perform justice and to make possible the forgetting of injury. Without this reaffirmation and forgetting, no moral authority, especially that of a democratic state, is realizable.

My argument up till now has been fourfold: (1) that accountability is central to the definition of democratic states, in contrast to the insignificance of accountability in dictatorships, monarchies, and other political forms; (2) that accountability is established in part through retributive justice: a reckoning with the past where the government ritually purifies itself in periodic prosecutions of actual wrongdoing in the center; (3) that retributive justice necessarily links prosecution of wrongdoing to the fate of victims, whose dignity is reestablished through social and jural processes, and whose trust in the legal system is a key index of state legitimacy; and (4) that failure to engage in retributive justice leads to cycles of retributive violence directed either against an internal scapegoat or an externally identified enemy.

Recall the three patterns of retributive justice that I sketched in Chapter 1. I will proceed by examining in turn the variety within each type of transformation, with no claim to comprehensiveness or thick ethnographic descriptions. My comparisons are consciously premature, for the short duration of the transition processes precludes any definitive claims about their directionality. I will not provide the same detail on every country for the simple reason that I do not have access to the same kind of detail. I have done extensive ethnographic work only in Germany. I have visited Poland, Hungary, the Czech Republic, and Russia, and I established contacts with scholars in those places. But my information on the rest of East-Central Europe is secondhand, which calls for heightened skepticism in anthropological comparison. To the extent I have tried to include more detail in description of events in Bulgaria and Romania, for example, I have encountered contradictory accounts. With no personal base from which to evaluate these differences, I have chosen to offer cursory accounts of transformations in those places where I have no personal experience. Hence what follows are comparative sketches only five years into a process of transition, intended primarily to situate the East German transformation in the context of other East bloc states and to indicate the variability and directionality of jural change within and between types. These comparisons must be redone in another five years.

TYPE 1: SOME RETRIBUTIVE JUSTICE

Type 1 occurs where the legal regime has changed abruptly yet smoothly, with some restitution for victims of the old regime but hardly any reckoning with wrongdoing in the past—this has been the case in Slovenia, Hungary, Poland, and to a large degree in the Czech Republic. In Slovenia, Hungary, and Poland the regimes themselves initiated reform that enabled the participation of the opposition, making it difficult if not impossible to purge or prosecute former officials or public employees, or to review judges for past misdeeds. Subsequently, reform has been sequential, and there has been no radical break, in personnel or institutions, with the old regime. As mentioned in chapter 1, the Slovene government self-consciously promoted multiethnic statehood in a series of legal acts that built on codifications of indigenous minority rights already enacted in the 1950s (Minnich 1993: 90–99). Within this type, I will focus on Hungary, Poland, and the Czech Republic.

Hungary

Nineteen eighty-nine marked a formal symbolic break with the socialist state in Hungary, but it was the result of two decades of reform. Hungarian scholars tend to argue that except for some singular cases of illegality (such as the 1922 law dispossessing Jews), the period of a fascist government from 1944 to 1945, or the two weeks in the fall of 1956 when the uprising was crushed, Hungary has had a thousand-year history of constitutional rule. The most important changes resulting from the Roundtable discussion in 1989 were a multiple party system (substantive liberal democracy, with a freely elected parliament in mid-1990) and a Constitutional Court (which commenced its functions on January 1, 1990) with expanded jurisdiction, including a broad right of judicial review of legislative acts. The Constitutional Court itself has assumed legal continuity with the previous regime. It is asserting a position of supreme moral authority in the postsocialist state, meaning that it has tried to remain apart from partisan political decisions, which, due to the elimination of one-party rule and decentralization of the legislative system, have increased. Given this new institutional configuration, the court has tried to strengthen the legitimacy of the other branches of government in their obligation and right to make political decisions, even as it has ruled on the constitutionality of enacted law and thus necessarily limited the power of the other branches.

The post-1989 government has reviewed neither judges nor prosecutors, and there have been no disqualifications in these occupations. However, parliament passed a bill controlling and disqualifying from responsible positions those who had worked with the secret police, a process administered by a three-judge panel. About half of all those individuals in leading positions in the various ministries of government were initially subject to demotions, with only a few dismissed. However, about half those dismissed had returned to work in the government within several years of their dismissal.

In contrast to events in the other former socialist states, injuries resulting from arbitrary exercise of political power were relatively rare in Hungary, except for the squelching of the attempted revolution in 1956. Hungarian complicity with the Russian invasion of 1956 resulted in some immediate discrimination against the participants, but the Kader regime that followed sought not belief or subordination but merely cooperation from the people. This strategy, even though not democratic-participatory, resulted, many argue, in a legitimate rule. There has been a general rehabilitation of participants in the 1956 uprising (see below), and there were several prosecutions of those involved in its repression. But because of problems with finding evidence and of contradictory testimony by participants who are now relatively old, only soldiers and other low-ranking individuals were initially prosecuted.

In 1992, the Constitutional Court struck down a law that would have lifted the thirty-year statute of limitation on crimes of treason, murder, and fatal injury committed between 1944 and 1990. Hence prosecutions of those involved in the suppression of the 1956 uprising were stopped. No prosecutions of officials have been conducted for actions after 1956. Restitution bills here, as elsewhere, tend to focus solely on property and ignore other forms of harm. In Hungary, unlike in the Czech Republic, former owners were entitled to lay claim not to their old property but to vouchers pegged to the old value of the property, which could then be used to buy any state property that was put up for auction. Moreover, a ceiling was set on the amount of money any individual could claim. The Hungarian Supreme Court subsequently ruled this law constitutional, claiming that property claims had no a priori status but had to be balanced against other legitimate individual rights and social goals.

The one area of potential criminality prominent in the new Hungary (as in all of the former socialist states) is that of economic crime, mostly concerning what is called *spontaneous privatization*—the transformation of state property into private without proper legal procedures (which in any case were not yet written). Indeed, a special unit of "economic police" has been created within the Hungarian police force to investigate such acts. But the actual or potential illegalities in this area are both so widespread and so difficult to prove that only one person who worked for the privatization agency and who was caught taking a bribe has been successfully prosecuted.

With regard to victims, a 1989 law concerning compensation for unjust imprisonment or damages due to state policy enabled between two and three thousand individuals to receive monetary compensation. All of these claims had to do with damages suffered from the period of 1945 through the 1950s. Most petitioners were former prisoners of war who had been sent to work camps in the Siberia, or they had been imprisoned within Hungary for "oppositional" political behavior, most notably for the 1956 uprising. After 1989, these two groups of prisoners formed a political lobby (Union of Political Prisoners), and members frequently appeared on television. Only approximately fifteen thousand of those who suffered in the late 1940s (known as *malenki rabot*) are surviving, but most of those who fought in the uprising of 1956 are still alive; many individuals in both groups have received apartments and pension adjustments. The press published names of people who had been murdered by the state, its secret service, or Soviet agents. The state rehabilitated these people, along with others, in a manner similar to the East German commissions, by issuing official letters of apology signed by the president of the republic. Finally, a new oral history institute was founded, whose initial work focused on documenting these particular people's lives.

Poland

In Poland, two major reforms in the early 1980s set in motion the possibility for the realization of the more radical reforms proposed by the Roundtable discussions after 1989: the establishment of a Supreme Administrative Court in 1980 to engage in judicial review of the legality of actions of legislative acts, and of a Constitutional Court and a Tribunal of State in 1982, the latter to judge on the legality of actions of high-ranking government officials (see below). These courts had very limited and in a sense merely formal powers. The Constitutional Court, for example, has jurisdiction only over acts committed after 1982, and its decisions are considered not judgments but "opinions," which can be rejected by a two-thirds majority of the large chamber of the Seym (parliament). First in 1989 an Independent Council of Judiciary was set up, elected by judges and representatives of the Ministry of Justice, the Supreme Court, the Bar, and the president of the republic. In 1991 a clear separation of powers was written into the constitution, though in practice the balance of powers has been volatile, especially between the president and the Sejm. Although the Constitutional Court has been active in reviewing Sejm decisions, and has often ruled them unconstitutional, the Sejm itself has been able to vote to overrule these opinions, again limiting the authority of the court.

Following an agreement reached in the Roundtable discussions of 1989, state prosecutors were reviewed, with some dismissals, early retirements, and even prosecutions. No judges were reviewed, however, and therefore no disciplinary procedures have followed, though such a review has been periodically proposed. Some judges have voluntarily retired or left their posts to engage in private practice, but these decisions were sometimes prompted by poor pay and not due to questions of competency. The reason most often given for resistance to a review of judges has been that it would compromise the independence of the judiciary, one of the basic principles of the rule of law. Hence, many Polish reformers were put in a Catch-22 position, accused of violating the independence of the judiciary in order to establish its independence.

A Tribunal of State was set up within the parliament in 1982, and became operative in 1985, to investigate the suspected criminality of members of the executive branch of government. All cases taken up before 1989 have been either dropped or dismissed for lack of evidence, or the accused have been acquitted. Since 1989, six cases have been investigated, with a total of forty-seven individuals under suspicion. These investigations have also resulted in some indictments (of a former prime minister and three members of his cabinet for economic decisions considered to be illegal, of eight members of the last communist cabinet for violating the laws governing the importation of alcohol, of a former prime minister for removing two cabinet ministers from office). Most indictments have subsequently been dropped, and few observers expect any convictions. In fact, Jerzy Wiatr (1996: 45), a former chair of the Committee of Constitutional Accountability, has condemned the tribunal functions "as a political instrument of rivals seeking to perpetuate political vendettas."

Due to the cooperative nature of the transition, the different oppositional groups have had difficulty agreeing on a policy of prosecuting members of the former government, or even on defining an area of possible governmental illegality. It was former government officials who had initiated the reforms in the political system that enabled the participation of the opposition. Many of these officials never lost their posts in the government and its ministries. Hence, the first freely elected prime minister, Tádeusz Mazowiecki, warned in 1989 that any "witch-hunts" against former leaders would polarize the country and paralyze the government bureaucracy. The government had become more active already in 1990, largely because Solidarity was still united behind Lech Walesa, the union leader who had vowed during his campaign to bring to justice former officials who had abused their power. After the election, the ministry of justice began to take up questions of rectification.

In late December 1990, the military prosecutor's office arrested and charged eight army officers for firing on demonstrators (fifty were killed) in the Gdansk shipyard riots of 1970. Many former government ministers were investigated for corruption and abuse of office, and in 1992, after much debate, the Sejm passed a screening law requiring public revelation of secret service collaborators. However, this resolution was overturned by the State Tribunal within a month of its passage, and only a very few of the cases against former officials ever went to trial. Of those, there has been to date only one prosecution, for the murder of the priest, Father Popeluszko, which resulted in a sentence of only two years. This lack of a symbolic break with the old system has brought about extreme cynicism about the future and often a denial by former elites of any responsibility for past wrongs. The result, as Bronislaw Geremek stated (1992: 48), is that "little has changed at [the] provincial level, where the same people as before continue to make the decisions." The evident collapse of the moral authority of former oppositional groups, symbolized by Walesa's defeat in 1995 and the victory of a former communist, is evidence that little has changed at the national level as well, at least with respect to personnel.

Institutionally and in the ethos of everyday life, however, the picture of change is more complicated, for all of the principles of the rule of law have in some form been invoked. Despite historic tensions with minorities, including Belorussians, Germans, Jews, and Ukrainians, and Gypsies, attempts by isolated individuals and groups to use and exacerbate these tensions for political purposes have not been successful. Conflicts have been largely resolved through democratic and jural means without resort to extralegal violence (Rybinski 1990: 108–11; Gornicki 1990: 17–22; Gebert, Zozula, Datner-Spiewak 1991: 106–7).

In contrast to the other states included in this category of transformation, Poland has had the least extensive reaction to appeals for rehabilitation and vindication, largely because, as I argued earlier, the change has been within regime type and therefore the number of clearly identifiable victims is small. There has been no groundswell of support for redress of past harms at a public and/or state level, even though there were isolated cases of unjust imprisonment and discrimination in education or work. Four or five rehabilitation laws have been proposed, but none has passed both chambers of the government—and none is likely to be passed in the future. Nearly all of the appeals for rehabilitation have been for injuries suffered in the 1950s. Since this appeal was already available in the 1970s, rehabilitation did not receive much renewed attention after 1989. In 1989, a special simplified procedure was instituted, whereby individuals can make an extraordinary appeal directly to the Ministry of Justice or the Supreme Court, or they can petition directly the court that initially convicted them.

In conversations I had in Warsaw in the fall of 1994, most Poles argued that because a substantial minority of people could make some sort of claim about injury suffered under the old regime, the cost of redressing past harms was prohibitive. They then made a distinction between normal and extraordinary harm, with only the latter requiring legal redress. Moreover, they explained that, in contrast to Germany, "resistance" or "civil courage" in Poland is considered an aspect of everyday life and not an unusual achievement or a behavior that deserves special rewards. Poland's policy is similar to that of the former Czechoslovakia in that victims must prove that their harm resulted from an actual violation of law by the authorities. Moral wrongs or injuries inflicted that were not expressly forbidden by any particular law are not recognized. People are also discouraged from going to court because cases are expensive and time consuming, Nonetheless, some victim groups have been organizing in different parts of the country. And some individuals, supported by public pressure from an association for political prisoners as well as members of human rights groups, have been compensated in individual court decisions for unjust long-term imprisonment. Others have been unable to get any compensation nor have they been rehabilitated, but, it was explained to me, not because present criminal law is inadequate but because of the lack of witnesses, insufficient evidence, or a refusal of individual judges to support interpretations of the law that would recognize the act as victimization.

Czech Republic

The present state in the Czech Republic represents perhaps the most radical break, with the exception of the now-dissolved GDR, with the former socialist state. Personnel and structure changed radically in November 1989, then the Czech Republic divorced itself from the Slovak part of the state on January 1, 1993. From 1989 to 1993, the judicial system suffered a general delegitimation so that judges today speak of a common attitude of disrespect and insolence in this period. This disrespect was expressed toward judges in both criminal and civil courts, even though the latter had nothing to do with enforcing illegalities or disciplinary measures of the former state. Under the pressure of an increased caseload and this general loss of authority, one judge committed suicide. The fear and danger of a collapse of the judicial system therefore influenced the review of judges, and later of state prosecutors. One attempt to stabilize the judiciary was to raise wages two- to threefold in order to compensate some for the disparity with the private sector, where lawyers after 1989 were earning 100 percent more than before. Because of this pay differential, many judges also voluntarily moved into private practice, making it impossible to ascertain accurately who left for political and who for commercial reasons. Moreover, since judges were initially reelected and not reappointed, some judges chose not to seek reelection rather than be subject of review. Thus the effect of the official review and disqualification policy is impossible to determine when applied to individual cases.

The committee that reviewed judges was composed mainly of people who had been outside the state, including several individuals who had been unjustly imprisoned. In his opening state of the nation speech in 1990, Václav Havel stressed the fact that all citizens were complic-itous in the regime, and therefore within his talk about the responsibil-ity to "live in truth" was an assumption of collective guilt. If all judges were guilty, so goes the extension of this logic, then perhaps the system was at fault—and it became difficult to single out particular individuals as more responsible than others. On the other hand, Havel's goal was also to prevent an implicit presumption of guilt being assigned to cate-gories of people on the various lists of suspected collaborators with the Ministry for State Security.

In any case, the review of jural personnel was more systematic than of other occupational categories. Some members of the review com-mittee wanted to disqualify all judges, but the committee finally agreed to approve 90 percent of those on the list. However, in 1993 the Vaclav Klaus government, which replaced the first postsocialist government, approved a majority of those judges dismissed under the first review, so that today most former judges who desire to can, and are, again active. A full Constitutional Court first began meeting in 1994, and it has not yet played a significant role in the transition. Rather, political conflict has centered around the separation of the Czech state from Slovakia, and around the shaping of the executive branch and the divi-sion of powers between regional and federal administrations.

After June 1992, state prosecutors were subject to a review similar to that of judges. However, after 1989, the structure and powers of the state prosecutors had been substantially changed so that the abuses under the former system were thought to be no longer possible under the new structure. After the review some prosecutors were disqualified, meaning demoted and given positions of lesser author-ity. None has been fired. Several were prosecuted on various charges of illegality (e.g., drunkenness, breach of state security, money laundering).

A screening law or "lustration act" was passed by parliament in Oc-tober 1991, intending to disqualify former members of the state secu-rity from working in state agencies. This law differed substantially from the initial draft and was not supported by many members of gov-ernment, including President Havel. As in all of the former socialist states, individuals in the private sector are largely or wholly unaffected by this review. If the ministry of interior determined someone had been an agent of the state security (with no differentiation made as to degree of complicity), that person was to be removed immediately from his or her position of authority and relegated to a lesser position. This law potentially applied to up to a million persons. Approximately five hun-dred of the demotions resulting from evaluations by the ministry have been appealed. The lustration act itself was appealed to the governing body of the International Labour Organization in Geneva, which recommended substantial revisions, especially a strengthening of due process guarantees, and it was reviewed by the Czech Constitutional Court, which also amended the law. In addition, a special parliamentary committee was set up in 1990 to investigate the crimes of the state security. These investigations have resulted in fewer than ten prosecutions, with no convictions.

Maintaining a consistent position throughout, President Havel reiterated his earlier statement about preventing such a reckoning, arguing instead for both an initial presumption of innocence and a form of collective guilt: "When will it be recognized that each of us is guilty in some way? We were all [part of] communism, we all voted for the communists" (Battiata 1991: A1). Since all Czechs were involved, singling out individuals for punishment would be unfair and unproductive. Thus government form has changed while personnel, except at the very top, have remained the same. Judicial personnel were screened for secret police complicity, resulting in about 10 percent of the judges leaving service, with a smaller number of state prosecutors being demoted but not fired. Individuals working in state agencies have also been vetted, but the severest penalty has been demotion to a lesser position of authority; many of these cases have been appealed and most individuals reinstated. After 1992, the split of the Czech Republic from Slovakia distracted attention from internal cleansing. Since then, there have been fewer than ten trials and, to my knowledge, only two convictions.

Among all of the former socialist states, the former Czechoslovakia passed the earliest and most extensive rehabilitation/vindication law in May–June 1991. By the end of 1991, 202,295 citizens had received certificates of rehabilitation, enabling them to receive compensation, paid in cash over ten years, for wages lost. Dubbed the Large Restitution, law number 87/1991, it called for the rehabilitation of a narrow range of political prisoners and victims of communism (restricted to crimes against the state from 1948 to 1989) through an out-of-court settlement. The parliament established a monetary remedy for those who suffered unjust imprisonment; most other victims were given certificates of rehabilitation. From 1948 to 1956, the number of people given prison sentences on political charges numbered 100,000; of this number 40,000 were given prison sentences exceeding ten years; 232 sentenced to death; 8,000 to 15,000 beaten to death during interrogations or shot to death at escape attempts; and 22,000 deported to labor camps without trial. About 12,000 former prisoners, with the average age seventy-five formed a Confederation of Political Prisoners of the Czech Republic, with 4,000 members in Slovakia.

The Large Restitution Law had the effect of a preemptive strike, for it has since been very difficult if not impossible to obtain rehabilitation or remedy for nonpolitically motivated but nonetheless extralegally perpetrated harms suffered before 1989 (for example, for having been victimized by moral wrongs or by injuries not forbidden by any particular law, e.g., being blacklisted, refused access to the university). Consequently, some people who it is generally agreed were victimized under the old regime were required to go individually to the courts to obtain remedy. Such processes can be costly and time-consuming. Also, the widespread assumption of a general complicity with the old regime and the exteriorization of the enemy through the divorce of the Czech and Slovak Republics, as I mentioned in chapter 1, has made it difficult for victims to press claims for redress. Adding to the problem of internal reckoning with the past has been the difficulty in dealing with the injustices involved in expelling 2.5 million Sudeten Germans after World War II. Many of these individuals, who are well organized within Germany, have demanded restitution of property, others merely the right to return to their "homeland." Although President Havel issued an official apology, Czech government officials consistently refused to deal with claims before 1948, insisting that the Sudeten Germans handle their problems on a private basis. Meanwhile, the Czech government has pushed the German government to compensate some 13,000 Czech political prisoners and their widows and orphans for their imprisonment by the Nazis. The German expellees, in turn, have tried to link these two injustices with each other. In April 1995, a Reconciliation '95 initiative, signed by 105 Czech and Sudeten German intellectuals, called for a dialogue between the Sudeten German Party and the Czech government, with an agreed-upon focus of a right to return.

Finally, a third law passed in 1993 acted as a moral proclamation distinguishing good from evil. Called the Law on the Illegitimacy of, and Resistance to, the Communist Regime, it both declared the former Czechoslovak regime "illegitimate" and "criminal," and, as Havel asserted, "through this law, the freely elected parliament is telling all victims of communism that society values them and that they deserve respect" (cited in Siklova 1996: 59). While these acts of retributive justice are appreciated by some, they have not created a consensus in the Czech Republic. For one, "the former dissidents are clawing at one another while the former StB [State Security] is no longer the focus of anyone's attention" (62). For another, many of the designated "winners' of the Klaus-led government's economic reforms are former government officials. Yet these officials are now working in the so-called private sector and therefore not subject to the kinds of moral scrutiny given to small-time collaborators and to individuals working for lower wages in the public sector.

TYPE 2: LITTLE RETRIBUTIVE JUSTICE

In Type 2, there has been little reckoning with the past, little change, and much violence. Especially in the legal domain, regime change has been more apparent than substantive, with minimal recognition of victims and very little or no prosecution of wrongdoers. Included in this type would be the former Yugoslavia (especially Serbia and Croatia), Romania, Russia, and perhaps all of the former Soviet Republics except the Baltic states. Yugoslavia disintegrated into a genocidal war, centered in Bosnia, victimizing the majority of the population there beyond anything that had occurred under Tito. The disintegration of Yugoslavia has been widely explicated elsewhere (cf. Alia and Lifschultz 1993; Rieff 1995). Its breakdown presents an unambiguous and extreme illustration of retributive violence as an effect of the absence of retributive justice. More theoretically challenging and more ambiguous are other variations of type 2, of which the transformations in Romania and Russia present two alternatives.

Romania

The violent overthrow of the Ceausescu regime in November 1989 is perhaps the most important event in the transformation of Romania. At least one thousand people lost their lives in street clashes between loyalists of the old regime and the oppositional National Front-controlled army. The overthrow resulted in an inversion of insider/outsider categories without changing the way in which the line between the two is drawn or calling attention to the accountability of the center; this line is still drawn autocratically, largely without regard for due process. For example, in December 1989, the special elite units of the Securitate shot indiscriminately at soldiers and regular citizens alike. Approximately thirty members of the special units were Arab students, mostly Palestinian snipers trained in the techniques of urban guerilla–type warfare who had protected the means of communication and transportation from the popular uprising. These elite units were subsequently scapegoated and branded "terrorists." After being apprehended, most of them escaped through Hungary and Turkey, though some remained. Only a few of the commanding officers of the security apparatus were subsequently arrested and tried (Iaru 1990: 73–77).

Such quick inversion of categories also occurred on December 19, 1989. Nicolae Ceausescu and his wife were executed, in a parody of a trial in which lawyers and prosecutors cooperated to expose the misdeeds of the deposed tyrant. More procedurally correct trials have followed, notably those of Ceausescu's son and the remaining members of the Politburo, who were sentenced to from 15 to 20 years for a planned "genocide," as it was called, referring, in the case of the Politburo, to their final meeting where they planned to squash the demonstrations in the winter of 1989. These acts of revolutionary justice against a small elite have served largely as a substitute for further cleansing; the same government, state security, and public officials serve as before.

The Communist Party has since vanished (initially banned by the new leadership on January 12, 1990, but it later reversed its decision), and been replaced by a National Salvation Front under the leadership of a former propaganda boss; the Securitate was officially disbanded and renamed the Romanian Service for Information. Both changes resulted in cosmetic decentralizations of power. An opposition has formed, spearheaded by Civic Alliance, and it has promoted liberal democracy and legal reform (Tismaneanu 1991: 77–81), but with minimal influence on the political process. In order to prevent democratic reform, officials have resorted to fomenting ethnic conflict (especially against the Hungarian minority) or they have encouraged extremist groups. For example, the group that publishes the country's most popular periodical, *Romania Mare* (circulation 600,000), proclaimed 1991 "the year of international struggle against Hungarian terrorism." Jews and Gypsies are the other primary ethnic groups who are externalized and set up as the opponents of Romanian-ness in order to create an internal consensus (Tismaneanu and Mihaies 1992: 25–27).

In sum, even the limited prosecution of former governmental elites is a big change compared with justice under Ceausescu. In the 1970s, the Communist Party Central Committee had issued a secret order barring the prosecutor general from pressing charges against officials. After 1987, prosecutors were even required to get agreement of local party bosses before bringing charges against any party member (Dascalu 1990: 1). Given this history, the still understaffed and underfunded public prosecutors are not in a position to engage in any large-scale prosecutions. Since there has been no review of people in the legal profession for illegalities, and because of much continuity in political leadership, there may in fact not be much desire for a more thorough ritual purification.

Russia

The Soviet Union began undergoing political, judicial, and economic reform under Gorbachev in the early 1980s, and this reform has continued through the formal breakup of the Soviet Union into autonomous republics. Although the Russian federation adopted a constitution in 1993 that included all of the guarantees essential to the rule of law, including protection of basic human rights, the provisions of this constitution have not been observed. Even the Constitutional Court has violated these guarantees in a well-known case where it ruled on an oral decree by the president before the decree had been formally written, much less adopted as law. The problem of implementation of constitutional provisions exists at all levels, with continuous and blatant violations by the president, the Duma, regional and local political authorities, and the police. Moreover, the state has clearly lost its monopoly on the legitimate use of violence as well as its control of economic life, and organized extralegal and criminal groups have stepped into this void, making "crime" and its control the number one political issue.[2]

Criminal groups, often called the Russian Mafia, are disparate and competing networks comprised of highly educated and often skilled former KGB officials, government workers, policemen, and others displaced by the dissolution of the Soviet Union and reorganization of the state. Some Russian criminal experts estimate that 80 percent of the economy is now controlled by these groups. In the absence of a respected legal framework in which local political and economic activity can develop without fear of arbitrary violence, these new groups are creating the parameters of change and order if not often the actual agents. They are providing the minimal amount of security, and often capital, necessary for new businesses to establish themselves. Most businessmen apparently regard the state and its functionaries and not organized crime as the real hindrance to economic development, since state monopolies (e.g., the postal service, transportation, energy) are interested in neither profit nor change. At the same time, of course, Mafia bands, groups functioning outside any sort of democratic control, are therefore a potential if not actual amoral and violent force that corrupts the local political process.

The judicial system has not been an important factor in the transformations to date, though in its brief period of activity it did enter the political fray. A Constitutional Court was created in 1993 but then dissolved for an entire year (until the Duma confirmed all nineteen candidates). Neither judges nor state prosecutors have been reviewed for past illegalities, and therefore not a single judge or prosecutor has been accused of crime and dismissed. Over 90 percent of all former judges are still serving, with the rest having retired or moved to private business. Judges' pay is relatively low, and judicial buildings are delapidated and neglected in comparison to buildings of the executive or legislative branches. Moreover, in cases where state prosecutors or police have successfully built a case against some criminal activity, it is estimated that 80 percent of the accused are released within a day of the arrest. Judges apparently fear becoming victims of organized crime (although it is journalists that have been murdered), and in a country with no tradition of judicial independence, the majority of judges are not known for their civil courage.

The new Constitutional Court became active again in early 1995. It has a legal staff of 80, with a total staff, including secretarial, of 150. The court not only selects which cases to take up but also can be petitioned by private citizens who challenge individual laws. Some 90 percent of these petitions have been rejected on grounds that they do not involve constitutional issues. The court is also challenged by petitions from government bodies asking for interpretation of the constitution and of demarcations between federal, regional, and local authorities. Articles 7 and 13 of the constitution guarantee the autonomy of the Constitutional Court and grant judges immunity from prosecution. In addition, the material rewards for the judges are generous (e.g., high pay, state-owned apartments, country homes), and police protection is provided to secure the judges from the wrath and violence of individuals or groups whom they judge to be guilty of crimes.

In the future, it appears that an independent judicial system with moral authority will not be created until the development of a relatively prosperous middle class (probably quasicriminal) that needs such a system. The current motors of change—for example, political parties, organized crime—benefit too much from legal disarray to respect or encourage the development of an autonomous judiciary. In light of the continued antagonism between the executive and the parliament it is likely that the Constitutional Court will continue to be forced to choose sides and that its decisions will be understood to be based on partisan politics. Only when a large group of individuals comprising a relatively stable middle class has a stake in legal security and continuity—regardless of the content of any particular legal or political decision—will the Constitutional Court and the principles of the rule of law, especially a consensual division of powers, achieve respect. The absence of such a consensus will tend to strengthen forces supporting a fascist political form that promises to eliminate chaos and guarantee order.

Rehabilitation in Russia entails compensating victims of various waves of political persecution since the 1917 Revolution. Such victims number around 100 million persons and include three generations of individuals, each persecuted under different laws yet frequently imprisoned in the same institutions. Members of the first generation were persecuted between 1917 and 1945; of the second between 1945 and 1955 or to the death of Stalin, after which the "first perestroika" began under Khrushchev; of the third from 1955 to 1987, when Gorbachev released two to three hundred prisoners and the media began a public reexamination of Stalin's crimes. Thus, primarily for administrative reasons, rehabilitation has been restricted to individuals who were sent to work or prison camps and to those who were incarcerated in psychiatric wards.

People in Moscow who want rehabilitation need to apply to a special center where the state prosecutors who control the former KGB files direct their special advisers to research the validity of claims. In restoring the dignity of the victim, the compensation law does not go so far as to allow the prosecution and punishment of the perpetrator. To process an application for compensation through the various bureaucracies can take years, depending on the cooperation, or lack of it, provided by state officials. Individuals at both the Memorial Society and the Moscow Research Center for Human Rights stressed to me that the difficulty in being rehabilitated is due less to the state of the law than to lack of official political support (from someone like Yeltsin, for example) and resistance by bureaucrats and law officers in enforcing or respecting its provisions. Within Russia but outside of Moscow it is reportedly extremely difficult to be rehabilitated, and some of the kinds of compensations offered to individuals in Moscow are not generally available elsewhere. Policy regarding rehabilitation in other former Soviet republics (Ukraine, Georgia, Belarus, Khazikistan) is similar to the Russian federal policy, with no substantial national differences. Former prisoners in these republics share similar injustices with Russians and maintain contact with those in Moscow.

The Russian federation policy calls for the issuing of an identification card that specifies one as a "disabled" person. It offers the following benefits: (1) a one-time compensation for imprisonment at approximately ten dollars per year imprisoned, (2) a 50 percent reduction in rent in a state-owned apartment, (3) free medical care without a wait, (4) food bonuses on special holidays, (5) priority in the purchase without a wait of certain household appliances, (6) a yearly visit in a state-sponsored health spa. Additionally, in Moscow individuals are granted free public transportation within the city. Realization of these benefits varies depending on the discretion of the individual or office in charge of administering them. The two human rights groups mentioned above are continuing to push for organization of the different victims groups and for more government benefits directed to the actual needs and disabilities of victims.

TYPE 3: EXTENSIVE RETRIBUTIVE JUSTICE

A type 3 kind of transformation is taking place in the Baltic states, Bulgaria, Albania, and Germany, where there has been radical regime change with extensive prosecution of the old elite along with retributive justice for many of the victims. Jural reforms in the Baltic states (Latvia, Lithuania, Estonia) continue to be in such a state of flux that they do not yet exhibit a discernible pattern. They have been intricately tied to an ongoing separation from the Soviet Union, formalized by independent statehood in 1991, and from internal ethnic Russian (among other) "minorities," along with the corresponding creation of ethnic majorities. Such majorities have often made people of Russian descent, who after World War II resettled in these regions as part of a Russian-Soviet colonial policy, into scapegoats for all the wrongdoing of the Soviet regime. However, many of these Russians have since been fully integrated into local structures, with many intermarriages. In Latvia, for example, where the move to deny Russians citizenship rights has been the most radical, around a quarter of all marriages are interethnic (Grigoriev 1992: 73–74). Although Latvia has been perhaps the most radical of the republics, all three states have passed laws enabling prosecutors to arrest former KGB agents and government/party officials suspected of carrying out persecutions in the past. The contradictory aspects of the Baltic transformations—extensive retributive justice with new injustices in the domains of corrective and distributive justice and an increase in nonstate violence—does not necessarily place them outside the framework I am proposing, but it will require watching these reforms unfold over a longer period of time before stable patterns emerge.

Bulgaria

Bulgaria and Albania are unique among the Balkan states in that they began a regime transformation without resort to internal scapegoating or external aggression, and they did this under circumstances of a declining economy. In other words, there have been prosecutions but no substitute victims. In Bulgaria much of the success must go to the initial reforms of the Bulgarian Socialist Party (BSP), which introduced the first privatization law; to the Union of Democratic Forces (UDF), which won the October 1991 elections; and to the leadership of Bulgaria's large Turkish minority. The UDF used its election victory to confiscate what it called "stolen assets" belonging to the party, and to introduce a lustration act similar to the one in the Czech Republic. Both measures were attempts to penalize the communists and to remove the massive material advantages and benefits of the networks of the old regime. The screening law, initially conceived broadly and supposed to be effective for five years, was applied for fewer than three years and ultimately restricted to administrators of scientific institutes and organizations (Yankova 1992: 44–45).

Members of the Supreme Judicial Council were replaced, along with the head public prosecutor, in the hopes of making the judicial branch more independent of the executive. An independent Constitutional Court was also created, which has consistently strengthened the power of the Supreme Court and struck down laws of the parliamentary majority. In several cases the Constitutional Court declared laws unconstitutional, which were then readopted by the parliament and struck down a second time by the court. In the spring and summer of 1992, there was a widespread purge of former party officials from the civil service and academic institutions and a vetting of thousands of others (Smollett 1993: 13). At the same time, several top government officials were put on trial, including three former prime ministers. These three each received sentences of up to seven years for charges ranging from embezzling state property, inciting racial hatred, and forced assimilation to creating concentration camps. On February 10, 1996, however, Todor Zhivkov, the last prime minister, was acquitted by the Collegium of the Supreme Court.

An important element in the initial success of the UDF, which was a coalition of nineteen different parties, was its ability to create alliances between groups with different ends. During the dictatorship, the government expropriated much property and wealth from rich landowners and businessmen, who were frequently also excluded from power. This group largely formed much of the leadership of the UDF. Since their own record of persecution was clear, they garnered support from economically poorer strata by blaming the present poverty on the old guard's squandering of state funds. Paradoxically, support from the Movement for Rights and Freedoms, a Turkish party led by Ahmed Dogan, also helped in legitimating the transformation.

Unlike most of the other East bloc states, Bulgaria had enjoyed no dissident community. Although many Bulgarians reportedly view the

Turks as unjustly privileged, they are also generally seen as inferior. At the same time, the Christian identification of Bulgarians was not easily convertible into an anti-Islam sentiment. Moreover, most Turks were already integrated at some level into the Bulgarian social and economic life. Hence in the early 1980s, when the government began persecuting the large Turkish minority (10 percent of the population) in what was officially called a "renaissance process," large numbers of people identified with Turkish resistance because it was seen as anticommunist but not anti-Bulgarian (Anguelov 1992: 28–31).

From the start, the Turkish-led Movement for Rights and Freedom stressed not ethnic but human rights in the widest sense. Hence demands for religious freedom, for reclaiming old Turkic-Arabic names, and for optional teaching of the Turkish language in the schools were largely seen not as separatist or antimajoritarian but as rights that the majority of Bulgarians also wanted. In sum, the first several years of the Bulgarian transformation involved an affirmation of minority (human) rights as part of a rectification of past injustices, prosecution of the political elite, and an attempted invocation of many of the principles of the rule of law. Central to these principles has been the establishment of an independent judiciary. As *communist* became an offensive word, the former communist party renamed itself. The judicial reckoning stopped when many members of the former elite returned to power, under nationalist banners. Because the post-1990 governments have not engaged in much economic reform, foreign investment has been minimal. Corruption among the elite has become rampant, and living standards for the majority have declined. This has a potentially destabilizing influence on the government, but the process of judicial reform has already gone far and is still supported by most of the parties across the political spectrum.

Albania

Of all the European socialist regimes, the dictatorship in Albania had been most isolated from international movements. It had had a disturbing record of human rights violations, with political prisoners numbering in the thousands, many sentenced for so-called agitation and propaganda against the state (Puto 1991: 115–16). With the regime change in 1990, and under pressure from local and global human rights organization, most of these prisoners have since been released. No national program of retributive justice for the various victim groups has been enacted, but local and diverse forms of retribution have been practiced. Trials against former leaders began several years later than they did in the other states, due largely to the lack of judicial experience and of machinery necessary to investigate and prosecute. Once begun, however, there have been fairly extensive examples of ritual purification under the rule of law. Nexhmije Hoxha (widow of the longtime Stalinist ruler Enver Hoxha), Kino Buxheli (party secretary), Ramiz Alia (the last communist president), Hekuran Isai and Manush Myftiu (Politburo members), along with ten senior members of the former Labor Party of Albania were charged (and most found guilty and sentenced) with corruption, abuse of power, or embezzlement. Although large demonstrations were organized in 1991 to support calls for prosecution, the trials appear to have had little immediate effect on justice at the local level or on the legitimation of the new state. The one counterexample is in Shkoder, northern Albania, where police and local authorities were found guilty of ordering shots fired into crowds in the April 1991 anticommunist demonstrations.

Noteworthy is that the first wave of trials did not involve the prosecution of substitute victims. Actual perpetrators of wrongs were identified and tried with due process. Problems in the institutionalization of a multiparty electoral system, however, threaten to instrumentalize the use of retributive justice in order to prevent an opposition from organizing. In the fall of 1995, the parliament passed two new lustration laws, appropriately titled, On the Verification of the Moral Character of Officials and Other Persons Connected with the Defense of the Democratic State, and On Genocide and Crimes against Humanity Committed in Albania during the Communist Regime for Political, Ideological, and Religious Motives. A commission is now authorized to "verify" the moral character of candidates for elective office, and individuals already tried for crimes, such as former president Ramiz Alia and more than two dozen former communist functionaries, are now subject to double jeopardy and tried again. President Alia is being tried this time for embezzlement—defined as a crime against humanity. Such cynical manipulations of retributive justice vitiate the early normative achievements of the regime.

What role these trials might play in future jural reforms as part of a historical memory is an open question. In anthropological terms, Albania is perhaps the single Balkan state that was truly isolated from global legal and economic exchange. The rule of law and democratic political form were relatively foreign, and the dictatorship had appropriated forms of customary law to produce an unusual version of totalitarian legality. Hence to the extent the new regime seeks legitimacy without resort to arbitrary force and without accommodation to local custom, it operates in a vacuum. All told, the attempt to invoke the principles of the rule of law has been simply too abrupt and novel to allow reasonable predictions about long-term outcomes. Moreover, the long-term effects of the attempts at retributive justice may depend more on the geopolitical importance of Albania to Europe, and on processes of external legitimation, than on internal dynamics.

Since 1990, the incidents of criminality of all kinds have reportedly increased by an estimated 500 percent. The opposition "Democrats" who now control the state initially maintained that this increase was the fault of the communists. Yet once in power, they have also been unable to stop the escalating violence and crime. Apparently the political transformation begun by reform communists at the end of 1990 was accompanied by a pillaging of state property (schools, depots, shops, irrigation canals, trains, factories) comparable in degree to the damage suffered during the Second World War. The state is now allegedly bankrupt, making it difficult if not impossible to engage in costly jural reforms. Many commentators maintain that Albania's economy is largely dependent on gifts and loans from global nongovernmental organizations, mostly from the European Union, northern Europe, or Italy. This dependence, in turn, may be conducive to further reform by facilitating contacts and forcing compliance with Western European legal norms, at least in the spheres of contract and property law (for a related argument concerning China, see Upham 1994).

Because of the increase in local violence, the new state's assertion of law and justice has been widely perceived as ineffectual, leading many people to return to the principle of blood vengeance, embodied in the Canon of Lek, set down by the chieftain Lek Dukagjini in the fifteenth century. Up to communist rule, this canon had regulated relations between self-governing, patriarchal, democratic tribes and kinship groups. At its core was the idea of conflict resolution through purification by blood. In the face of the delegitimation of the communist state, many Albanians have attempted to reassert other, older traditions that had been repressed—such as the blood feud. Although the totalitarian state denied the traditional principles of the canon, it in fact selectively employed them and kept them alive, for example, by consistently punishing an entire family for the crime of any individual. Competing claims over state-controlled land, 70 percent of which has been redistributed by the government, has led to violent fights between families and gangs, frequently "resolved" in blood feuds outside the state's jural system (Lloshi 1992: 66–68). A new nongovernmental organization, called the Mission to Resolve Blood Feuds and led by a Catholic priest, which obtained funding in part from a Danish civil society project, claims to have resolved 168 feuds in its several years of operation. It uses elaborate ceremonies in which documents are signed, songs sung, and oaths chanted (Sampson 1995: 23). Needless to say, the state has not immediately established itself as a moral authority for the entire community. Hence, despite prosecution of wrongdoing at the political center and rectification of victims, cycles of private or family vendettas and retributive violence are likely to continue as modes of justice at the local level.

CONCLUSION

My own argument in this book about the principles of the rule of law has been both descriptive and prescriptive. Not only do regimes transform in different ways, but some states are transforming better than others: better because they are more successful at establishing themselves as legitimate moral authorities that provide the possibility of justice; better because it is more likely that those political communities that invoke the principles of the rule of law will not disintegrate into cycles of violence. What is the key to such a transformation, which, I repeat, has no endstation, but requires intermittent ritual purification of the political center? *The key is the state's assumption of accountability for retributive justice*: the rectification of past injuries through prosecution of wrongdoers and restoration of the dignity of victims. This means neither that the criminal justice system is the sole arbiter of all conflict nor that it will eliminate all violence and wrongdoing. Instead its legitimacy must be based on a re-location of accountability in the center of the regime itself—no displacement to the periphery, no scapegoating, no substitute victims—through periodic ritual purification of wrongdoers. Hence my prescriptive conclusion: the long-term legitimacy of democratic states, to the extent states in East-Central Europe take this form, will rest centrally on belief in the morality expressed by the principles of the rule of law.

Although this work focuses on the use of retributive justice in democratic states, my conclusions are equally relevant to nondemocratic regimes. By extension, my argument would predict that trials in monarchies and dictatorial states would often be counterproductive, leading not to justice, but to cycles of revenge. If political regimes are not founded on principles of accountability, their legal systems will tend to function as arms of the executive branch of government, violating one of the fundamental principles of the rule of law. Without formal separation of the executive and judicial and guarantees of the independence of the judiciary, jural systems will most likely be used to harass opponents of the regime. The wrong people will be rewarded, the wrong people punished. Such injustices will delegitimate the political regimes that fail to invoke the principles of the rule of law, and some groups of people will likely feel compelled to use their own devices to seek substitute victims. The dynamics I describe are becoming commonplace; states lacking a higher authority that one can trust, such as Rwanda, Burundi, and Nigeria, for example, will probably turn the current investigations and trials into political farces. Leaders will find substitute victims, aggrieved parties will perform acts of vengeance, possibly turning to forms of modern terrorism. In Bosnia-Herzegovina, due to the international controls on the use of justice, the effects of retributive justice are fully open. If, however, there is no legal retribution in Bosnia-Herzegovina, it is likely that injured parties will pass on to their children a sense of obligation to seek personal revenge. I am hopeful that these comparisons will provide new directions for descriptive and theoretical work on legal systems. Moreover, perhaps the insights I present here will contribute to the global invocation of the principles of the rule of law.

Notes

Chapter 1
Framing the Rule of Law in East-Central Europe

1. Max Weber (1978: 874) argued that the rejection of "all transcendental law, especially natural law" was a major characteristic of "Continental jurisprudence" generally. "Even up to the most recent times, [it] proceeds on the basis of the largely unchallenged axiom of the logical 'closedness' of the positive law." Before National Socialist rule, Gustav Radbruch, perhaps the leading legal philosopher of the Weimar Republic and former Social Democratic minister of justice, had argued that in the case of a conflict between claims for justice (or morality) and the law, one should always decide positively—that is, for the law. After witnessing Nazi illegalities, however, he formulated in 1946 what has become known as the Radbruch Formula: positive law has priority even when it is wrong and inexpedient; however, when the contradiction between the positive law and justice reaches an unbearable degree, justice may be used to negate the law as a "wrong law." Perhaps the leading legal theorist of positivism in this century, Hans Kelsen (1967), who emigrated from Germany in 1933, had always separated positive law from morality, insisting that since the law could have any content, a legal sentence that follows the norm of valid law is separate from the political justification for the law. The conclusion that he drew from this was that all legal systems are coercive orders (*Zwangsordnungen*) with their own norms of justice, and therefore their legitimacy could not be invalidated by criticism based on criteria of justice (see Hart 1958; Loos and Schreiber 1984: 301–9; Meier: 514: 75–78)

2. Problems of distributive justice, such as those explored by Bruce Ackerman (1992) and Michael Walzer (1983), follow a logic closer to that of corrective than restitutive justice. Walzer has consistently argued from a position of cultural relativism in comparisons of judicial systems and conceptions of justice, often borrowing from anthropological representations of the closed nature of cultural belief systems. If applied to Eastern Europe, his relativism would seem to support the assertion that socialist legal norms were separate and autonomous from liberal democratic legal norms, making prosecution of wrongdoing extremely difficult if not impossible. In his most recent book, Walzer (1995) complicates his earlier position, arguing for a distinction between thick and thin moral standards, without, however, abandoning his earlier position regarding the autonomy of cultural systems from which a relativistic moral position follows.

3. Perhaps the leading exponent of this school, Clifford Geertz (1983: 170), stated that his goal in an anthropological explanation of law was neither to "infuse legal meanings into social customs [nor] to correct judicial reasonings with anthropological findings [but to look] first one way, then the other, in

order to formulate moral, political, and intellectual issues that inform [both disciplines, law and anthropology]." This is a statement with which one can hardly disagree, but it both assumes the separateness of domains (legal and social) and disciplines (law and anthropology) in order then to bring them together, and it avoids justifying which way to look. In order to maintain an absolute relativism, culturalist accounts tend to focus on initial positions and not on the political consequences of taking up certain questions for research and rejecting others, as well as on the outcomes and effects (or lack of effects) of interaction between domains or disciplines.

4. We are also not helped much by the work of the most well known liberal political theorist of justice, John Rawls. His initial presumption of a "veil of ignorance" between past and present as a necessary condition to constitute the political community assumes what in Eastern Europe has to be first established: At what point does the present begin? Rawls does not fundamentally alter this framework in his most recent book. He still assumes that the "basic structure is that of a closed society" with citizens who are "free and equal persons" oriented toward "a fair system of cooperation over time" (1993: 14, 12). But most of the problems installing the rule of law have to do precisely with the fact that East-Central European societies are heterogeneous societies, strongly influenced by an ambiguously defined "outside"; that they have no clear "original position" separating former or future members from present ones, and that their members are highly unequal, often illiberal, and intent on deceiving or coercing each other.

5. Bloch's fascinating analysis of "rebounding violence," which maintains that religious ritual transforms "prey into hunter," holds at a general level for the current jural transformations that are the subject of this book. Following the revolutions of 1989, many former "prey" in East-Central Europe suddenly sat in parliament or on committees to "hunt" criminals, who themselves had been the former hunters. However, his interpretation of this violence as "itself a result of the attempt to create the transcendental in religion and politics" simply inverts the usual causal explanation: now religion and jural systems are instigators instead of responses to violence (1992: 7). The attempt to create transcendent moral systems such as the Rechtsstaat in former socialist regimes cannot be said to have instigated the violence found in most of these places. Neither, however, are the new moral systems the result of current patterns of violence. Rather, wherever the principles of the rule of law are being invoked, their invocation is a reaction to past and not present violence. This invocation theoretically eliminates neither the sacrificial process nor the need for retributive justice; only personal vengeance and the use of the substitute victim are theoretically eliminated. The attempt to establish transcendent "Big Other" signifiers (e.g., the State, Morality, Family, Law, Religion) and the proliferation of violent acts (e.g., ethnic cleansing, forced partition of peoples, persecution of minorities, crimes against private property) are part of a chain of signifiers where there is no identifiable originary or prior link. To be sure, the rule of law is also a transcendent, but it is directed to the regulation of self more than the other. My claim is more limited and specific: the principles of the rule of

law, once invoked, are a means of stopping interminable cycles of retributive violence.

6. The issue of accountability has been frequently discussed in ethnographic monographs, but it has usually been presented within discussions of rationality (e.g., whether the reasoning used was formally consistent and logical) or within discussions of human agency. For example, Evans-Pritchard's (1976) account of Azande causal reasoning has been used in both discussions. For an exception to this, see James Ferguson's (1993: 78–92) pointed critique of technicist reasoning in "structural adjustment" programs, where he redirects the discussion to one of human responsibility—or, as I am arguing, accountability—for the moral outcomes of economic policies.

7. Among the many scholars arguing from a property-first position, see Cepl (1992b), Posner (1992), Sunstein (1993), and Weigel (1992).

Chapter 2
Comparing: Decommunization—Recommunization—Reform?

1. This chapter is primarily based on fieldwork undertaken in Germany for approximately twelve months between June 1992 and August 1995. Most of the research in Hungary, Russia, Poland, and the Czech Republic was completed in October and November 1994; in those countries I conducted interviews in either German or English, with translators in a few cases. Also, I have relied on letter exchanges for some information. I am most grateful particularly to Masha Gesson in Moscow, Peter Gedeon in Budapest, and Irek Krzemin'ski in Warsaw for insights and linguistic clarifications of arguments made in this paper, and to Stefan Senders for substantive criticisms and comments.

Chapter 3
Historicizing the Rule of Law

1. In this historical summary, I have borrowed liberally from the following texts: Berman 1983; Boldt 1990a, 1990b; Loos and Schreiber 1984: 231–311.

2. U.S. citizens have a written constitution that binds all legal norms and institutions. Unlike European countries, the American colonists after the War of Independence did not have an absolutist state against which they needed protection. Given different colonies with conflicting religious creeds, the European colonists generally distrusted homogeneous majorities and were concerned with the protection of themselves as minorities. They also emphasized the necessity of general participation over a "social contract" of the sort Europeans presupposed, since that contract had yet to be formed. With no single group having a priori dominance over the others, "division of power" became a central principle holding the colonists together. The constitution, then, favored mutuality of recognition, compromise, and coalitions, and emphasized diffuse, decentralized power and state over federal rights. Limitations on exercising power made it difficult to act forcefully or radically; it also initially made self-government at a local level more possible.

3. Contained in article 20(1), read with article 28(2), of the Grundgesetz, or Basic Law, of 1949.

4. Although the Basic Law has been retained since 1949, the preamble has in fact been changed several times. For my purposes here, the most significant changes have been in what constitutes the "German people" and the territory of the German state.

Chapter 4
The Invocation of the Rechtsstaat in East Germany:
Governmental and Unification Criminality

1. After the fall of 1989, East German courts were literally inundated with demands for justice. For example, the number of cases in labor courts increased by 742 percent in 1990 alone. The case overload, and accompanying backlog, continued to grow after unification. In the province of Brandenburg, for example, between 1991 and 1992 the total number of cases delayed because of court overload increased 57 percent, from 9,145 to 16,000 (*Berliner Zeitung*, January 20, 1992, 14). Meanwhile, by the end of 1994, the number of East Germans going to court began to reach West German proportions. In Berlin, for example, the number of civil cases rose 273 percent between 1991 and 1994 (*Der Tagesspiegel*, October 10, 1994, 10).

2. The dis- and requalifications for civil servants (criteria for disqualification in private businesses were not covered by the law) were uneven between and within the new Länder (provinces). Only in East Berlin were the criteria fairly uniform, and there, as explained above, only judges and state prosecutors were dismissed; other civil servants, including police officers and teachers, remained in their posts though most were later vetted for Stasi activity by the Gauck-Authority. This was possible only because West Berlin had a large enough staff and was physically close enough to take over the jural administration of the entire eastern part of the city.

The fate of occupational groups who were subject to disqualification varied: among teachers in Berlin, 4.7 percent were implicated but only 0.99 percent dismissed (Gauck 1995a: 5); among lawyers in private practice, of 304 reviewed, 4 were disqualified (*Der Tagesspiegel*, October 1, 1994, 10). The Unity Treaty of August 31, 1990, envisioned continuity in civil servants but also obligated the new Länder to review civil servants for qualification and suitability for the position. Unlike "de-Nazification" following World War II, political party affiliation was not used as a criteria (given that 97.6 percent of all GDR judges were members of the Socialist Unity Party, this would have made reappointment all but impossible [*Berliner Zeitung*, January 15, 1992, 10]). A single criterion was listed as ground for dismissal: *Tätigkeit*, activity connected with the Stasi. It did not specify whether this included those who merely had contact (*Kontakt*) or those who worked with (*Zusammenarbeit*) or those who worked for (*Mitarbeit*) the Stasi. The Unity Treaty did, however, rule out consideration of political party membership (which had been the U.S. criteria for de-Nazification). The different review commissions shared an assumption of an "objective" perspective, which entailed the search for an "objective" criterion from which to review GDR personnel. Although this insistence upon an objective standpoint intended to take into consideration conditions in the GDR, instead, it meant, as Diemut Majer has pointed out, that historically specific circumstances of behavior were ignored. On the other hand, resistance to forming a "catalog of criteria" (because it was impossible to arrive at or agree on an "objective" one) facilitated arbitrary and variable application of standards for review (1992: 147–67).

3. The same trend holds for state prosecutors and judges sent to Berlin. Since February 1991, when the first person from one of the western Länder was assigned to Berlin, eighty-six prosecutors and judges arrived to work on governmental criminality. From that first group only four remain. In 1994, the number assigned from outside Berlin was reduced to forty-five. The permanent part of the group "governmental criminality" includes seven from the city of Berlin and nine from the federal government. In addition to problems in continuity, the public prosecutor's office also must deal with a very young and inexperienced staff (Schaefgen 1994: 157).

4. In late 1995, Geiger was promoted to be head of the *Verfassungsschutz* (Office of Constitutional Protection). Many people suspect him of having removed Stasi documents implicating West Germans in criminality to West German archives in Cologne and Pullach, where the public has no access (Andreas Förster, "Ein perfekter Staatsdiener," *Berliner Zeitung* 174, July 28, 1995, 3).

5. By the end of June 1995, the Gauck-Authority had completed 89 percent of the 1.63 million requests for vetting individuals for public service, and they had completed 8,500 requests for vetting from private companies. Stasi complicity was found in 7 percent of those vetted for public service, in 12 percent of those vetted for private companies. Both the government and private companies tend to continue to employ a majority of the people who are found to have worked for the Stasi. For example, although approximately 4.5 percent of East Berlin's teachers were found to have worked for the Stasi, only 0.9 percent were fired (*Berliner Zeitung* 150, June 30, 1995, 5). If the vetting resulted in dismissal from the job, it was justified in terms of *Ungeeignetheit* (unsuitability), which was tied to proof of work for the Stasi. Fired individuals had four weeks to appeal to a labor court. But few East Germans knew about the protections of West German labor law; thus few appealed. Of those who appealed, nearly all courts initially approved the dismissals. However, all decisions on second appeal (to my knowledge), which first began being handed down in 1993, reinstated those dismissed. Justification for the reversal has been that one must prove that work for the Stasi resulted in a *Nachteil* (shortcoming or harm). Since 1993, even first courts of appeal are no longer upholding the dismissals.

6. There are several exceptions, all involving an individual's spying on the Federal Republic as an IM, undercover collaborator for the GDR. The unusual cases of Dr. Gabriele Gast, sentenced in 1991 to six years and nine months prison, and Klaus Kuron, sentenced in 1992 to twelve years in prison for spying, stand in stark contrast to the fates of other spies investigated, who largely were full-time Stasi agents or worked for other spy organizations. In May 1995, the German Constitutional Court issued an important ruling holding several

leading GDR spies innocent and encouraged lower courts not to continue trying former GDR spies.

7. The common assumption of theorists using hermeneutics or system theory in postunity debates has been that the GDR's legal system was a closed system of rules that could only be criticized narrowly in its own terms. Concerning the limits of hermeneutics, Habermas had already in the late 1970s criticized Gadamer for limiting "meaning" to the actor's own horizons of understanding (see the summary in Teigas 1985). Luhmann's (1985: 186ff) positive theory of law insists that the development of legal positivism is part of an evolutionary social process, an accomplishment to be protected from, and not balanced against, arguments for suprapositive judicial norms (supranational or natural law perspectives). Luhmann argues that since in modern societies law is made through the iteration and reiteration of decisions, and since laws are at any time changeable, their inner legitimacy is never in question. Therefore, he concludes, legal legitimacy is a product of legal process alone and does not depend on either historically specific intentions or outcomes. This model presumes what is clearly not the case: that "politics" is demarcated clearly from law, so that legal process can operate autonomously.

Chapter 5
Accountability on Trial

1. Neither the prosecution of criminality nor categorization of victims in any particular East bloc state is typical of the others. Vogel's trial for extortion, for example, is a consequence of the symbiotic policies of the two German states and made possible by the restrictive travel policies of the GDR. Travel was much freer in other East bloc countries; and everywhere it was restrictive, there was no West German state waiting to welcome them.

2. Professor Vogel is also charged with other sundry crimes, such as tax evasion and perjury.

3. In the early years of the exchange, the Federal Republic paid between DM 40,000 and DM 50,000. The total sum paid to the GDR over fifteen years was DM 3.5 billion (Grasemann 1992: 59).

Chapter 6
Democratic Accountability: Results, Evaluations, Ramifications

1. Another argument often put forward is that property owners should be preferred for restitution claims because at least it is possible to determine the amount of damage they suffered, whereas intangible forms of harm are impossible to compensate for fairly. Offe and Bönker counter: "It would be morally irrelevant to let the choice of rectificatory strategies be guided and distorted by the morally irrelevant fact that property can be given back, while years lost in prison cannot" (1992:31).

2. Holy reports that in opinion polls carried out in 1991, "92 percent of Czechs were of the opinion that the Slovaks benefited more from the common

state than they did themselves and 86 percent of Slovaks expressed the opposite view" (1994: 810).

3. *Week in Germany*, November 12, 1992, 1.

4. There have been twenty-six Enquete-Kommissionen during the history of the Federal Republic. After gathering testimony and evidence, their function is to assess the findings and propose a remedy to parliament.

Chapter 7
Justice and Dignity: Victims, Vindication, and Accountability

1. The concept *dignity* comes from the Latin *dignitas*, meaning "intrinsic worth." A violation of dignity is behavior that demeans or humiliates, where one's value or worth is diminished. The two conventional grounds most frequently used to talk about human value are membership in collective identities (e.g., ethnic or religious majorities or minorities) or residency. The former is called a peoples approach, the latter a territorial one. Both of these conventional rights approaches derive value from a notion of equality (equal rights, equal worth). By contrast, reliance on dignity uses a notion of freedom that is intrinsic to the person, independent of community, state, or external authority. As Hans Kelsen (1967) warned during the Weimar period, if democratic decision making is to be defined by the majority principle, it must emanate out of freedom, not equality. Therefore, unlike a "right," dignity can neither be measured nor taken away or granted, nor can it be denied particular humans. In legal dogma, the concept of dignity relies on the Kantian injunction that every human should be treated as an end and not a means. Therefore, there is an initial presumption for individual consent and against coercion of any sort. This also means that a definition of dignity and its protections can never be reduced to legalistic formulations, for it can be realized only in social processes that always exceed legal process In sum, while the peoples and territorial approaches may guarantee an individual rights to a community and to the protection of its laws, a dignity approach justifies value claims that may have validity independent of the community or its laws (Schachter 1983: 848–54).

In terms of international law, the Helsinki Final Act (principle 7) of 1975 offered the latest advance in elevating dignity as a concept above the peoples or territorial approaches, claiming that all human rights and fundamental freedoms "derive from the inherent dignity of the human person." The very vagueness of the concept is one of its advantages over the peoples and territorial approaches. The International Human Rights Covenant, signed by two-thirds of all member states of the United Nations, the Declaration on Principles of International Law, the African Charter on Human and Peoples Rights, and the International Covenant on Civil and Political Rights (1984), to list but some of the postwar international accords, all base the principle of rights on the concept of "the right of self-determination." This necessarily implies a people with territorial rights if not with the more usual claim to its own territory, which in turn is a state-centric definition. Today the peoples approach tends to legitimate oppressive governments operating within unjust state boundaries for it begs the question of what is a people. As McCorquodale writes, it "upholds the perpetual power of a state at the expense of the right of the inhabitants" (1994: 868). The territorial approach has an even more telling problem in that it is totally indifferent to the issue of who is determining the self or the nature of the people.

In sum, a right to self-determination must not be seen in isolation or as the source of other rights, for out of this principle individuals have no claim to rights against the groups to which they belong. Moreover, any group that can clearly demarcate itself has theoretically a right to secession. A more flexible approach, such as one based on "human dignity," is needed so that citizens of one state or members of one group of people can live in another state or with another people without compromising anyone's dignity or their right of self-determination. In other words, individuals and groups must be protected against "oppressive acts in the name of self-determination" (McCorquodale 1994: 878; see also Koskenniemi 1994: 241–69)

2. Article 1 states: "The dignity of man shall be inviolable. To respect and protect it shall be the duty of all state authority." Article 14 explicitly guarantees "property and the right of inheritance." In post-1989 East Germany, the issue of correcting past injustices and righting wrongs always concerned two sets of self-identified victims, which correspond to these two bases of dignity: one involving violation of property rights, the other violation of human rights or acts whose wrongness have resulted in nonmaterial damages. Hence it is no wonder that injustices suffered in one domain have been frequently confused with those in the other. This confusion is by no means limited to Germans, for social scientists as well as others in former socialist states tend to collapse the two types of rights into one.

3. Much of the information presented here comes from an interview conducted on June 15, 1993, with Herr Grollmitz, chair of the Rehabilitierungskommission des Rundfunk und Fernsehen der DDR, the Commission of Vindication of the former state television and radio, the last acting commission of this sort in the former GDR.

4. German courts have only occasionally reaffirmed the importance of the apology as a remedy for a moral injury. As important as such an apology might be to the resolution of conflict, it is rarely given any legal significance. And although the meetings of victim and perpetrator have been relatively rare (in or out of court), even less frequent have been those where the perpetrator acknowledged his/her wrong. I suspect that without such an acknowledgment, the final goal of a jural process—reconciliation—is rare. In one unusual legal case following such an apology, which was accepted by the victims, the head judge in a Berlin court, Rainer Pannek, squashed the indictment of a former GDR Supreme Court judge. Alfred T., now eighty-two years old, had participated in 1950 in sentencing to life imprisonment nine members of the Jehovah's Witnesses on trumped up charges of spying and inciting war. The case was legally complicated by the fact that in 1952 Herr T. had fled to the West. Two previous attempts to prosecute him, in 1953 and in 1966, were stopped, each for a different reason, but with the end of the Cold War, public prosecutors were again obligated to investigate judicial illegality. Given his longtime residence

in the West, however, it was unclear whether East or West German law applied to him. Judge Pannek applied West German law, and accordingly ruled that the statute of limitations had already been exceeded—thus avoiding a decision on the issue of "judicial illegality." Both the defense and prosecution intended to appeal the decision, the former because it wanted an acquittal, the latter because it wanted a one and one-half year suspended sentence.

5. In response to the first question, whether they felt the commission had handled their cases correctly/justly (*gerecht*) and if not, whether it could have served them better, seventeen of the twenty-one felt that they were handled correctly, four felt they were not. The criticisms of three of those four were concerned not with the performance of the commission but with the lack of legal measures that would recognize its work. Only one person criticized the commission's proceedings as unfair. The second question asked whether and in how far the remedy proposed by the commission had been realized. Answers ranged from "100 percent" to "partially" to "not at all." Six people indicated that the commission had promised them nothing (other than a written confirmation of their unjust treatment). Seven respondents said the proposed remedy had been realized, while seven others said it had not been realized. One person did not respond. The third question asked whether the commission was an appropriate means to actualize the *Rechtsstaat*. Seven respondents answered the question affirmatively, eleven negatively, with the other three not answering. The fourth question asked whether they would like to pursue their cases in court if the appropriate laws were passed making it possible to do so. Twelve responded affirmatively, seven negatively, two with no answer.

Chapter 8
The Rule of Law and the State: Violence, Justice, and Legitimacy

1. Using a framework of "path dependency," David Stark (1992) makes a similar argument for Eastern European political transformations.

2. Statistics on crime are notoriously unreliable. But by all accounts, the amount of criminal activity in Russia has increased tremendously in the 1990s. The Russian prosecutor general recently estimated that the actual number of crimes is three times the number reported, and that by the year 2000 (within the next four years) he expected crimes to rise 2.5 times ("Rising Crime in Russia," *New York Times*, May 7, 1996, A8).

Bibliography

Ackerman, Bruce. *The Future of Liberal Revolution*. New Haven: Yale University Press, 1992.

Alexy, Robert. "Walter Ulbricht's Rechtsbegriff." *Recht und Politik* 29 (1993): 207–12.

Alia, Rabia and Lawrence Lifschultz, eds. *Why Bosnia?: Writings on the Balkan War*. Stony Creek, Conn.: Pamphleteer's Press, 1993.

Anguelov, Zlatko. "No Identity Problems." *East European Review* 5 (4, 1992): 28–31.

Ash, Timothy Garton. *The Magic Lantern: The Revolution of '89 Witnessed in Warsaw, Budapest, Berlin, and Prague*. New York: Random House, 1990.

Aubert, Vilhelm. "Law and Social Change in Nineteenth-Century Norway." In *History and Power in the Study of Law*, edited by June Starr and Jane Collier, 55–80. Ithaca: Cornell University Press, 1989.

Averesch, Sigrid. "Versöhnung im Gerichtssaal." *Berliner Zeitung*, August 18, 1995, 4.

————."Willige Glieder der Bürokratie." *Berliner Zeitung*, November 30, 1997, 7.

Bahr, Egon. "Drei Jahre nach der Einheit-Für oder gegen eine Amnestie." *Neue Justiz* 12 (1993): 537–40.

Barthes, Roland. *Mythologies*. New York: Hill and Wang, 1972.

Battiata, Mary. "East Europe Hunts for Ex-Reds: Police List Used as Tool in Purge." *Washington Post*, December 28, 1991, A1.

Becker, Werner. "Strafjustiz—Politische Justiz—Weltanschauungskritik." *Berliner Debatte* 2 (1993): 23–28.

Benda, Vaclav. "Protecting the Revolution or Perverting it? Interview with V. Benda." *East European Reporter* (March/April 1992): 42–43.

Berman, Harold. *Law and Revolution*. Cambridge: Harvard University Press, 1983.

Bisky, Lothar, Uwe-Jens Heuer, and Micahel Schumann, eds. *Rücksichten: Politische und juristische Aspekte der DDR -Geschichte*. Hamburg: VSA-Verlag, 1993.

Blaau, Loammi. "The Rechtsstaat Idea Compared with the Rule of Law as a Paradigm for Protecting Rights." *South African Law Journal* 107 (1990): 76–96.

Bloch, Maurice. *Prey into Hunter: The Politics of Religious Experience*. Cambridge: Cambridge University Press, 1992.

Blok, Anton. "The Symbolic Vocabulary of Public Executions." In *History and Power in the Study of Law*, edited by June Starr and Jane Collier, 31–54. Ithaca: Cornell University Press, 1989.

Blumenwitz, Dieter. "Die juristische Problematik strafrechtlicher Verfolgung von DDR-Regierungskriminalität—Konsequenzen für den inneren Frieden des deutschen Volkes." In *Die Kriminelle Herrschaftssicherung des kommunistischen Regimes der DDR, 3. Bautzen Forum in Bautzen*, edited by Friedrich Ebert Stiftung, 65–72. Leipzig: Friedrich Ebert Stiftung, 1992.

Boldt, Hans. *Deutsche Verfassungsgeschichte, Band 1. Von den Anfängen bis zum Ende des älteren deutschen Reiches 1806*. Munich: Deutscher Taschenbuch Verlag, 1990a.

———. *Deutsche Verfassungsgeschichte: Politische Strukturen und ihr Wandel, Band 2. Von 1806 zur Gegenwart*. Munich: Deutscher Taschenbuch Verlag, 1990b.

Bönker, Frank, and Claus Offe. "Die moralische Rechtfertigung der Restitution des Eigentums." *Leviathan* 3 (1994): 318–52.

Borneman, John. *East Meets West in the New Berlin*. New York: Basic Books, 1991.

———. *Belonging in the Two Berlins: Kin, State, Nation*. New York: Cambridge University Press, 1992.

———. *Subversions of International Order: Studies in the Political Anthropology of Culture*. Albany: State University of New York Press, 1998.

Bourdieu, Pierre. *Outline of a Theory of Practice*. Cambridge: Cambridge University Press, 1977.

Bundestag, Deutscher. *Bericht der Enquette-Kommission. Aufarbeitung von Geschichte und Folgen der SED-Diktatur in Deutschland*. 12 Wahlperiode Bonn: Deutscher Bundestag, 1994a. 12. Drucksache 12/7820.

———. *Beschlußempfehlung und Bericht des 1: Untersuchungsausschusses nach Artikel 44 des Grundgesetzes*. Bonn: Deutscher Bundestag, 1994b. Drucksache 12/7600.

Buruma, Ian. *The Wages of Guilt*. New York: Farrar, Straus, and Giroux, 1994.

Cepl, Vojtech. "Ritual Sacrifices." *East European Constitutional Review* 1 (1, 1992a): 24–26.

———. "Retribution and Restitution in Czechoslovakia." *Archives europeanne de sociologie* 32 (1992b): 202–14.

Clastres, Pierre. *Society against the State: Essays in Political Anthropology*. New York: Zone Books, 1974.

Dascalu, Roxana. "Romanian Prosecutors Face Legacy of Communist Interference." *Reuters Library Report*, April 20, 1990, 1.

Däubler-Gmelin, Herta. "Erwartungen an den Deutschen Bundestag zur Rehabilitierung und Entschädigung." In *Gerechtigkeit den Opfern der Kommunistischen Diktatur, 2. Bautzen Forum in Bautzen*, edited by Friedrich Ebert Stiftung, 23–26. Leipzig: Friedrich Ebert Stiftung, 1991.

Derrida, Jacques. "For of Law: The 'Mystical Foundation of Authority.'" In *Deconstruction and the Possiblity of Justice*, edited by Michel Rosenfeld, Drucilla Cornell, and David Carlson, 3–67. New York: Routledge, 1992.

Detienne, Marcel. "Pratiques culinaires et esprit de sacrifice." In *La Cuisine du sacrifice en pays grec*, edited by J.-P. Vernant and M. Detienne Vernant. Paris: Gallimard, 1979.

Dirks, Nicholas. "Ritual and Resistance: Subversion as a Social Fact." In *Culture/Power/History: A Reader in Contemporary Theory*, edited by Nicholas Dirks, Geoff Eley, and Sherry Ortner. Princeton: Princeton University Press, 1994.

Dönhoff, Marion Gräfin. "Gerechtigkeit ist nicht Vergeltung." *Die Zeit*, January 6, 1995, 1.

Elster, Jon. "On Doing What One Can." *East European Constitutional Review* 1 (2, 1992a): 15–17.

———. "On Majoritarianism and Rights." *East European Constitutional Review* 1 (3, 1992b): 19–24.

Evans-Pritchard, E. E. *Witchcraft, Oracles, and Magic among the Azande*. Oxford: Clarendon, 1976.

Faust, Siegmar. "Ist der Rechtsstaat ungerecht?" *Recht und Politik* 3 (1994): 170–74.

Ferguson, James. "De-Moralizing Economies: African Socialism, Scientific Capitalism and the Moral Politics of 'Structural Adjustment.' " In *Moralizing States and the Ethnography of the Present*, 5th ed., edited by Sally Falk Moore. 778–92. Arlington, Va.: American Anthropological Association, 1993.

Foucault, Michel. *Discipline and Punish: The Birth of the Prison*. New York: Pantheon, 1977.

Fuller, Lon. *The Morality of Law*. New Haven: Yale Univeristy Press, 1969.

Gabriel, Oscar. "Institutionenvertrauen im vereinigten Deutschland." *Aus Politik und Zeitgeschichte* B 43 (1993): 3–12.

Gauck, Joachim. "Wut und Schmerz der Opfer." *Die Zeit*, January 20, 1995a, 5.

———. "Der Schlußstrich erfreut das repressive Establishment von Herzen." *Frankfurter Rundschau*, January 28, 1995b, 10.

Gebert, Konstanty, A. Zozula, and H. Datner-Spiewak. "Being a Jew in Poland." *East European Review* 4 (4, 1991): 106–7.

Geertz, Clifford. *Local Knowledge*. New York: Basic Books, 1983.

Gellner, Ernest. *Nations and Nationalism*. Oxford: Basil Blackwell, 1983.

Geremek, Bronislaw. "Communists and Caesuras: Another Round Table." *Eastern European Review* 5 (2, 1992): 47–48.

Geyer, Michael. "Historical Fictions of Autonomy and the Europeanization of National History." *Central European History* 22 (3/4, 1989): 316–42.

Girard, René. *Violence and the Sacred*. Baltimore: Johns Hopkins University Press, 1977.

Gluckman, Max. *Politics, Law, and Ritual in Tribal Society*. Oxford: Basil Blackwell, 1965a.

———. "Introduction." In *Political Systems and the Distribution of Power*, edited by Michael Bantan. London: Tavistock, 1965b.

Göhler, Reinhard. "Die Verpflichtung von Staat und Gesellschaft gegenüber den Opfern der kommunistischen Gewaltherrschaft." In *Gerechtigkiet den Opfer der kommunistischen Diktatur, 2. Bautzen Forum in Bautzen*, edited by Friedrich Ebert Stiftung, 27–32. Leipzig: Friedrich Ebert Stiftung, 1991.

Gornicki, Grzegorz. "Poland: Her Minorities and Neighbours." *East European Review* 4 (3, 1990): 17–22.

Grasemann, Hans-Jürgen. "Der Beitrag der zentralen Erfassungsstelle Salzgitter zur Strafverfolgung—Beispiele menschlicher Schicksale." In *Die Kriminelle Herrschaftssicherung des kommunistischen Regimes der DDR, 3. Bautzen Forum in Bautzen*, edited by Freidrich Ebert Stiftung, 55–65. Leipzig: Freidrich Ebert Stiftung, 1992.

Grigoriev, Alex. "Latvia in Limbo." *East European Review* 5 (2, 1992): 73–74.

Habermas, Jürgen. "Law and Morality." In *The Tanner Lectures on Human Values*, vol. 8, edited by Sterling McMurrin, 217–80. Salt Lake City: University of Utah Press, 1988.

———. *Between Facts and Norms*. Cambridge: MIT Press, 1996.

Hampton, Jean. "Correcting Harms versus Righting Wrongs: The Goal of Retribution." *UCLA Law Review* 29 (1992): 1659–1702.

Hart, H. L. A. "Positivism and the Separation of Law and Morals." *Harvard Law Review* 71 (4, 1958): 618–20.

Heitmann, Steffen. "Gerechtigkeit und Wiedergutmachung von Unrecht unter der kommunistischen Diktatur—Möglichkeiten und Grenzen der Justiz." In *Gerechtigkeit den Opfern der Kommunistischen Diktatur, 2. Bautzen Forum in Bautzen*, edited by Freidrich Ebert Stiftung, 18–22. Leipzig: Freidrich Ebert Stiftung, 1991.

———. "Drei Jahre nach der Einheit—Für oder gegen eine Amnestie." *Neue Justiz* 12 (1993): 537–40.

Henkin, Louis. "Revolutionen und Verfassung." In *Zur Begriff der Verfassung*, edited by Ulrich Preuß. Frankfurt: M. Fischer, 1994.

Herzfeld, Michael. *The Social Production of Indifference: Exploring the Symbolic Roots of Western Bureaucracy*. New York: Berg, 1992.

Herzog, Felix. "Zur strafrechtlichen Verantwortlichkeit von Todesschützen an der innerdeutschen Grenze." *Neue Justiz* 47 (1, 1993): 1–4.

Holmes, Stephen. "Introducing the Center: A Project to Promote Clear Thinking about the Design of Liberal-Democratic Institutions." *East European Constitutional Review* 1 (1992): 1.

———. "Back to the Drawing Board." *East European Constitutional Review* 2 (1, 1993): 21–25.

———. "The End of Decommunization." *East European Constitutional Review* 3 (3, 4, 1994): 33–36.

Holy, Ladislav. "Metaphors of the Natural and the Artificial in Czech Political Discourse." *Man* 29 (4, 1994): 809–29.

Hondrich, Karl Otto. "Das Leben ist ein langer ruhiger Fluß . . ." In *Wir Kollaborateure*, edited by Cora Stephan, 34–49. Hamburg: Rowohlt, 1992.

Hubert, Henri, and Marcel Mauss. *Sacrifice: Its Nature and Functions*. Chicago: University of Chicago Press, 1964.

Huntington, Samuel. *The Third Wave: Democratization in the Late Twentieth Century*. Norman: University of Oklahoma Press, 1991.

———. "Clash of Civilizations?" *Foreign Affairs* 73 (3, summer, 1993): 22–49.

Iaru, Florin. "Bad to Worse." *East European Reporter* 4 (3, 1990): 73–77.

Imholz, Kathleen. "Can Albania Break the Chain? The 1993–94 Trials of Former Communist Officials." *East European Constitutional Review* 4 (3, 1995): 54–60.

Ismayer, Wolfgang. "Enquete-Kommissionen der Deutschen Bundestages." *Aus Politik und Zeitgeschichte* B27 (1996): 29–41.

Jahberg, Heike. "Die Treuhand im Abschlußjahr: Flops und Erfolge." *Die Zeit*, January 2, 1994, 25.

Janis, Mark. *An Introduction to International Law*. New York: Little, Brown and Company, 1993.

Janka, Walter. *Schwierigkeiten mit der Wahrheit*. Hamburg: Rowohlt, 1989.

Judt, Tony. "Nineteen Eight-Nine: The End of Which European Era?" *Daedalus* 123 (3, 1994): 1–20.

Kähne, Volker. *Gerichtsgebäude in Berlin: Eine Rechts- und Baugeschichtliche Betrachtung*. Berlin: Haude & Spener, 1987.

Kelsen, Hans. *Pure Theory of Law*. Berkeley and Los Angeles: University of California Press, 1967.

Kennedy, Duncan. "The Structure of Blackstone's Commentaries." *Buffalo Law Review* 28 (205, 1979):

Kertzer, David. *Religion and Political Struggle in Communist Italy*. New York: Cambridge University Press, 1980.

———. *Ritual, Politics, and Power*. New Haven: Yale University Press, 1988.

Kittlaus, Manfred. *Bericht zum Aufbau der Dienststelle ZERV*. Berlin: Der Polizeipräsident in Berlin, 1993.

———. *Die Akten müssen offenbleiben, die Strafverfolgung ist Verpflichtung gegenüber den nachfolgenden Generation*. Speech to the Bürgerkomittee, Leipzig, 1994. Berlin: Der Polizei President in Berlin.

Kleine-Brockhoff, Thomas, and Oliver Schröm. "Innerdeutsche Beziehungen." *Die Zeit*, August 28, 1992, 12.

Koblitz, Donald. "Keine Elster, sondern eine Nachtigall." *Die Zeit*, January 19, 1996, 5.

Konrad, Georg. "Authority and Tolerance." *East European Reporter* (March/April 1992): 40–41.

Koskenniemi, Martti. "National Self-Determination Today: Problems of Legal Theory and Practice." *International and Comparative Law Quarterly* 43 (2, 1994): 241–69.

Leciejewski, Klaus. "Mangelware Marktwirtschaft." *Die Zeit*, February 24, 1995, 24–25.

Leggewie, Claus, and Horst Meier. "Zum Auftakt ein Schlußstrich? Das Bewältigungswerk 'Vergangenheit Ost' und der Rechtsstaat." In *Wir Kollaborateure*, edited by Cora Stephan, 51–79. Hamburg: Rowohlt, 1992.

Leicht, Robert. "Auf der Grenze." *Die Zeit*, January 19, 1996, 1.

Limbach, Jutta. "Justizpolitik in Berlin nach der Einheit." *Berliner Anwaltsblatt* 4 (1993): 97–101.

Lloshi, Xhevat. "Looking Backwards to Move Forwards." *East European Review* 5 (3, 1992): 66–68.

Loos, Fritz, and Hans-Ludwig Schreiber. "Recht, Gerechtigkeit." In *Geschichtliche Grundbegriffe*, edited by W. Conze, E. Brunner, and R. Koselleck, 231–311. Stuttgart: Klett-Cotta, 1984.

Lüderssen, Klaus. *Der Staat geht unter—das Unrecht bleibt? Regierungskriminalität in der ehemaligen DDR*. Frankfurt am Main: Suhrkamp, 1992.

Luhmann, Niklas. *A Sociological Theory of Law*. Boston: Routledge and Kegan Paul, 1985.

MacCormick, Neil. "Der Rechtsstaat und die rule of law." *Juristenzeitung* 39 (1984): 65–70.

Macke, Peter. "Zur Rolle der Gerichte in den neuen Bundesländern." *Deutsche Richterzeitung* 72 (April 1994): 136.

Majer, Diemut. "Ein halbierter Rechtsstaat für Ostdeutschland?" *Kritische Justiz* 25 (2, 1992): 147–67.

Markovits, Inga. "Wo bleibt die Gerechtigkeit." *Die Zeit*, May 13, 1994, 2.

———. *Imperfect Justice: An East-West Germany Diary.* New York: Oxford University Press, 1995.

McCorquodale, Robert. "Self-Determination: A Human Rights Approach." *International and Comparative Law Quarterly* 43 (4, 1994): 857–84.

McIntosh, Simeon. "Continuity and Discontinuity of Law: A Reply to John Finnis." *Connecticut Law Review* 21 (1, 1988): 1–48.

Medish, Mark. "Russia: Lost and Found." *Daedalus* 123 (3, 1994): 63–90.

Meier, Horst. "Reigierungskriminalität im SED-Staat." *Merkur* 514 (1991): 75–78.

Merry, Sally. *Getting Justice and Getting Even: Legal Consciousness among Working-Class Americans.* Chicago: University of Chicago Press, 1990.

———. "Sorting Out Popular Justice." In *The Possibility of Popular Justice*, edited by Sally Engle Merry and Neal Milner, 31–66. Ann Arbor: University of Michigan Press, 1993.

Minnich, Robert. "Reflections on the Violent Death of a Multi-Ethnic State: A Slovene Perspective." *Anthropology of Eastern Europe Review* 11 (1–2, 1993): 90–99.

Moore, Sally Falk. *Law As Process: An Anthropological Approach.* Boston: Routledge and Kegan Paul, 1978.

———. *Social Facts and Fabrications: "Customary Law" on Kilimanjaro, 1880–1980.* Cambridge: Cambridge University Press, 1986.

Müller, Ingo. *Hitler's Justice: The Courts of the Third Reich.* Cambridge: Cambridge University Press, 1991.

———. "Die DDR—ein 'Unrechtsstaat'?" *Neue Justiz* 7 (46, 1992): 281–83.

Münkler, Herfried. "Weimarer Republik, Faschismus and Nationalsozialismus." In *Pipers Handbuch der politischen Ideen*, edited by Irving Fetscher and Herfried Münkler, 283–310. Munich: Piper, 1987.

Offe, Claus. "Bestrafung Disqualifizierung, Entschädigung? Strategien rechtlicher 'Vergangenheitsbewältigung' in nachkommunistischen Gesellschaften." *Berliner Journal für Soziologie* 2 (1992a): 145–51.

———. "Coming to Terms with Past Injustice." *Archives europeanne de sociologie* 32 (1992b): 195–201.

Offe, Claus, and Frank Bönker. "The Morality of Restitution. Considerations on Some Normative Questions Raised by the Transition to a Private Economy. Draft Paper, June 18–19." Paper presented at a conference, Restitution in Eastern Europe, Budapest, Hungary, 1992.

Osang, Alexander. "Unzumutbar." *Berliner Zeitung*, February 20, 1995a, 3.

———. "Merkblatt, Vorgang, Rücklauf." *Berliner Zeitung*, February 25–26, 1995b, 5.

Osiatynski, Wiktor. "Decommunization and Recommunization in Poland." *East European Constitutional Review* 3 (3, 4, 1994): 36–41.

Ott, Hermann. "Die Staatspraxis an der DDR-Grenze und das Völkerrecht." *Neue Justiz* 8 (1993): 337–43.

Pawlik, Michael. "Das Recht im Unrechtsstaat." *Rechtstheorie* 25 (1, 1994): 101–17.

Posner, Richard A. Review of *The Future of Liberal Revolution*, by Bruce Ackerman (Yale University Press, 1992). *East European Constitutional Review* 1 (3, 1992): 35–37.

Preuß, Ulrich. "Der Begriff der Verfassung und ihre Beziehung zur Politik." In *Zum Begriff der Verfassung*, edited by Ulrich Preuß. Frankfurt: M. Fischer, 1994a.

———. ed. *Zum Begriff der Verfassung*. Frankfurt: M. Fischer, 1994b.

Puto, Arben. "Human Rights—The Most Serious Issue: Interview with Arben Puto." *East European Review* 4 (4, 1991): 115–16.

Radbruch, Gustav. "Gesetzliches Unrecht und Übergesetzliches Recht." *Süddeutsche Juristen-Zeitung* 1 (1946): 105ff.

Rautenberg, Erardo Christoforo. "Täter-Opfer-Ausgleich im Land Brandenburg." *Neue Justiz* 7 (1994): 300–303.

Rawls, John. *Political Liberalism*. New York: Columbia University Press, 1993.

Renesse, Margot V. "Eine unabhängige Justiz gibt es nur bei echter Gewaltenteilung." *Neue Justiz* 9 (1993): 409–11.

Rieff, David. *Slaughterhouse: Bosnia and the Failure of the West*. New York: Touchstone, 1995.

Rosenfeld, Michel. "Dilemmas of Justice." *East European Constitutional Review* 1 (2, 1992): 19–20.

Rybinski, Maciej. "Germans in Poland." *East European Review* 4 (2, 1990): 108–11.

Rzeplinski, Andrzej. "A Lesser Evil?" *East European Constitutional Review* 1 (3, 1992): 33–35.

Sampson, Steven. "The Social Life of Projects: Bringing Civil Society to Albania." In *Civil Society: Anthropological Approaches*, edited by Chris Hann. New York: Routledge, 1995.

Schachter, Oscar. "Human Dignity as a Normative Concept." *American Journal of International Law* 77 (1983): 848–54.

Schaefgen, Christoph. "Die Strafverfolgung von Regierungskriminalität der DDR—Probleme, Ergebnisse, Perspektiven." *Recht und Politik* 3 (1994): 150–60.

Schätzler, Johann-Georg. "Die versäumte Amnestie." *Neue Justiz* 2 (1995): 57–62.

Schlink, Bernhard. "Rechtsstaat und revolutionäre Gerechtigkeit." *Neue Justiz* 48 (10, 1994): 433–37.

Schröder, Michael. "Fahnenflucht als regelmäßiger Rehabilitierungsgrund?" *Neue Justiz* 8 (1993): 350–55.

Schroeder, Friedrich-Christian. "Als es den roten Teppich für Honecker gab." *Frankfurter Allgemeine Zeitung*, November 9, 1992, 12–13.

———. "Die Übernahme der sozialistischen Rechtsauffassung in ihrer Stalinschen Ausprägung in der SBZ/DDR." *Recht und Politik* 29 (4, 1993): 201–6.

Schulze-Fielitz, Helmuth. "Der Rechtsstaat und die Aufarbeitung der vorrechtstaatlichen Vergangenheit." *Deutsches Verwaltungsblatt* 106 (17, 1991): 893–906.

Schwager, Christian. "Von Freispruch bis zu mehrjährigen Haftstrafen." *Berliner Zeitung*, November 4, 1994, 2.

Schwanitz, Rolf. "Rehabilitierung und Entschädigung der Opfer—Auftrag an den Gesetzgeber." In *Gerechtigkeit den Opfer der kommunistischen Diktatur, 2. Bautzen Forum in Bautzen*, edited by Freidrich Ebert Stiftung, 33–40. Leipzig: Freidrich Ebert Stiftung, 1991.

Senatsverwaltung, für Justiz. *Aktueller Stand und Bewältigung der Regierungs- und Vereinigungskriminalität sowie des Justizunrechts—Jahresbericht*. 67 Konferenz der Justizministerinnen und -minister, Wiesbaden, Germany, 1996.

Shklar, Judith. *The Faces of Injustice*. New Haven: Yale University Press, 1990.

Siklova, Jirina. "Lustration, or the Czech Way of Screening." *East European Constitutional Review* 6 (1, 1996): 57–62.

Smollett, Eleanor. "America the Beautiful: Made in Bulgaria." *Anthropology Today* 9 (2, 1993): 9–13.

Stark, David. "Path Dependence and Privatization Strategies in East Central Europe." *East European Politics and Societies* 6 (1, 1992): 17–51.

Starr, June, and Jane Collier. "Introduction: Dialogues in Legal Anthropology." In *History and Power in the Study of Law*, edited by June Starr and Jane Collier, 1–30. Ithaca: Cornell University Press, 1989.

Sunstein, Cass. "Against Positive Rights." *East European Constitutional Review* 2 (1, 1993): 35–39.

Tagesspiegel, Der. "Mehr Todesopfer an der Mauer als bisher bekannt." December 13, 1992, 2.

———. "Berliner Justiz zieht Bilanz." October 1, 1994, 10.

Teigas, Demetrius. *Knowledge and Hermeneutic Understanding: A Study of the Habermas-Gadamer Debate*. Lewisburg, Penn.: Bucknell Press, 1985.

Tismaneanu, Vladimir. "Reform and Truth." *East European Reporter* 4 (4, 1991): 77–81.

Tismaneanu, Vladmir, and Mircea Mihaies. "Infamy Restored: Nationalism in Romania." *East European Reporter* 5 (1, 1992): 25–27.

Todorov, Tzvetan. *Facing the Extreme: Moral Life in the Concentration Camps*. New York: Metropolitan Books, 1996.

Trubek, David. "Where the Action Is: Critical Legal Studies and Empiricism." *Stanford Law Review* 36 (1984): 575–622.

Unger, Roberto Mangabeira. *The Critical Legal Studies Movement*. Cambridge: Harvard University Press, 1983.

Upham, Frank K. "Speculations on Legal Informality: On Winn's *Relational Practices and the Marginalization of Law*." *Law and Society Review* 28 (2, 1994): 233–43.

Verdery, Katherine. *What Was Socialism, and What Comes Next*. Princeton: Princeton University Press, 1996.

Walzer, Michael. *Spheres of Justice*. New York: Basic Books, 1983.

———. *Thick and Thin: Moral Argument at Home and Abroad*. Notre Dame, Ind.: University of Notre Dame Press, 1995.

Weber, Hermann. "Politische Verfolgung im kommunistischen Herrschaftssystem." In *Gerechtigkeit den Opfer der kommunistischen Diktatur, 2. Bautzen Fo-*

rum in Bautzen, edited by Friedrich Ebert Stiftung, 41–45. Leipzig: Friedrich Ebert Stiftung, 1991.

Weber, Jürgen, and Michael Piazolo, edited by *Eine Diktatur vor Gericht*. Munich: Olzog Verlag, 1995.

Weber, Max. *Economy and Society*. Vol. 2. Edited by Guenther Roth and Claus Wittich. Berkeley and Los Angeles: University of California Press, 1978.

Weigel, George. "Their Lustration—And Ours." *Commentary* (October 1992): 34–39.

Wesel, Uwe. "Da lachen die sozialistischen Hühner." *Die Zeit*, January 21, 1995, 2.

Wiatr, Jerzy. "Constitutional Accountability in Poland after 1989." *East European Constitutional Review* 5 (1, 1996): 42–45.

Winn, Jane Kaufman. "Relational Practices and the Marginalization of Law: Informal Financial Practices of Small Businesses in Taiwan." *Law and Society Review* 28 (2, 1994): 193–232.

Yankova, Veneta. "Democracy's First Steps." *East European Review* 5 (2, 1992): 44–45.

Yngvesson, Barbara, and Christine Harrington. "Interpretive Sociolegal Research." *Law and Social Inquiry* 15 (winter 1990): 135–48.

ZERV. *Zentrale Ermittlungsstelle Regierungs- und Vereingigungskriminalität: Jahresbericht*. Berlin: Der Polizeipräsident in Berlin, 1993.

ZERV. *Zentrale Ermittlungsstelle Regierungs- und Vereinigungskriminalität: Sachstandsbericht*. Police Publication 147. Berlin: Der Polizeipräsident in Berlin, 1994.

ZERV. *Zentrale Ermittlungsstelle Regierungs- und Vereinigungskriminalität: Jahresbericht*. Berlin: Der Polizeipräsident in Berlin, 1995.

ZERV. *ZERV Bulletin*. Berlin: Der Polizeipräsident in Berlin, 1996.

Index

Name Index

PRINCETON STUDIES IN
CULTURE/POWER/HISTORY

High Religion: A Cultural and Political History of Sherpa Buddhism
by Sherry B. Ortner

A Place in History: Social and Monumental Time in a Cretan Town
by Michael Herzfeld

The Textual Condition *by Jerome J. McGann*

Regulating the Social: The Welfare State and Local Politics in Imperial
Germany *by George Steinmetz*

Hanging without a Rope: Narrative Experience in Colonial and
Postcolonial Karoland *by Mary Margaret Steedly*

Modern Greek Lessons: A Primer in Historical Constructivism
by James Faubion

The Nation and Its Fragments: Colonial and Postcolonial Histories
by Partha Chatterjee

Culture/Power/History: A Reader in Contemporary Social Theory *edited by*
Nicholas B. Dirks, Geoff Eley, and Sherry B. Ortner

After Colonialism: Imperial Histories and Postcolonial Displacements
edited by Gyan Prakash

Encountering Development: The Making and Unmaking of the Third World
by Arturo Escobar

Social Bodies: Science, Reproduction, and Italian Modernity
by David G. Horn

Revisioning History: Film and the Construction of a New Past
edited by Robert A. Rosenstone

The History of Everyday Life: Reconstructing Historical Experiences and
Ways of Life *edited by Alf Lüdtke*

About the Author

John Borneman is Associate Professor of Anthropology at Cornell University. He is the author of *After the Wall: East Meets West in the New Berlin*, *Belonging in the Two Berlins: Kin, State, Nation*, and *Subversions of International Order: Studies in the Political Anthropology of Culture*. He is the coauthor, with Jeffrey M. Peck, of *Sojourners: The Return of German-Jews and the Question of Identity*.